I dedicate this book to the memory of three leaders and directors of the social theatre in the thirties: Garfield King of Vancouver, Lilian Mendelssohn of Montreal and Jim Watts of Toronto.

Contents

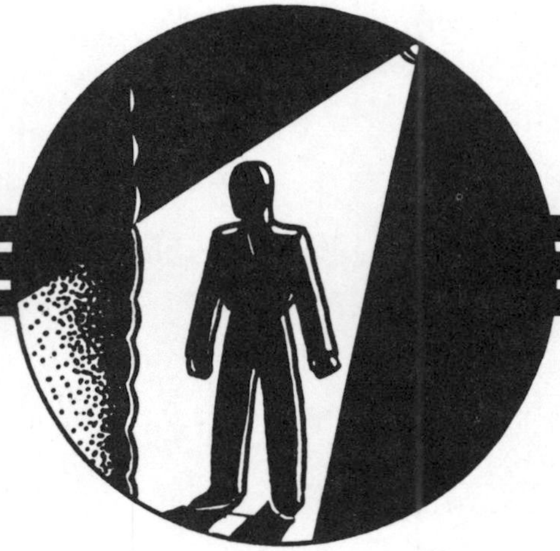

StageLeft

CANADIAN THEATRE IN THE THIRTIES

A Memoir

By Toby Gordon Ryan

CTR Publications

Toronto

1981

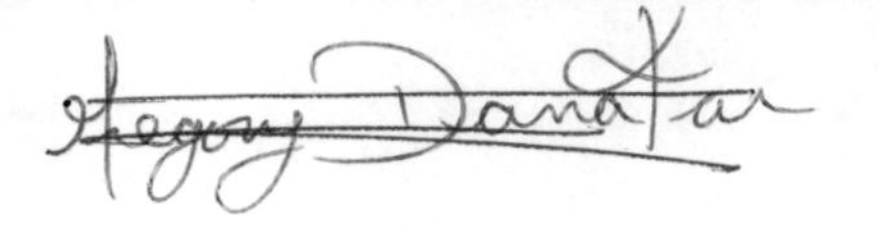

"Love the art in yourself
and not yourself in art."
— Stanislavski.

Cover design by Bryan Mills & Associates.

ISBN 0-920644-53-8 (hardcover); 0-920644-51-1 (softcover).

Part Three: Theatre of Action

Part Four: Appendices

Illustrations

Introduction

IN THE FALL OF 1975, I was approached about doing an oral history project for the government of Ontario. I was told that up until that time, the project had focussed on political figures. Now entering a new phase, the project — officially called the Ontario Historical Studies Series — would now include people in other areas of endeavour including the arts. Was I interested in organizing and conducting interviews in the theatre area?

The idea, I must admit, intrigued me enormously. My ignorance of all but the most well-known aspects of Canadian theatre history was equal to anyone's in the profession and probably much greater than many. Like others, I had worked for years under the delusion that the Canadian theatre had *really* only begun when I had become a part of it.

My own specific interest in the subject had been sparked the previous year at a University of Toronto conference called *Canadian Theatre Before the Sixties.* It was there I met Merrill Denison for the first time and it was there as well that I made my first contact with the unique theatre that had been attempted so many years before by Herman Voaden. As a result of that conference, the *Canadian Theatre Review* (which I edited) published a special issue on the subject. The issue seemed to strike similar chords of interest in others. I began realizing for the first time just how much we didn't know about what — and who — had come before.

I was eager therefore to improve my own understanding of our theatrical past and I simply couldn't resist the opportunity being presented to me. Over the next few weeks, I met with the OHSS people to agree on terms of reference. The project was to be open-ended and I was to interview one person per month, a number that proved to be wildly optimistic. The people to be interviewed could be of my own choosing though OHSS retained a kind of veto power if the subject was not felt to be of sufficient import. Each interview would be taped (the average length turned out to be about three hours), then transcribed, corrected by the subject and later deposited in the Ontario Public Archives. A researcher was hired to work with me — for the early interviews it was Forster Freed; for the later ones, Therese Beaupre — and we were encouraged to begin work as soon as possible.

Over the next four years, some two dozen interviews were carried out both in and outside of Ontario. It turned out to be extremely difficult to limit people in the arts to a single province. It also turned out to be one of the great learning experiences in my professional life. I often felt like Emily in Wilder's *Our Town* exclaiming after *her* chance to go back in time, "So all that was going on. . . ."

Among those interviewed were some who have since died — Earle Grey and Dora Mavor Moore. There were many others who were and still are quite active in our theatre scene — Herbert Whittaker, Mavor Moore, Donald Davis, Amelia Hall, George Luscombe, Robert Christie, Len Peterson, Jane Mallett, Paul Kligman. Others had moved through the years into related fields though retaining certain ties with the theatre — Lister Sinclair, Robertson Davies and Herman Voaden. Some had even left the country entirely — Bernard Slade and John Colicos among them.

Two who stood out from the others were Oscar and Toby Ryan, both of whom had been active in left wing, socially-rooted theatre work in the Depression era. Oscar, a member of Toronto's Progressive Arts Club and its Worker's Theatre, was, in fact, still active as a theatre critic for the *Canadian Tribune* (he wrote until recently under the pseudonym Martin Stone). Toby, a member of the Toronto Theatre of Action's original executive and active with the company as an actress until its dissolution, was working at the time of the interview in the area of developmental drama with inner city children.

Both, I think, were somewhat suspicious when I first contacted them. After all, why would a Canadian government agency want to give them an opportunity to put the record straight about their theatre activities and the unique relationship of those activities to Canadian society in the thirties, forties and fifties? Happily, trust was established. The interview took place in their apartment in the Annex area of downtown Toronto and, by the time we finished talking, almost five hours had passed.

We spoke of many things that day and many people. They told me of such things as the Red Squad and police harassment of theatrical activities in the thirties. They told me of men and women out of work all across the country coming together to produce pro-union plays such as Odets' *Waiting For Lefty* and anti-war plays such as Irwin Shaw's *Bury the Dead*. Perhaps even more interesting than the works themselves were the responses these works engendered in Canadian society at the time. One simply didn't say those sorts of things in polite society. Nevertheless, these things *were* said and they were said by many whose names subsequently became part of Canada's cultural establishment — Johnny Wayne, Frank Shuster, Lou Applebaum, Lou Jacobi, Basya Hunter, Ben Lennick, Sydney Newman, Syd Banks. We spoke too of the school they started for young actors and the name of one of their early instructors could not be ignored — Lorne Green.

In the years since that interview with Oscar and Toby, and its subsequent publication in severely edited form in *CTR*, a number of essays have appeared about Theatre of Action. But the full story of this fascinating group and this fascinating period has never really been told. For Theatre of Action and similar theatre companies in Vancouver, Winnipeg and Montreal were engaging their audiences in ways that had never been attempted before in this country.

Subsequently, Toby realized the need to fill in the details of this story and, thanks to a Canada Council grant, she travelled across Canada interviewing those who had shared in it. The result — *Stage Left: Canadian Theatre in the Thirties* — turns out to be a fascinating theatrical and social memoir which documents for the first time this most unique of Canadian theatrical episodes. It is at once a moving personal story and a rich history of a period and a theatrical movement that few people — in or out of our theatre — know or fully understand. It is a story that clearly needs to be told. It is also one which very much still needs to be heard.

Don Rubin
Toronto
October 1981

Preface

IN 1929, THE STOCK MARKET crashed on Wall Street. The whole world was affected by that dramatic event.

Within a couple of years, the Progressive Arts Club and the Workers' Theatre were born in Canada to give voice to the shock of mass unemployment and the misery it brought to millions of people.

Theatre of Action was part of this response and it provided a strong voice of awareness and hope during a period when people were finding ways to struggle against the worsening crisis, the rise of fascism, and the danger of world war.

Ten years later, in 1939, war was declared. It was this dramatic event that over-shadowed and eventually cut short the life of Theatre of Action. It is fitting somehow that such a theatre should be born at a very troublesome time in Canada, when the need for its positive contribution was important. By the same token, its demise took place when events of world proportion took precedence over any contribution a theatre might make.

In the years between those two major upheavals, Theatre of Action, as well as the progressive theatres in Vancouver, Winnipeg and Montreal, had a strong impact on their communities, on Canada's drama festivals and, generally, on people who were part of their audiences, or were involved in their productions.

I was part of those theatres and this book is my attempt to repay all that I gained from them. Because these groups grew from their time, this story is then both about the world I found myself in and the world of theatre in Canada in the thirties.

It was not an easy story to write. It took me, in fact, two years. In doing it I spoke to thirty-nine people in 1978 and 1979 and had the help of their recollections of the various theatres. I thank them for the time given me.

I wish also to express my thanks to the Explorations Program of the Canada Council and the Ontario Arts Council for their contribution to the research required in producing this memoir. I would also like to acknowledge the initial interest in this subject by the Ontario Historical Studies Series.

Last, but not least, my gratitude to my husband, Oscar, who encouraged me to undertake this project and gave me enormous assistance in its completion.

— T.G.R.

Part One:

A NEW KIND OF ARTS ORGANIZATION

I

An Important Decision

IN THE FALL OF 1929 there was "The Crash" on Wall Street — a suitably dramatic description of what was to affect millions of lives in the Western world for ten long years before the start of the second World War.

For me, at sixteen, that decade, while difficult, was nevertheless full of youthful excitement, activity, growth and great satisfaction.

I was part of a theatre movement which was new in form, progressive in outlook, socially aware of the times and of the need for reflection.

How did it happen that the daughter of an immigrant worker grew up with the strong conviction that a career in theatre was what she wanted most of all?

My parents, like so many immigrants, came to Canada to improve their lives — but more important, when children came along, to make sure that those children would be well-educated, that they would not spend their years in a shop. For me, that meant going to a commercial school to be trained as a white-collar office worker.

How could they know that by the time I graduated in 1929 it would be very hard to find a job? With some "pull," however, I did manage to get one. The salary? Ten dollars a week.

To understand my decision to be in the theatre, as well as my social conditioning, I have to go further back in time.

I grew up in Toronto. My father was a worker in the needle trades. An early union organizer, he understood the need for a union, especially for immigrants being employed in the many sweatshops. I became aware, early in my life, how hard a job and how dangerous it was to organize a union. I had only to listen to the conversations at home to know what was going on.

As the daughter of a union man, I also learned very early in life what strikes were about and what they meant for my family. We knew them as a time for belt-tightening. We couldn't have all the things we wanted. I don't remember being unhappy about the situation — it was just something we accepted. It was part of our background.

The rich cultural life we enjoyed compensated for what we might have lacked in material things. Besides, life was simpler for children when I was growing up. We made our own street games and we didn't need as many things to have fun.

One important element my parents did provide, and which was to play a major role in my future plans, was the enrollment in the Workmen's Circle school. As immigrants, they were determined to give their children an opportunity to enrich their education by sending them to a Jewish school to learn about history and literature in their parents' language.

The Workmen's Circle school was itself both socialist and secular in outlook. We developed a fine background in classical Yiddish literature and a firm grasp of Jewish history. On the other hand, there was no attempt to turn this into a chauvinistic or nationalistic view. On the contrary, we were encouraged to look on the world around us with a true internationalist spirit motivated by social awareness.

I recall a warm summer evening at the Pickering camp run by the Workmen's Circle school — the night of August 22, 1927. Sacco and Vanzetti had just been executed. We had been following their arrest and trial. Their execution was a deep emotional blow. All the campers and staff were assembled on the camp grounds and we formed a large chain circle. In song, movement and words we honored the two Italian immigrant workers who had been put to death in spite of massive world protests. That night we shed tears for two men we had never known. We felt their loss as though they had been close relatives.

The school also laid great emphasis on the arts as part of our enrichment. We had choir, folk dancing and — most important to me — a yearly concert for which we prepared dramatic presentations. That's where I discovered the excitement of theatre. That's where I learned to memorize lines in a play, to give recitations and readings, to stand on a stage and give enjoyment to an audience.

During that period, in fact, I was booked by various organizations to entertain (without fee, of course) at their functions. Usually, I would read and recite. I wasn't always happy doing this — I preferred being part of a play — but I did get a lot of experience with audiences at a young age. It must have gone over well. I was asked to perform again and again. Clearly, I was developing a strong love for what I was doing and I knew I wanted to pursue it further.

In addition to these early experiences on stage, I also attended the theatre. On most Saturday evenings in the winter, our family would go to the National, on Bay and Dundas or the Standard Theatre on Spadina, where leading Jewish companies from New York brought in a variety of theatrical fare. (My father refused to attend Friday night shows, but not for religious reasons. "All the butchers and storekeepers go on Friday!" he would say, scorning those merchants who were given free passes in exchange for displaying window posters).

The plays we saw ranged from Sholem Aleichem to Shakespeare, the poetic dramas of Hirshbein to Goldfadden's musical comedies. Maurice Schwartz (and his Art Theatre), Jacob Ben-Ami, Paul Muni, Jacob Adler (whose family later became important members of the Group Theatre in the States), Molly Picon and many, many other stars of the Yiddish theatre brought their companies to Toronto. Whole families fed hungrily on tragedy, comedy, intrigue and romance. And often they fed on cold chicken or salami too as their hearts broke and tears ran down their cheeks.

Since money was tight in our house, only three tickets were purchased for our family of five. My parents each had their own seat while my sister and I shared one. My brother, the baby of the family, took turns sitting on laps. Because it was cheapest, we always sat high up in the "gods," but I recall vividly how rivetted I was to the stage and how involved I became in what was being played so far down below.

Once I was actually invited backstage by a benign old character actor from the Standard who had previously visited our Workmen's Circle class. I stood entranced in his dressing room and witnessed the magical ritual as he applied make-up. The fragrance of the greasepaint seemed to me to be like ambrosia.

Of the plays I saw, I was especially affected by *The Dybbuk,* the classic Jewish play about the supernatural possession of a soul and its subsequent exorcism. It was a frightening drama for a young child and its spell stayed with me for quite some time. Despite this, I couldn't resist the strong urge to act out some of the more scary moments from time to time. At one point, we actually transformed our backyard into a theatre. For the performance, I draped myself in a white sheet and brought to life the possessed soul with a strange and eerie voice.

Another theatrical highlight of my childhood was seeing the Yiddish-language *King Lear*. I didn't grasp all its implications, but I was certainly caught up in the realistic storm, the high drama and the tragedy it portrayed.

My mother, however, took it another way and all the way home she expounded on the suffering that children bring to their parents. The whole experience left me with a conviction of how effective theatre can be — and of the marvellous emotional and intellectual effect it could have on people.

As I grew up, I knew that somehow I had to be in the theatre. It is interesting to note that of the group of senior students at the Workmen's Circle school, three of us — Eva Langbord, Paul Mann and I — did wind up in the theatre while another chose dance (Saida Gerrard), one became a sculptor (Helen Nelson) and her sister (Lillian) became a fine pianist. Among the others, there were also two social workers and a physician.

My interest in theatre was further crystallized in high school — playwright and director Herman Voaden was my English teacher and I looked forward to his classes with great excitement. Voaden through the years has made many contributions to Canadian theatre, but perhaps his finest was, indeed, as a teacher, particularly in introducing Shakespeare to students.

His approach to plays on the curriculum was always as a theatre person, a unique slant for that time. He departed from the usual practice of simply memorizing. He brought the plays to life. Each play was acted out in class, with stops for discussion of what we were saying, of what the lines meant, what the characters were doing.

We did that with *Romeo and Juliet* (in which I played the Nurse), *Julius Caesar* (in which I played Caesar because none of the boys would do it) and Goldsmith's *She Stoops to Conquer*. The two latter productions we did for other students at the school. We got to understand Shakespeare's language. More important, we came to know these plays as part of a living theatre tradition rather than as classics only to be read. What marvellous luck it was that Voaden, a truly creative teacher, should have been guiding me in this way when I was so close to making important decisions about my future.

Voaden became head of the English Department at Central High School of Commerce in 1928. Fifty years later, I read a piece that he wrote in which he said that he saw teaching as a mandate to try to win students to a love of the arts, particularly books and the theatre.

During my years in high school where I was prepared for office work, my life was enormously enriched not only by Voaden but by my own regular theatregoing. With my friends, I saw many of Shakespeare's plays at the Royal Alexandra starring Sir John Martin Harvey and his company of English actors. The Princess Theatre (now demolished) featured some new American plays (most memorably, a production of Eugene O'Neill's *Strange Interlude*). Locally, Vaughan Glazer ran a company at the old Victoria Theatre (also now gone). The Empire Theatre (vanished as well) imported a stock company which played a great number of plays in repertory. True, theatre was, for the most part, imported. There was little indigenous work then, except for the non-professional "little" theatres. At that time, most everything and everyone in the theatre was British or came from New York.

We also attended concerts. I heard Paul Robeson on one of his early visits to Toronto. It was a memorable occasion — so much so that we went backstage after to get the autograph of this handsome and impressive man.

Books too became a large part of my life — both prose and poetry. In addition to the classical Russian writers, I got to know the writing of Flaubert and Zola; of Galsworthy, Hardy and D.H. Lawrence. I was deeply affected by Romain Rolland's great novel, *Jean-Christophe*, the story of the development of a creative artist in a particular society; I discovered Thomas Mann, Theodore Dreiser, Sinclair Lewis, Upton Sinclair's revealing social studies (*The Jungle, King Coal, The Goose Step, Oil*).

My understanding of war was deepened when I read *Under Fire* by Henri

Barbusse; I was moved by the new Black poets of the United States — Langston Hughes, James Weldon Johnson and Paul Dunbar. All of this reading opened my mind to the world, to the people everywhere who suffered injustice, poverty and discrimination, and to the role of creative people who had so much of value to contribute to society.

The sum total of these experiences led me to pursue the theatre. I understood as well how important it was to study in a professional theatre school. Excellence required further development. At sixteen, I got my first job. I took it with the notion that I would work for a year, save a little money and go to New York to study. My friend Saida Gerrard, the dancer, had made a similar decision. We agreed to go to New York together.

Somehow, though, I had to break the news to my parents. I put it off as long as I could. I had no illusions about their reaction to my decision. Finally, however, the time arrived when I simply had to tell them. As I had suspected, there was an explosion. They could not understand why I would want to leave Toronto for wicked New York. As well, my wanting to be an actress was to them almost tantamount to becoming a fallen woman. They threatened, they argued and they fought me until the day I left.

In hindsight, I realize I must have had a very stubborn will and strong convictions. My parents couldn't and wouldn't support my decision. The little bit of money I had saved would not take me very far. None of that, though, seemed to matter at the time. I just had to try.

I had, in the interim, made inquiries about a theatre school in New York and discovered one that was not too expensive and which also offered part or full scholarships for theatre study. I wrote to the Workers' Theatrical Alliance (Artef, as it was called) and arranged to have an audition.

In the Fall of 1930 at the age of seventeen, I bought a bus ticket for New York. I arrived there, after a tiring trip, in time for my audition. I had an aunt in Brooklyn and she agreed to put me up for a while.

Why did I need to go to New York? The explanation is simple. There just were no schools of drama in Canada at the time. For young people in the thirties, the choice was to go to New York or to London, England. It was that clear.

II

New York City — Artef

ON THE DAY OF MY AUDITION I arrived at the Artef studio full of confidence. I had prepared one of my successful, memorized readings for the audition. I guess my ignorance and lack of maturity prevented me from feeling fright or nervousness.

The room I saw was not very large. Across one side was a long table with four or five people behind it. I only knew Benno Schneider, the director of the school and a former member of Stanislavski's Moscow Art Theatre.

After a preliminary interview about my background, education and financial condition, I was asked to perform. I started off with great zest. After all, I told myself, hadn't I entertained many audiences with this solo performance?

The reading I had chosen had some humorous moments. I remember hearing laughter. When I looked at Schneider, I saw a small smile on his face. I thought I was doing very well.

When I had finished, I was thanked warmly and told to call in two days for their decision. They were, of course, auditioning other candidates. I was confident, judging by their responses, that I would be accepted. I look back on that now as the sheer brashness of youth.

I spent the next two days just looking at New York. I had read and heard about the famous Times Square and Broadway and all the thoroughfares adjacent to that hub of theatre life, avenues of dreams for young hopefuls. I wandered down Fifth Avenue with its sumptuous stores and the streets branching out from it. I visited art galleries and museums, Carnegie Hall and the Metropolitan Opera House.

The complicated subway system, the traffic, the wall-to-wall people, the restaurants, stores and the flashing neon lights were all pretty heady stuff for a fairly sheltered 17-year-old from Toronto where, nights and Sundays, everything closed down.

As counterpoint to all this was the fact that it *was* 1930. The Depression had settled in. Unemployment had a firm grip on the city. On Sixth Avenue you could see large crowds of men and women, young and old, standing in front of the employment agency hoardings which advertised the few menial jobs that were available. (Of course, they got a cut from the job seekers when a job was found).

There were also the first appearances of apple-sellers on the streets. In spite of the toney restaurants and sumptuous stores, people crowded the Automat and Klein's department store on 14th Street for the bargains they offered. Generally, I thought the people looked frightened and more than a little shabby.

I reacted to what I saw with a mixture of excitement at the possibilities and some fear about how I would manage. On the whole, though, my youthful optimism took over. I knew that I had to get into the Artef school and that I had to start working. The rest would somehow work out.

In two days when I phoned Artef about the results of my audition, I was asked to come in and discuss it. I met Benno Schneider again and was told by him that they had accepted me. In view of my financial situation, and the fact that I was from out-of-town, they were prepared to let me take the courses without the usual fees. In return I would help the theatre with office work, as well as ushering at performances.

I was deliriously happy and accepted the offer eagerly. My schedule would be a full one. I would have two acting classes a week with Benno Schneider; a voice and diction class once a week with Sergei Radamsky, with great emphasis on choral speaking to develop color and vocal variety; modern dance movement once a week with Sophie Berenson; as well as seminars and discussions on theatre in modern society and how best it could reflect the times we lived in.

The acting classes were, of course, the most exciting. Here I got my first introduction to the Stanislavski school of acting. I was struck by how little I knew, how shallow and superficial my approach had been.

I discovered what a fine line there was between being an actor — exploring the truth and reality of a character in a dramatic situation — and being a show-off. It was a revelation for me. It was also extremely hard to undo my many bad stage habits.

Schneider, who I think enjoyed the challenge I presented, was a patient but persistent teacher who insisted on stripping away phony effects. I worked hard with him to achieve the degree of honesty he wanted, especially in the improvisations he set. He was hard to satisfy but he gave his students a standard by which to measure their work.

Schneider didn't make a gimmick of the techniques Stanislavski had developed to help actors (as was to happen later in New York when "The Method" got to be distorted and the butt of jokes). On the contrary, in Schneider's approach, technique was the tool to discover and explore true human emotion and how best to express it; a technique to help actors relate to each other in dramatic situations on stage so as to reveal the playwright's intention clearly and honestly.

When we began scriptwork, all of this came together for the most important reason: to give audiences the finest emotional and intellectual experience possible in the theatre. I was fortunate to have this experience so early in my theatrical education.

As students in the Artef school we were welcome to attend rehearsals of the acting company and to see our work taken further by professional actors. As a bonus, from time to time, some of us were given the opportunity to perform in productions needing crowds, or in small roles that Schneider felt we were ready to handle.

It was fascinating to see him at work on a play. In addition to his fine, solid work with actors on characterization, he was a thoroughly creative director. He stylized his productions where it was right to do so with movement and unusual stage pictures. His forte was satire, in which he was able to stylishly underscore the pretensions of the East European *nouveau riches* in such plays as Sholem Aleichem's *200,000* and *The Aristocrats.*

Yegor Bulichev and *Dostigayev* by Maxim Gorki were filled with extraordinarily fine character studies of Old Russia and beautifully orchestrated ensemble acting. In addition to modern Soviet plays, this company also did modern American pieces such as *Drought* by Hallie Flanagan, *Jim Copperhead* by Godiner, *The Third Parade* by Charles Walker and Paul Peters, *Haunch, Paunch and Jowl* by Samuel Ornitz, Beinesh Steiman's *At The Gate,* and Cherner's *In The Roar of Machines.*

In addition to the strong ensemble work of the acting company, Schneider nearly always employed music and dance as part of his directorial style. In Solotaroff he found a fine designer who brilliantly enhanced the work on stage.

Always this theatre and its director underscored the social place of theatre in the struggles of people both past and present. Thus my education in Artef included not only theatre training but an education in social consciousness as well.

My theatre studies were hard work and time-consuming — but I thrived on them. Apart from that, my life in New York was difficult. I was scrambling for part-time work as a typist to earn enough at least for food. I had fortunately made some close friends who shared their meagre accommodation with me, but I also had to eat. Most of the time my diet consisted of *Oh Henry* bars — filling but fattening. Occasionally I ate a cheap meal in the Automat or cheese-and-nut sandwiches at Nedicks or Chock-Full-O'Nuts. Being invited out for a real meal at someone's home or in a restaurant was a great celebration. Unfortunately, when this did happen I discovered that the meals were generally too rich; I couldn't absorb them well.

It's hard to describe the psychological effect of being poor and living in New York during the Depression. Luxury lived side by side with poverty. And the wealth of theatre was certainly not financially accessible. Yet, the desire to see the many plays available exerted tremendous pressure.

When I didn't have money, I could only yearn for a chance to go to Carnegie Hall and hear all the world-famous artists and orchestras. One theatre critic for whom I did some typing invited me to the theatre occasionally. My voice teacher presented me with a ticket to the Metropolitan Opera (high up in "the gods") and it was a grand opportunity to visit this famous opera house where I saw a production of *Wozzek*.

These windfalls provided some enrichment to my personal life. On the whole, though, everyday living was a struggle, aggravated by the extremes of unattainable good living that New York offered.

My social awareness was certainly sharpened considerably when I found a job in a ribbon factory. I had heard my father describe the word "sweatshop" but had no actual experience to define what it meant. I arrived at a loft in which the smell of glue was overpowering. The loft was claustrophobic and an obvious fire trap. The man who owned the factory was old and very bad-tempered and thought nothing of showing it. When I arrived, he made it clear to me that he was doing me a great favor by hiring me.

He took me into a large, smelly, dirty space where I saw young men and women working. Some were my own age; all were terrified to take their eyes off their work. Some stood in front of machines where the ribbons were cut; others rolled ribbons on cardboard spools and pinned the ends down. Hours to be worked: 8 in the morning to 5:30 in the afternoon with a half-hour for lunch. Lunch had to be eaten in the shop. I was shown the washroom, a disgrace even in the most backward country. The boss darted in and out of the shop all the time watching everyone. Going to the washroom seemed like committing a criminal offense.

I was living then in Brighton Beach, a section of Brooklyn. In order to report for work on time, I had to be up at 6. Subway cars were crowded with people half asleep, pressed together in mutual distaste.

For me, this was a particular ordeal because evenings were busy with theatre classes. I would arrive home very late at night and find it almost impossible to wake in the morning. Then to watch ribbons coming through roller machines. It was inevitable that I would doze off. Some of the ribbon would inevitably get caught in the roller. When this happened, the boss had such a tantrum that it seemed he would have a stroke on the spot.

I put up with it for a while, but then came the fateful day when I had been humiliated and shouted at once too often. I just didn't care anymore. I shouted back and told him what he could do with his job. Of course I was fired. I looked around at all my co-workers whose faces reflected the pleasure they felt at my daring. It was as though I had shouted back for all of them. That was small comfort for me. Still . . .

The experience, however, was a valuable one. I now knew something of the exploitation and humiliation suffered by workers who stood alone. They really had nothing to put against the power of an employer. It was a great education in social awareness and one which I have never forgotten.

III

New Year's Eve — 1930-1931

FOR SOME STRANGE REASON which I cannot now recall, I found myself alone on the one night of the year when you want to be with people you care about. What to do? I checked my finances: I had just over two dollars.

I knew I couldn't just sit in a room all evening. I thought carefully. I had read about New Year's Eve on Times Square. A subway ride and back would cost ten cents. A ticket to a midnight show at one of the movie houses there would be a dollar. I might even be able to treat myself to a box of popcorn. My decision was made.

I went by subway to Times Square. As I came out of the station, I could believe neither my eyes nor my ears. The noise was deafening. I had never seen so many human beings together in one place before in my life. Cars and people all mixed up together. Horns honking, bells ringing, noise-makers chattering non-stop. The neon lights made the square seem as bright as daytime.

I suddenly realized that in that sea of humanity, I probably didn't know a single person.

When the Times Building clock struck twelve, the noise, which had been deafening, became impossible. People were hugging and kissing and hopping up and down to greet the new year.

I have never felt so sad and miserable as I did at that moment. The phrase "alone in the crowd" had specific meaning for me. Nor could I see, at that moment, why I should celebrate this new year. My prospects were none too hopeful.

I pushed my way across the square to a movie theatre — any one would do. The picture was *Dr. Jekyll and Mr. Hyde*. The midnight showing was about to begin. I bought my ticket, went in, got my box of popcorn and made my way to a seat in the dark house. As the film began, sitting there in the dark, I began to cry. It came effortlessly. The whole evening somehow meshed together in that dark theatre and the tears just came.

It was now 1931 . . .

As part of the Artef detachment that year, I paraded on May Day, the traditional workers' holiday and ended up at Union Square for a program and speeches. It was there I saw Prolet-Bühne, the German agit-prop theatre which had come to visit New York. John Bonn, the director of the group, later became an active leader of the New Theatre League in the States. I was fascinated with this company and its techniques.

The performance by this small acting troupe was fascinating to me. Their theatre was completely mobile. They wore a basic neutral costume adding props and bits of clothing for each characterization. Their mass recitations were beautiful and well expressed their feelings. They spoke directly to the large audience about the then current social problems. The theatricality and emotional impact were quite exceptional. Audiences in return, responded spontaneously and with feeling.

This New York appearance by Prolet-Bühne — and several additional performances I saw later — shed light for me on a new and dynamic form of theatre. The experience certainly helped broaden my own view of the stage as a potent instrument for change and a voice through which one could reach and affect people.

At that time, the place for young actors waiting for their big chance was Walgreen's Drug Store on Broadway. I visited several times and, sure enough, it was always full of young men and women still in theatre school, or just graduated, discussing which producer was casting for what. As we sat there over cups of coffee, rumor flew from table to table. When any news surfaced for even the smallest walk-on, there would be a dash for the telephone — everyone scrambling to get there first.

Somehow, though, I couldn't get caught up in the race. I had neither the aggressiveness nor the desire to push my way into that hard and unfeeling theatre atmosphere. I had already absorbed, through my training, a different attitude to what theatre was about. I felt alien — or was it Canadian? — in that milieu. But what was it I wanted?

I was beginning to find out at Artef as I watched the acting company there building a theatre for workers despite great financial hardships. It was a theatre to make them laugh, and, at the same time, to make them aware of their strength and purpose in a period of economic hardship and social ferment. I began to appreciate how important and necessary this theatre was.

At about the same time, sparked by left-wing magazines, arts workers generally were beginning to speak directly about conditions of life around them. The Depression and the social misery it caused were subjects for new writers, many developing new techniques, who spoke for social change; artists and cartoonists who portrayed reality in exciting new ways; theatres and dance companies using new techniques to entertain as well as to sharpen awareness.

As my own economic condition became more desperate, the need to return home grew stronger. My love for — and desire to be part of — theatre remained undiminished. What had been added was the excellent training I had received at Artef, both theatrical and intellectual. I had absorbed much in a short time and I knew what I wanted to do on my return to Toronto.

IV

Toronto — Depression and Repression

CITIES, I HAVE FOUND, never look their best in the gray, cold winter. My home town was no exception in the Depression year 1932.

At first, I felt disoriented; I had been away for several years and busily occupied. Suddenly, here I was with lots of time on my hands. I was living with my parents again and my immediate needs were being looked after. I didn't seek work — I had to have time to adjust. I had, on the other hand, lost contact with the old friends who had remained here.

For a while I just walked, revisiting familiar places, trying to get my bearings. It was damp, it was cold. Dirty snow lay around in mounds. People moved quickly on the streets, bundled up and curled up in themselves to keep warm. The lines of men waiting for a meal at the Scott Mission were longer than usual.

It was while taking a short-cut through Queen's Park, from College Street to Bloor, that I became aware of an unusually large crowd. Many were holding banners. On the stone base of one of the statues a man was making a speech. Suddenly, the sound of motors, masses of men — on foot, on horseback, on motorcycles — converged on the crowd and on the speaker.

Frightened, I ran to the first tree I could find and stood behind it, hoping I wouldn't be seen. Police on horseback did not discriminate between those attending the meeting and those who just happened to be in the park at the moment.

It was at that moment that a frantic woman, holding her baby, joined me under the tree. The motorcycles continued to roar while people screamed and jumped to get out of the way. Police on foot continued to swing their clubs. As my fear mounted, a policeman galloped toward us, then, at the last minute, pulled in the reins. His horse reared up within inches of my face. The woman beside me was shrieking hysterically, her baby crying.

Having achieved his purpose, the policeman galloped off to repeat the performance elsewhere. It was a scene I couldn't easily forget.

As the Depression deepened, the unemployed began to organize and speak up in ever larger numbers, urging governments to act on their behalf. This was invariably met with harassment and harsh repression. I began to feel that it was time for me to add my voice to the sound of the times. I was nineteen years old.

One of the first people I met at the time was an artist named Avrom Yanovsky and we became very close friends. I spent a great deal of time in his College Street front room which served also as a studio.

Avrom was becoming rather well-known for his extremely clever political cartoons in various labor papers. He also sketched and painted. On the walls of the room were drawings of the many people he knew or who had visited him.

I asked a lot of questions about happenings in Toronto and the people pictured on his walls. I got to know a fair number this way, including Oscar Ryan, later my husband. As Avrom talked, he usually held a charcoal stick in his hand and sketched rapidly. I still have a sketch of me he drew one afternoon.

Many years later, he talked about the Police Department's "Red Squad," and how they would come to labor meetings watching and listening. And once, Avrom was picked up by the police.

"I was coming from the Canadian Labor Defense League office," he said. "I was doing cartoons for their publication, *The Labor Defender*, and I was on my way home. As I turned the corner at Spadina to go along College Street where my house was, one of those little old cars with a canvas top pulled up and there were members of the Red Squad in it. They asked me to get in and I was taken to the Police Station. They took me into a special room and on the walls they had 'trophies' of things they had taken away from meetings.

"They searched me and took out of my pockets clippings, as well as a typewritten copy of the Negro work song, *Water Boy*. They threatened me with eight years in prison. I kept thinking they would beat me. They did question me, particularly about the typewritten song which was on onion-skin paper. They examined it very closely, looking for 'something secret.' They kept that.

"I then told them I had to get home for supper as I had to go somewhere else afterwards. When one of them asked where I was going I told them there was an opening at the Art Gallery and I had an invitation. He muttered, 'You artists stick together.'"

In our talks together he also told me of a new arts organization of which he was a member — the Progressive Arts Club. He thought I would meet some interesting people and find the discussions worthwhile. I agreed to go along with him to a meeting in a room the club rented in an attractive old three-storey house near the Grange.

What was the Progressive Arts Club? Oscar Ryan, an editor, author and theatre critic, was one of the founders. He recalled that during the late twenties, a number of people had been saying, "Wouldn't it be great if we had something positive to counter the current cultural climate?" That was around the time of *The Crash.*

"In the early thirties we began to do something a little more positive and the Progressive Arts Club (PAC) was formed in 1931 by a small group of interested people.

"We were ambitious. We wanted to cover every area of the arts. But at the beginning it was largely a discussion group. We talked about writing, about literature and poetry and the graphic arts and theatre. We formed a writers' group and read each other's manuscripts and discussed them. We invited lecturers from time to time to discuss trends in Canadian literature. Prof. Felix Walter was one speaker and he spoke about Meteorological Poetry, something detached from life. We attracted such people as Dorothy Livesay, the poet, and Stan Ryerson, the historian, and Ed Cecil-Smith, the Toronto newspaperman who later commanded the Mac-Paps in Spain.

"We held well-attended gatherings on Saturday afternoons and Sunday evenings. We attracted musicians, sculptors, painters and dancers.

"Among those who joined PAC were Cecil-Smith's wife, Lillian, and his friend David Hogg, and Norm Bowles, a cheese salesman who wrote protest plays on the side and acted in them.

"We had a fairly interesting cross-section of young Canadian artists, including better-established people who were sympathetic, like Florence Wyle and Frances Loring. Most interested were the younger artists — Helen Nelson and Sam Kagan, both sculptors; and Avrom Yanovsky and Richard Taylor, the celebrated *New Yorker* cartoonist; and quite a few others from the Toronto area.

"Those who came together in PAC were dissatisfied with the established cultural values of the country. We felt that literature, the graphic arts, theatre, etc., were merely reflections, and usually imports, from the United States and Great Britain.

"We thought two things — one, that we would like to see a more genuine Canadian reflection in the arts. But even more, because of the times we were living in, we especially wanted a more radical, a more basic outlook by artists, a more critical attitude to the society we lived in — and we didn't find such a viewpoint too prevalent. We felt that too few culturally active people were interested in social questions.

"Since this was the period immediately after the outbreak of the crisis — the big Depression — we thought it was terribly important to call attention to what was happening in our country and to encourage existing art workers, especially the young, to speak up.

"At first, PAC met in private homes. Later, when we had attracted sufficient membership to raise some rent money, we took a studio in a building now long ago razed, on Grange Avenue, behind the Art Gallery, on the top floor of a three-storey house. We had one of the larger rooms, where we met for discussion and lectures once or twice a week. (Another tenant, who occupied a studio on the second floor, was the musician and later orchestra conductor, Paul Sherman. He occasionally attended our meetings).

"As a practical way to express our views and attract wider interest, we started *Masses*, a national monthly printed magazine. Some twelve issues were published between 1932 and 1934. I was associated with it until the latter part of 1933. (I recall writing its first editorial, *We Present Our Credentials*).

"We carried discussions on esthetics in a fairly down-to-earth fashion, debated art viewpoints and printed good pictures, cartoons and illustrations, mostly linoleum cuts. Play scripts were printed, books were reviewed, and so on. We attracted people who were not 'signed-up' members, but who wrote for *Masses* and sometimes expressed views that didn't always jibe with those of the editors.

"Associated with the magazine at that time were the authors of a number of short plays — Stanley Ryerson, Frank Love, Ed Cecil-Smith, Dorothy Livesay, myself, Norm Bowles. We had national circulation in the principal Canadian cities and in some smaller ones. Our sales were modest, but we obviously created some interest, because it was the first magazine of its kind that I know of to be published in Eastern Canada."

Another person I spoke to in preparing these memoirs was Frank Love, electrician, trade unionist and author. In the thirties, he was out of work and on welfare. Nevertheless, he was very active in his union.

"I was taking an English course at the University of Toronto," he told me, "and a professor asked us to write some essays. I had attended a meeting in Queen's Park where Tim Buck was supposed to speak. I didn't know who Tim Buck was, but anybody that was advocating change — *that* I was in favor of.

"So we went down, another fellow and I, to the park to see. And, of course, Tim wasn't allowed to speak. He never got into the park, but we got out. We were driven out by the police. I wrote an essay on it, just as an exercise for the professor. Then I wrote another one, about the mounted police too, and the professor read them to the class. Somebody got up in the classroom and said, 'Nobody in this class could have written that.'

"Later, still out of work, I started to write a short story. I think I did publish one in *Masses*. The professor called me down, asked what I was trying to do and I said, 'Well, I might start writing, might earn a dollar.' So he told me that I had the touch, that I had the gift of expression there and I should keep on writing.

"Later, I met a fellow at the university, and I think it was he that led me to the Progressive Arts Club. We met in a house for quite a while. We would write something and you could read it there for approval. The idea was that others would criticise and tell you how to improve it.

"I don't remember exactly how I came to write the play, *Looking Forward*. I must have been asked to write it for the hunger march about to take place. The message was to be about unemployment insurance. It was to be taken on a trip to Ottawa and on the way it would be played in a hall, the back of a truck, on the ground, wherever the tour stopped. The idea was to build up the march.

"Apparently it was very successful. I remember Ed Smith telling me that in Gananoque it was presented in a hall and that it was very, very successful. The people there had never seen a live play and they loved it.

"The situation in *Looking Forward* was that the family — mother, father and daughter — were on welfare. The daughter had a boy-friend and he was a radical. He had influenced the daughter and their argument was that unemployment insurance was a necessity. They wouldn't have to be on welfare.

"At that time, welfare was very skimpy. You went down to the welfare office, and they gave you a bag of groceries and you carried it home — five or six miles, wherever you had to go.

"The play showed the father completely discouraged, but the daughter was after him to go out and advocate unemployment insurance on the street corners, or to organize the unemployed.

"The unemployed were organizing at that time, they had associations in various parts of the country. The best organization of the unemployed was in East York, a new Toronto suburb. Immigrants had settled there. The organization had about 600 members and I attended several of their meetings.

"I never saw the play till it was about six months old, when it was shown before the East York workers in one of the schools. I got a great laugh out of it because of the way it was presented. It ended up with a sort of a big laugh. I got the point across and everybody went home happy.

"I realize now that it was a straight propaganda play. I mean there wasn't much character work in it. They were real characters, but they didn't talk, you might say, in a normal manner. The actors had only a short time to get the message across. The daughter was an advocate of insurance and the father — he was an advocate of 'Drop dead'. But you have some of the same attitude today. There are people who say, 'What the hell difference does it make what I do? It's not going to change anything.' There were people like that then too.

"I think the audience felt they were real, all right. They saw themselves on the stage. Most of the people in the audience were out of work, or so close to being out of work that a lot of them were on welfare. They were just going through that themselves and they didn't consider it a propaganda play.

"I think the real success of *Looking Forward* was because there were real people in it. Up until that time, the Workers' Theatre had concentrated on the mass recitation, which was very, very effective. This play had real people on the stage.

"At that time in Canada the theatre was almost non-existent, nor were there many Canadian plays. So *Looking Forward* was one of the first Canadian plays to deal with a mass problem of the Canadian people."

V

A New Kind of Arts Organization

I WAS EXCITED BY MY CONTACT with the Progressive Arts Club. I met some very interesting people there. They were eager to pioneer a new kind of arts organization. Here, I felt, was the logical place to start a theatre — a social theatre that would reflect the times, that would contribute, in a theatrical way, to the protest movements then developing for civil rights, for jobs, for unemployment insurance, for union organization.

Once this idea crystallized in my mind, the group I immediately thought of, and which had left such a deep impression on me, was Prolet-Bühne. It became clear to me that this was not a time for a theatre in a special building, waiting for audiences to come and see plays. The times called for a theatre which would, as PAC was clearly doing, *go to its audiences* and speak to them directly about what was going on and what they could do about it.

The Depression not only affected workers in their jobs. It was so all-pervasive that even the students on the campuses joined the battles for a better future. At the University of Toronto, the newly-formed Students' League took part in awakening protest movements. Out of this socially-aware student organization came Jim (actually Jean) Watts, Dorothy Livesay and Stanley Ryerson. They had some student theatre experience and were anxious to become part of it.

Thus, this nucleus, and some additional young men and women, became the Workers' Experimental Theatre. In the writers' group of PAC, we now had people ready and anxious to provide plays suitable for a mobile theatre for the times.*

The Workers' Experimental Theatre (soon abbreviated to Workers' Theatre) had very little organization. All of us acted, directed, collected props, built and painted whatever little scenery there was, scrounged rehearsal space.

**See* Eight Men Speak and Other Plays of the Canadian Workers' Theatre *published by New Hogtown Press, Toronto, 1976.*

We had no money but many good friends and helpful organizations who wanted to see our theatre flourish. The Ukrainian Labor-Farmer Temple Association (ULFTA) on Bathurst Street welcomed us to their hall for rehearsals. Sometimes we could use their stage. It was not always available as the organization had a tremendous cultural program of its own which included music, dance and theatre.

When the stage was not available we used a dressing-room downstairs. Unfortunately, it was close to the men's washroom. It got to be very funny after a while to have our very serious dialogue about war, about unemployment, punctuated by flushing toilets and a small audience of bewildered men who couldn't imagine what we were so intense about. Nevertheless, we were deeply grateful to the organization for giving up some of their space to us.

The Jewish Labor League had a hall on Brunswick Avenue. They, too, helped us by allowing us to use their quarters from time to time. We rehearsed in large rooms in private homes. We used any available space we could find, providing it was free. In this way we built our repertoire of short plays and mass recitations and prepared them for performance.

We borrowed some ideas, at first, from the Prolet-Bühne. They were an excellent prototype for what we wanted to accomplish. In this sense, my seeing this fine troupe in New York helped Workers' Theatre to aim for high standards of presentation. We later created some of our own techniques to suit our situation.

Our actors wore simple black pant-and-blouse outfits, to which were added pieces of costume (hats, kerchiefs, aprons, gloves, etc.), to identify specific characters. We constructed flexible one-piece stage settings which could be put up quickly anywhere (and were portable) to identify locale. We had small props, which actors could handle easily and which helped the audience to identify character and situation (wooden rifles, canes, four wooden poles which could be turned into a prison cell, etc.). This made our theatre extremely mobile and one that could be taken anywhere on short notice.

We played in workers' halls, outdoors on trucks or on bandstands in parks. We played for trade unions, Workers' International Relief, the unemployed councils, Canadian Labor Defense League branches, Labor League, Ukrainian, Finnish, Macedonian and other ethnic organizations, May Day celebrations, concerts of cultural enrichment.

We charged a nominal fee for performances, just enough to cover expenses.

On the whole, we were kept very busy and participants found it exciting to pioneer this very special social theatre for a very special time.

A little extra spice was added to our rehearsals when they were visited frequently by three hefty men in overcoats and fedoras who stood at the back and watched us at work. It was fairly easy to identify them as police. At first, these visits were rather intimidating, as they were meant to be, but as time went on we simply accepted the harassment as a fact of life in the thirties.

Workers' Theatre was a truly collective effort, pooling all the creative resources we had. One person, though, stood out for her drive and commitment to this social theatre — Jim Watts.

Organizer, director, actress, spark-plug, Jim Watts was an unusual and dynamic young woman. This is how Jocelyn Moore, a close friend from university days, remembers Jim before her association with Workers' Theatre:

"She was in Medical School then. Afterwards she transferred out. We used to frequent a little lunchroom called Charlotte's Coffee Shop, down in the basement on St. George Street. I think perhaps I met her there. Dee Livesay was a year or two ahead of me, but she was still around at college. Stan Ryerson and others in the group, I somehow got to know them.

"I was drawn to them by the fact that I was very young and ignorant of their point of view. I can't remember how I became so friendly with Jim, but we just sort of clicked, I guess. I learned a great deal from her and she really taught me lots. I guess she enjoyed teaching me.

"Actually, the basis of our friendship over the years was that I was one of the few people who did not resent taking money and presents from her. I don't mean actual money, but she had this thing about having inherited money that she always called her 'unearned increment' and she had a kind of unreasonable need to give it away. Most of her friends, being poor and sensitive, couldn't take this. But I was quite rational about it. If it gave her pleasure to buy me an expensive book, then I was delighted to have it. I let her do it.

"I can remember rebelling once; this was sometime after I was married. She came into the house and I was waxing the floor with a hand waxer. She said, 'Oh, you can't go on like that — you've got to have an electric waxer.' I put my foot down and told her, 'I will not have an electric waxer. I can wax the floor very nicely. It's good exercise and I can't afford an electric waxer. I will not accept a gift of an electric waxer.' Even that did not break up our friendship.

"Jim was terribly attractive to everybody, not only in a feminine way. Men were always falling in love with her, but women liked her too, though they tended to shy away from her a little because she was different from other girls. She had so much of everything. I don't mean just money, but personality and looks and drive. She was strong in her convictions, but with an underlying insecurity too. The two were very much intertwined in her personality.

"I remember when she and Lon Lawson went to New York to study. When they came back she talked about it all the time. She went on about (Elia) Kazan, she had taken classes from him, so she was really serious. She talked a great deal about how we must do the same thing here.

"I also recall when Jim left the theatre to go to Spain, it might have been in 1936 or 1937. She joined the ambulance unit (organized by Norman Bethune) as a driver. She was a very experienced driver and that was to be her role. Having had a sort of pre-med course, I guess it would have been natural for her to think along those lines. I was trying to sort that out in my mind. I know she did send some articles from there as well, to both *New Frontier* and the *Daily Clarion*. I know she was in France for at least half a year, maybe more, working with Spanish refugees.

"Jim always had an apartment on campus and entertained a lot. Sunday brunches and things like that. All the most interesting professors, and a lot of the most interesting older students came. To be a member of that group was really something.

"I was in an awful lot of those, which made me realize not only what a terribly attractive person she was, and I mean attractive in the sense of drawing people in, but how much they valued her. They competed for invitations. Both Earl Birney and Roy Daniels were around a lot, brilliant young men. Jim shared these important people with her friends."

My own recollection of Jim is of a very dear friend and close colleague. I can still see this tall, slender, blonde young student with the expressive, piercing brown eyes as we planned and worked together in the Workers' Theatre. Whenever things looked just too difficult to cope with, Jim supplied that extra vitality to push ahead. We saw eye-to-eye on most creative and practical steps, with her sense of humor playing a large part in clearing up any disagreements that might arise.

Her generosity, both personally and to the theatre we were pioneering, was remarkable. On a personal level, I recall especially the fine Sunday brunches at her small but beautiful apartment on Elgin Avenue. You got to it by walking up a small driveway, where there was an outside staircase leading to the floor above. At the top of the stairs you stepped onto a lovely, cool veranda, with vines and plants all around for privacy.

Her apartment, though not lavish, was tastefully and comfortably furnished.

There was usually something to drink and the scrambled eggs, or bacon and eggs, always seemed more appetizing in these surroundings. There was good talk, some laughter and, many times, important discussions and dreams for the future. Sometimes other members of the PAC were invited, sometimes some special friends from college. Jim was always a most efficient and marvelous hostess.

I recall staying overnight at her apartment. That was particularly pleasurable for me. I was living in a furnished room, where having a bath once a week was a luxury, particularly when the landlady decided to turn off the hot water because she felt you had used enough. How luxurious to stay at Jim's apartment where you could have a bath and a shower!

When Workers' Theatre planned its various tours, it was Jim's car (a small coupe with rumble seat) we used to transport actors and props. It was Jim who rented and paid for the first office we occupied at 989 Bay Street so we could have some sort of basic headquarters.

When David Pressman, our first professional director, came to Toronto to teach Summer School, Jim invited him to stay at her cottage in Rouge Hills, where she made him comfortable. Many of her friends, including my husband and I, were invited for weekends — a refreshing oasis away from the city's hot summer. She was very sensitive to people's needs and offered hospitality without fanfare and with great good humor.

Jim prepared herself for her work in the theatre by travelling to New York in the fall of 1934 to take classes at New Theatre School. When she returned to Toronto a year and a half later, she introduced *Waiting For Lefty* to Toronto audiences.

Jim joined the Canadian Women's Army Corps as a driver in 1940. She did some teaching at Ste. Anne de Bellevue and was subsequently commissioned a lieutenant. She served as personnel officer at the Kingston army base.

It is interesting to note that in her later years she devoted her time, as a member of the Voice of Women, to the battle against militarism and for peace in the world.

I pay this special tribute to Jim because she was such a driving force in the whole social theatre movement in this country. I know we could not have succeeded as we did without her ability and creativity. It seems a terrible injustice that she died comparatively young and couldn't take part in this memoir, as she should have. It should rightfully have been told by both of us, and I sorely miss her.

In telling this story now, I am therefore also honoring the person who gave so much of herself to the times in which she lived, and especially to the theatre which was such an integral part of those times.

Reports on the activities of Workers' Theatre in Toronto appeared most frequently on the pages of *Masses,* the magazine of the Progressive Arts Club. Its June 1932 issue, for instance, reported:

"Workers' Experimental Theatre of PAC gave its first performance. The play presented was *Deported,* a realistic play depicting a family of foreign-born workers, celebrating the betrothal of their eldest son, when they are served notice they are to be deported as charges of the State."

The same issue also mentioned a short play we did called *Solidarity, Not Charity* on June 3, 1932, "in aid of Workers' International Relief."

And from *Masses,* December 1932 issue:

"During the past month, Workers' Theatre of PAC gave a performance of mass recitation, *Theatre — Our Weapon*, at a PAC social, as well as a short play, *Relief*, a satire on the devious ways of charity organizations in distributing their funds. The following week at a concert arranged by the United Workers' Association in Mount Dennis, the Workers' Theatre of PAC gave three plays and two mass recitations."

Enthusiasm for Workers' Theatre plays grew in Toronto as the group's repertoire expanded. Our reception encouraged us to attempt a tour of the Niagara Peninsula. Here was a new audience, many of whom had never seen any live theatre. More particularly, we would bring them a social theatre with a challenge that spoke directly to their concerns.

We chose St. Catharines, Port Colborne, Thorold, Welland and Niagara Falls. Letters were dispatched to interested labor organizations and by the summer of 1933 we were able to start our travels.

Five actors (Jim Watts, Percy Mathews, J.P. Smith, myself and Izzy Levine) plus Avrom Yanovsky, plus props and other necessary materials and clothes, were jammed into the battered roadster owned by Jim. She loved the little car. Affectionately and almost apologetically, she had christened it Jesus Chrysler.

Ours was a unique, explorative touring company, a small group of "strolling players," plus the artist-cartoonist-designer-muralist, Avrom, whose light, incisive and comic chalk-talks charmed audiences everywhere we went.

What was a chalk-talk? Avrom himself described it best.

"You have an upright easel on the stage, a large one, with a large board on it, maybe two feet by three feet, with sheets of newsprint on it, and lecturer's chalk — one-inch-thick sticks of charcoal.

"I had prepared in my mind humorous cartoons of political events and I talked about each one. My habit was to combine it with a play on words — puns.

"I originally got the idea from the Canadian cartoonist, Bengough, from the early time of Sir John A. MacDonald. Bengough used to tour Canada at that time doing chalk-talks. I picked up an old book, a reprint, where he talked about doing chalk-talks and how he did them. I studied it and that's what really gave me the idea.

"At the time, I used to get a lot of typewritten or mimeographed material from New York from the John Reed Club, where William Gropper explained his chalk-talks.

"It was that, plus Bengough's book in Canada, that gave me the idea. Bengough also published a magazine called *Grip*. He did cartoons on political life in Canada. I picked up a copy in an old bookshop."

We played, for the most part, in workers' halls — some with a proscenium stage and backstage facilities, others with just a slight rise from the floor platform. Everywhere the people in charge of these halls greeted us warmly when we arrived to set up and rehearse our program. They stayed to help in any way they could to make the performance as effective as possible.

For many of our ethnic audiences, our visit was the first experience with a theatre doing English plays that were direct and contemporary.

As a travelling troupe without funds, we depended on local people to put us up and feed us and this was one of the more delightful aspects of our tour. We got to know and were treated royally by many kind, warm people in the cities we visited, people who often were on relief themselves but shared their food with us and gave up the most comfortable bed in the house. They were delighted to entertain the young roaming actors. We were very touched by their hospitality.

For Jim, I think, this was a very special experience. She had never come into such close contact with ordinary working people. I recall the first night she and I shared a room in a Ukrainian home. We climbed into an ample bed and under a mountainous, soft featherbed such as many Europeans enjoy. But it was summer and very warm. The two of us, practically submerged under this down-soft cover, laughed most of the night every time we realized what a picture we must have made with just our heads showing from the billows of bedclothes.

For our late supper that evening we were honored guests. We were treated to large bowls of thick cabbage soup and delicious black bread and butter, plus a very tasty home-made coffee cake for dessert. My background had prepared me for the lovely meal. But for Jim this repast was a first and I must say she enjoyed it thoroughly. All these pleasant experiences made us feel truly like a roving people's theatre.

It was summer. All of us enjoyed the outdoors. As we went from city to city, we would stop near water, have a swim and do a little sunbathing, then continue on our way refreshed. The memory of the six of us, working and playing together, and the receptions we were given, on and offstage, are still fresh and pleasurable.

One of the highlights of this tour was our participation in a cannery workers' strike, while we were playing St. Catharines. The workers were, for the most part, immigrant women whose wages and working conditions were pretty dreadful. Union organization was the issue and most labor bodies in the city were supporting the strikers. Since jobs were scarce, the company was able to recruit scabs to replace striking cannery workers.

An appeal was made at the concert where we performed for support for that night's picket line to block the entrance to the factory. The plan was to move a freight car in front of it so that the strike-breakers would be prevented from entering.

We had already entertained the women on the picket line with some of our plays. The police had been out and had watched our performance. After the concert we too responded to the appeal for help and joined that night's picket line. We were later taken to the police station and given a strict deadline to leave town. The police criticized Jim Watts for being there because she was a university student who "should have known better." We were all questioned, but they really went after Jim.

The next morning we read that the mayor had described us as out-of-town "agitators." He threatened dire consequences if we didn't leave. We took his advice and left. We still had the greater part of our tour to complete.

This incident must surely have been a first time for a theatre company to be given such importance in our country.

In addition to playing for audiences on tour, we also tried to meet people in various towns and cities who were interested in forming local workers' theatres. We tried to help with advice, scripts and general encouragement in the short time at our disposal.

Our repertoire for this first tour, as reported in *Masses*, consisted of seven short plays:

— *Solidarity, Not Charity* — a one-acter taken from the U.S. *Workers' Life*.
— *Eviction* — a mass recitation written by two members of Montreal PAC about the murder of Nick Zynchuk.
— *Farmers' Fight* — one-act play, Montreal PAC.
— *Labor's Love Lost* — one-act satire, adapted from U.S. *Workers' Theatre* magazine.
— *Meerut* — mass recitation on the trial and sentence of the Indian trade union leaders, by the WTM of England.
— *Joe Derry* — written by Dorothy Livesay, member of PAC, for the tour.
— *War In The East* — a play in four scenes on the war against the people of Manchuria and China, written by Stanley Ryerson, member of Toronto PAC.

From *The Niagara Falls Gazette,* June 9, 1933:

SHOW FOR WORKERS

Workers' Theatre To Give Performance in Jubilee Hall Saturday.

Niagara Falls, Ont., June 9 — The Workers' Theatre, a new organization devoted to the production of plays illustrating "the hopes and aspirations of the great mass of workers in every sphere of activity, by depicting the struggle of the working class for political and economic emancipation," will give one of its performances here in Jubilee Hall, Valley Way, on Saturday night at 8 o'clock. The presentation Saturday will consist of a series of plays, sketches and mass recitations.

The Workers' Theatre is making its first tour of Ontario. Organized six months ago in Toronto it is composed of "young working-class men and girls who give their time and talent voluntarily to the work," it is explained by T. Kelagher, representative of the Progressive Arts Club, of which the theatre is a branch. The parent club receives no financial backing from any individual or group, Mr. Kelagher says.

The magazine *Masses* played a very important role in publicizing the activities of Workers' Theatre. More than that, the magazine provided the stimulus for theatres of this kind to be organized in other parts of Canada. A great deal of correspondence and many scripts were sent out all over the country. The record of the numbers of such theatres and what they did is unfortunately not to be found anywhere now. We have only some notes from *Masses* to provide some idea of the extent of the activity stimulated.

From the May-June 1933 issue of *Masses*:

Workers' Theatre group of the Toronto PAC filed an application to the local committee (of the Dominion Drama Festival) but was politely informed that "it was too late."

May 1 performance of a play called *Unity* by Oscar Ryan at Hygeia Hall.

Two Canadian Labor Defense League branches and the Jewish newspaper *Der Kamf* banquet, also assisted by Workers' Theatre.

Concert of PAC on May 26 where Workers' Theatre presented three plays.

Workers' Theatre in Toronto now has membership of 17.

Letter from Mulvihill, Manitoba, about organizing workers' theatre.

Ukrainian Labor-Farmer Temple Association in Rycroft, Alta. writes to say they have a workers' theatre group of about 25 members.

Canadian Labor Defense League in Winnipeg has started some dramatic activities in their branches. Workers' Theatre in Toronto has supplied material.

Coleman, Alta., has workers' theatre group of about 30 members.

Finland, Ont., has small workers' theatre group of young workers.

Workers' Theatre, section of PAC in Winnipeg, is newly organized. Have membership of 20 and have performed at a Workers' International Relief concert and several smaller affairs.

Youth Section of ULFTA of Moose Jaw, Sask. has workers' theatre group.

Workers' Theatre of the Montreal PAC reacted to murder of the unemployed worker, Nick Zynchuk, by presenting a mass recitation, written by two members of PAC in Montreal, at a protest meeting against his murder.

From *Masses*, September, 1933:

A week or so after the first tour of Workers' Theatre ended, the second tour began with a new cast. This tour included London, Windsor and East Windsor. In East Windsor, there was so much enthusiasm over the possibilities of workers' theatre, they asked for some people to stay awhile to help them set up their own branch of PAC. Two members were loaned to them for a couple of weeks. There is now a functioning PAC there.

In London there are no less than four workers' theatre groups which may come into existence as a result of this tour. Workers of this city gave Workers' Theatre the best reception received anywhere, packing a fairly large hall and assisted the actors by actually being part of the presentations. As a result, when a PAC organizer managed to get to London for a couple of days, he learned that the Unemployed Councils and the CLDL were all interested in forming their own dramatic groups. Avrom, Toronto PAC artist, accompanied the group on both tours and his chalk-talks at each performance were enthusiastically received by audiences.

Toronto has produced three new plays recently. One is a satire on the Economic Conference and was presented at the PAC picnic on Aug. 6, 1933. One is a play new to Toronto, called *Joe Derry*. The third, called *Looking Forward,* is a two-act play depicting the struggle for unemployment insurance.

Toronto Workers' Theatre has arranged for a third tour. This time, Gananoque and Ottawa are included in the itinerary. *Looking Forward* will contribute the main feature of the program, supported by shorter plays and mass recitations. Our cartoonist, Avrom will be along also. They will be in Ottawa (for the mass gathering of the hunger marchers) Sept. 4-8.

A drama tournament is being planned for the first week in November. Program will be divided into three sections. 1. Agitprop plays. 2. Legitimate drama. 3. Children's groups. Watch for further details.

Another tour of Niagara District is in prospect for the Fall. A northern tour, as far as Timmins, is in the embryo stage.

A loud EUREKA is heard from the new branch in Windsor. They have produced mass recitations at park meetings, picnics and various events.

The PAC Writers' Group in Montreal have produced a mass recitation for Sacco-Vanzetti and the drama section will be in action with it. Unfortunately, the recitation was written too late for distribution this year. It will be printed and distributed from coast to coast for presentation next year.

Youth Section of the Farmers' Unity League at Radway, Alta. is organizing a dramatic section this Fall and expects to start work on material received from Toronto. Some members have had previous theatre experience before they joined the FUL.

Winnipeg sends a good report. Are rehearsing four plays, one of which they wrote themselves. Have accepted several assignments and are planning a district tour for the Fall. Also begun working on setting up drama groups in the northern part of Winnipeg.

From *Masses,* January, 1934:

East Windsor Workers' Theatre has active membership of 18. Very well-known in district. Doing a great deal of outdoor work at demonstrations, picnics and mass meetings. Farmers of Leamington area got to know them well. Played in Chatham on Nov. 19, putting on ten sketches, short plays and mass recitations. They played to full house there and have been invited back.

Kivikoski, a farming centre 10 miles north of Port Arthur, is a Finnish community which carries on regular dramatic activities. They have used a number of short sketches issued by Workers' Theatre, as well as plays supplied by the Finnish organization.

Plans are being made in Toronto for short courses to improve stage work. Diction, voice culture and plastic movement lectures are being arranged.

During recent Stratford furniture strike, a troupe was sent from Toronto and played several plays and sketches in an evening to raise money for the strike fund. Close to 3,500 people jammed into the old Brooks Motors plant to see the performance.

Success of membership drive in Montreal makes it possible to divide into two theatre groups. Many more requests for assistance can be filled. They have been forced to refuse a number of requests — so popular have they become. There are now a number of French members in the group and the need for material in French dealing with specific Canadian situations is needed. These will have to be written in Canada by French-Canadians themselves.

Winnipeg Workers' Theatre has been more active in the early part of the winter than at any time. *The Two Destroyers, Looking Forward, Labor's Love Lost* and other short plays and sketches have been presented. They have formed a Supporters' Club, which will meet every month, to act as a contact with their audiences. Preparing for a concert during February to mark anniversary of the PAC in Winnipeg. Three plays will be presented.

I would like to refer here to one incident of police harassment which was especially effective against our theatre. In 1933, the May Day Committee in Toronto invited Workers' Theatre to provide some dramatic content at a concert meeting being arranged for Hygeia Hall on May First.

Oscar Ryan, member of the Writers' Group of PAC, wrote a play for that occasion and called it *Unity*.

The group held a dress rehearsal early in the afternoon of May Day at the Hall. Members of the theatre then left with the understanding that we would all gather there again in the evening in good time for the performance.

As some of us walked away to cross the street, we saw two of our leading actors talking to two rather tall and beefy men in front of a parked car. We smelled trouble: they were being questioned by the notorious Red Squad. They soon hustled our actors into the car. They were obviously headed for the police station.

Those of us who saw what had happened were first gripped by panic. How could we do our play in the evening without these actors? We had no extra people or understudies. But we recovered soon enough to get on the phone to the Canadian Labor Defense League and tell them what had happened. We conveyed our sense of urgency to them. They succeeded in winning the release of our two actors. Our show went on.

There were no charges, of course. This police action was intended simply to intimidate us and to interfere with our work. Perhaps we should have felt complimented at the importance placed on our activities by the police authorities. Perhaps they figured that we should have been frightened enough to give up Workers' Theatre. In fact, however, we were neither flattered nor frightened. It should have been clear to the powers-that-be that young people who have a strong commitment to something they consider important don't give up easily. If anything, harassment of that kind usually has the opposite effect. We were very angry and we persisted more stubbornly than ever in our theatre activities.

As for the quality of our work, it really requires the view of someone not involved directly in the performances. Oscar saw most of the short plays. His feelings were generally positive.

"Audiences found that these plays, produced in a very direct yet very imaginative fashion, had an immediate impact. They excited a big response. People sometimes cheered and shouted support in the course of the performance.

"There were a number of innovations in staging methods. These weren't the sort of frothy traditional plays that Canadians had seen in church basements. They dealt with urgent questions — unemployment, human rights, war, strike situations, whatever — and spoke in very direct terms to the people involved.

"And the people, for the most part, responded enthusiastically.

"Apart from content, the staging stressed theatricality. They introduced some innovations to Canada — the use of mass chants, of stylized motion, of satire and caricature, and even the uniform group costume, as well as living tableaux, and even a kind of choreographed movement, sometimes exaggerated, sometimes simple and direct — but never above the heads of the audience."

VI

Eight Men Speak

THE HIGH POINT, the most challenging experience in the life of the Workers' Theatre, was the production of *Eight Men Speak*. The script was a co-operative effort by four members of the PAC Writers' Group — H. Francis (Frank Love), Mildred Goldberg, Oscar and E. Cecil-Smith.

The play was in six acts and called for a cast of over thirty. We had to find additional actors to augment the small Workers' Theatre company. We approached the Unemployed Council for help. The response was terrific. We didn't know there were so many single unemployed men interested and excited about being in a production of this kind.

I was impressed with the loyalty of these young men who, in spite of their own desperate situation, came regularly to rehearsals. It was, for them, no easy matter. Since the single jobless received no state assistance, they had to spend much of their time lining up for mission or soup-kitchen meals, and then finding a place to bunk, especially in the cold weather. None thought of dropping out. They were real troupers.

It should be remembered that most of the men had never acted before; many of them had not even seen a live play on a stage. It meant learning in rehearsal as they went along. What marvellous, diligent students they were! When they were not involved in a scene, they sat and closely watched everything else as it took shape, so as to learn and improve their own skills.

In view of all these circumstances, I would say the production of this play was a great achievement. Oscar, as co-author, describes how this all came about:

"*Eight Men Speak* resulted from a very critical civil rights situation in Canada. In 1931, eight leaders of the Canadian Communist Party were arrested in simultaneous raids across the country. It was the culmination of a period when people were being picked up on the street, in their homes, at meeting halls, simply because they had no visible means of subsistence; in other words, they had no jobs. Many had no homes, so it was common practice for policemen simply to pick them up and take them to police stations, and sometimes rough them up.

"It was a very violent period with wholesale and sustained attacks on civil rights across the country. The climax, of course, was the arrest of the Communist leaders. But even this outrageous Section 98 violation of civil liberties was peaked with the attempt to murder Tim Buck, national leader of the Communist Party, by firing shots into his prison cell at Kingston Penitentiary.

"At the time I was publicity director for the Canadian Labor Defense League. Its principal objective was repeal of Section 98 of the Criminal Code, under which almost anybody could be arrested for almost anything — doing anything or doing nothing. It was introduced at the time of the 1919 Winnipeg General Strike by Arthur Meighen.

"We in the CLDL felt that something had to be done to rouse public sentiment against Section 98 more effectively than through leaflets, mass meetings, petitions and other traditional ways.

"We thought, *Why not have a play*?

"I took our proposition to the Progressive Arts Club writers' group. We discussed the possibilities. Would we be able to produce a script and mount it in a hurry — immediately? Four of us volunteered to write it collectively. We worked out a sketchy outline, and assigned scenes and acts among ourselves. Within a few weeks we had the first scripts to read, discuss and revise.

"At first, our intention had been to do a dramatized mock trial in a large theatre. But we wanted something with greater impact. We felt it needed intensity, color, conflict, theatricality. We added blackouts and mass recitation and some light humorous elements. We introduced, I think fairly effectively, new staging effects which were not then commonly employed in Canada, but had been pioneered in some of the European experimental theatres. We soon had a script ready to put into production. That's where Workers' Theatre took over.

"Jim Watts directed the early rehearsals and, when the load became too big, turned over the job to me but continued as assistant. Rehearsals were held almost daily. Our cast, many of them unemployed, could not afford carfare; they walked to and from the rehearsal halls each time.

"There was one performance — December 4, 1933 — at the Standard Theatre on Spadina at Dundas, in the heart of the city. Some 1,500 people crowded in. They were a tense and exceptionally responsive audience. Again and again and again throughout the evening people cheered and applauded and cried out their support. The final curtain brought a sustained ovation, an emotional outburst. For audience and actors alike, it was a rare theatre experience not soon forgotten.

"We decided on a repeat performance. No sooner did we announce it than the police threatened to cancel the theatre's license. The owner backed down."

Eight Men Speak's premiere received only scant critical reviews from Toronto's daily papers, which were more interested in political hysteria than in production values, especially after the banning.

Frank Love, another co-author, recalled:

"I was surprised that the press should not be impressed (by the production) even though they disagreed, but why weren't they stirred by it? I remember one girl, she came from a fairly well-to-do family. She was working as a secretary and she was a very knowledgeable girl. She told me she was never so stirred in her life. Too bad it couldn't have been put on again and again to see the reaction from more people. When we announced a second performance, the whole university was down there buying tickets. But nobody else got a chance to see it. I don't know whether they would have been stirred by it or not. If they would have, maybe this was a good technique to follow again."

In a foreword to the first printed edition of *Eight Men Speak* in 1934, Ed Cecil-Smith placed the ban in its political context:

"Why are the Canadian authorities afraid of this play? Why do they move heaven and earth to prevent it being presented for a second time? Why has the order gone out from the Ontario parliament buildings that any theatre which is rented for the showing of *Eight Men Speak* shall at once lose its license? Why did the Winnipeg police and the Manitoba government swoop down on the Walker Theatre and remove the license the day before the play was to appear there?

"The answer is not far to seek. It lies in the essential truth of every word of these six acts. These things which are dramatized in the following pages must not be allowed to be played in public, if the government concerned can do anything to prevent it. . . .

"It was played to a house seating 1,500 which was sold out long before the curtain was scheduled to rise. It received an ovation from the working class audience which was reflected by scare headlines in the bourgeois press. The Toronto Police Commission held secret sessions and consulted the crown attorney and city solicitor to see what legal action would be taken against the authors, producers or actors. For fear of dragging the facts to light in an even more public manner, these upholders of law and order decided not to make such a frontal attack.

"By methods well known to capitalist lawyers and lobbyists it was finally decided that the attack should be made by the provincial inspector of theatres with a perfectly safe threat of license cancellation.

"While these discussions were going on in secret, there was an enormous demand that the play be repeated. Owing to a difficulty in securing a theatre (it was only possible to rent one for one night a week) the Standard was again rented for January 15, 1934. Two days before this the manager of the theatre was hauled to the office of the inspector of theatres and given the ultimatum. He at once broke his signed contract with the PAC. . . .

"It was finally disclosed that Prime Minister R.B. Bennett himself had been sent a copy of the stenographic report of the play by the RCMP. He could not understand, he is quoted as saying, how on earth the Toronto public ever allowed this play to be produced at all. So now we find that this attack on the freedom of the stage and the freedom of criticism of the government has a very highly centralized beginning.

"In other cities and towns, plans went ahead for presentation of *Eight Men Speak*. In fact, since the ban was pronounced in Ontario, it has actually been presented in part on at least six occasions, and never once has the government dared to prosecute the producers or actors. . . ."

This production was a turning point for me, as well as for others in Workers' Theatre. As a member of the cast, I was reminded again of how potent an art form theatre can be.

The audience reaction was very emotional — cheering, laughing, booing — as their involvement grew. There was active rapport and participation between actors and audience, such as I have always believed good theatre should have. Without this, theatre becomes an exercise in escape and one never knows what the audience is feeling, or whether they are even entertained.

I believe good entertainment in the theatre includes audience involvement — whether they are moved to laughter, or to tears, or caught up in mystery and revelation.

I began thinking at about this time that it was no longer enough to do short plays which appealed only to particular people. It wasn't enough any more to have simplistic characterizations and situations. We had to go further.

It occurred to me therefore that it might be possible to combine two kinds of theatre into our organization in order to appeal to many more people. Such a theatre could devote part of its time to short, mobile plays which could be taken out to various audiences. But the greater part of our effort would be given to longer scripts, still concerned with contemporary social themes, but which were more complex in production and in the development of characters and ideas.

I wanted to draw on people who seriously wanted to study their craft and who would work at developing themselves as actors and directors. It would obviously take more time and effort to produce such plays, plays which would speak to the major issues and conflicts of the times in a deeper, more theatrical way. It did, though, seem possible to reach out to newer and broader audiences with a theatre of high artistic standards, innovative in technique and in subject matter.

I began to think this way as I saw what was happening to Workers' Theatre. People involved began to drift away, many of them for personal reasons. Only a very small nucleus had the commitment needed to keep it going.

In discussion with Jim Watts and several other members I found that there seemed to be agreement on what we needed now to advance social theatre. Jim herself decided to go to New York to enter theatre courses at the New Theatre League school.

This was also the time when there was an explosion of social theatre in the United States, partly as a result of the Federal Theatre Project. New Theatre League was organized as the centre for new playwrights writing on contemporary themes. Publication of *New Theatre* magazine kept everyone in touch with new developments. The best known of the new writers of the period was, of course, Clifford Odets, author of that legendary play of the thirties, *Waiting For Lefty*.

The few of us who were interested in a permanent theatre such as we were projecting met to search for a name which would express the kind of group we were to be. We searched long and hard, with dozens of names being suggested. Finally, we agreed: Theatre of Action.

We knew there was such a group in New York, but no matter how hard we tried to think of some other name, we could not improve on Theatre of Action, which expressed so well the dynamic nature of our planned theatre.

Jim went off to New York to study. Shortly afterwards, I left Toronto with my husband to live in Winnipeg, where we spent close to a year.

On Jim's return to Toronto, she set up our first "headquarters," a small office in a building on Bay Street, from which correspondence was carried on, new members enrolled, some attempts to raise money made and a school launched.

Thus did Theatre of Action come into being.

It has been claimed in some quarters that in the transition from Workers' Theatre to Theatre of Action some watering down of principle took place and that there was less militancy shown. I find it hard to understand on what basis such claims are made, or for what reason. They are certainly far from the truth.

As an active member of both groups, I found this transition both natural and right for the future development of our social theatre.

We needed to attract people who would be committed to some permanence for the group, who would study their craft and gain experience to produce work of a high standard in a unified ensemble. It was time to enrich our work and grow — something all living theatres must seek. It was particularly necessary for those of us who wished to bring the new plays of our turbulent times to larger audiences than we had been able to reach before.

Part Two:

THE IDEA SPREADS

VII

Vancouver — Progressive Arts Players

. . . Twice to tea at Government House . . . and I was still on relief. . . .

— Denny Kristiansen, in Vancouver Province *interview, March 5, 1976.*

AMONG THE DIFFICULTIES Canadians encounter even now, in getting to know this vast country of ours, are the great distances between east and west.

In the Depression years the problem was almost insurmountable. Few could travel from Toronto or Montreal to the west coast to see what was happening there. It was simply a matter of money. Contact between the social theatres of that period was, accordingly, confined to some sparse correspondence.

We were aware, of course, in Toronto by 1936 that a Vancouver group had mounted a super production of *Waiting For Lefty*, had taken it to Ottawa to the Dominion Drama Festival finals and had there won the award for the best play in English.

To write this memoir I had, therefore, to seek out those who had been active participants in that unique Vancouver theatre.

Harold Griffin was a founding member of the Vancouver Progressive Arts Club, a newspaperman, playwright, poet, author of two histories (one on the Canadian Northwest, the other on the early labor movement in British Columbia) and of three books of poetry. In his youth he worked on Fleet Street in London. Migrating to Canada, he traveled widely. A veteran journalist, he was the very knowledgeable editor of *B.C. Fisherman*, a lively and influential trade union publication.

In 1935 he was production editor of *B.C. Workers' News*. Forty-three years later, looking through its files, he traced for me the beginnings of the Progressive Arts Club of Vancouver. From its pages of July 12, 1935:

"A group of workers interested in the presentation of plays of social significance have taken permanent headquarters and rehearsal rooms at 404 Homer Street.

"The first play to be put on is *Waiting For Lefty* by Clifford Odets. The Progressive Arts Club is the Vancouver branch of the movement which has active units in most Eastern Canadian cities."

"PAC," Griffin told me, "was originally intended in Vancouver to be a unity of all the arts. There were a few aspiring playwrights, writers who were reasonably well established on the left — I had some hand in it — but we felt closer to the theatre. Production was the focal point. We had various people with various talents, but actually it became a theatre organization.

"For the most part the people around PAC were unemployed. The moving spirit in the whole thing was Garfield King, a lawyer who took an interest primarily because his brother Earl had been one of the victims of the old Ramsay-Palmer case in San Francisco. He became very much interested in civil liberties. He had long been associated with the progressive movement. He was also active in local amateur theatricals and had been so disgusted by a little theatre production that he told whoever was producing it that he could go out on Skid Row and find among the ranks of the unemployed a cast which could do a much better job, given a suitable vehicle.

"At that time *Waiting For Lefty* was the script which had cut quite a swath through the American and Canadian social theatre movement. It was the logical play. As a result of King's interest and his associations with the left, there came an announcement that a group calling itself the Progressive Arts Players was being formed and anybody interested was welcome to come along and take a hand."

Griffin showed me the August 9 issue, which reported that "the PAC Players are now preparing to stage *Waiting For Lefty*." He added, "So we were in the process of organizing in August. But there were not many people involved in those days."

A report in the October 14 *Workers' News* said: "The stage and auditorium of the Ukrainian Labor Temple will be converted into a labor theatre . . . The theatre is ceasing to be a toy for the rich."

"I didn't go to the first performance of the play," Griffin said, "because I was just too busy at the time. I would think the audience would mainly be people who were around the political left and a sprinkling of intellectuals, those who were curious and those who were attracted by the publicity. There had been a lot of publicity."

Then came crisis, the heavy hand of the law.

The November 22 issue of *B.C. Workers' News* reported: "The police of Vancouver have served notice on the ULFTA (Ukrainian Labor-Farmer Temple Association) in whose theatre the play, *Waiting For Lefty* was produced on five occasions to packed houses, that its hall license would be cancelled if they permitted the play to be produced again in their theatre."

Griffin showed me the 1935 paper. "That gives you the flavor immediately — fine productions, packed houses — and they were still filling the cast in October. In five weeks, they had played five times. So while the play was in constant rehearsal and polishing, it was also being played.

"The police threatened to cancel the hall's license, but that didn't stop performances at new quarters. The theatre decided to enter *Waiting For Lefty* in the local Drama Festival which was to take place in the Empress Theatre on the nights of January 30, 31 and February 1."

Then *B.C. Workers' News* reported: "An intimation has been received from Ottawa that no objection will be taken to the staging of *Waiting For Lefty*. This is in striking contrast and a rebuke to the attitude of the local police and License Inspector Urquhart."

"In looking over the list of plays in competition," Griffin commented, "it is clear that *Waiting For Lefty* was the only one with any real content, with meaning for people."

The February 7 issue carried this item: "The official housewarming of the new PAC clubrooms at 326 West Hastings took place with 150 people attending, taxing the accommodation to capacity and they were treated to an exceptionally well-rendered program of musical numbers, recitations and singing of an international character."

"The ethnic groups, as you call them now, participated in that," Griffin recalled. "They had a very rich culture. There was the Finnish Organization, which had been staging lengthy three-act plays in Finnish for years, the drama of their national cultural heritage. The Ukrainians, with dance and music, also had a particularly rich heritage and a very large following."

Griffin drew my attention to the economics of the group in 1935 — "A financial statement signed by Edward Lauk and Arthur Stirling Murphy, the auditors. Lauk was the father of an NDP Minister of Trade, Industry and Commerce. He was in *Waiting For Lefty*. 'We have examined the accounts, the books of the PAC, and find them in A-1 order. Gross income $1,524.99. Cash on hand, $2.45. Bank $202.61. Properties $185.43. Expenses, Royalties, etc. $1,120.50. Library $14.00. Total of $1,524.99.'

"Most of the money for the theatre was raised by donations, solicited or contributed voluntarily, by well-wishers and those who happened to have a dollar or two and from performances, for which there was a minimum charge. Remember, at that time, the unemployed, if they got it, were getting $3.05 a week, a meal ticket and $2 for their room.

"Here's an account, dated March 13, 1936, that 'hundreds were turned away last Wednesday night from the Empress Theatre (which seated, I should think, at least 1,200 people) when the PAC Players presented *Waiting For Lefty*, the 16th performance in the city. After the play, three speakers — Professors Sedgewick and Clarke of U.B.C. and the Rev. Mr. Constable — gave a symposium on the question of Art and Propaganda, as applied to the play, with Brigadier-General Victor Odlum as chairman.'

Waiting For Lefty had won in the Dominion Drama Festival regionals by then.

"I attended that DDF performance," Griffin recalled. "My impression was that this was avant-garde theatre. While still in England, I had been a member of a small group in Dulwich and we used to put on plays in a theatre that had room only for ten or twelve people, in part of a house that a man had converted into a small theatre. If any place was suited for audience participation, that was it. We were also sitting on the stage.

"*Waiting For Lefty* was my first experience with such extensive audience participation. I had to break with all my concepts of traditional theatre. There was a complete rapport between audience and actors. The actors were living out a fiction on the stage, which corresponded to their experience in real life, and the audience was witnessing a fiction on the stage which was almost a mirror of what they personally had lived through. The actors lived their parts, they really did. They didn't have to act, they merely had to intensify their own experiences, or so it seemed.

"The press reaction was mixed. Nobody could deny the achievement. Vancouver was a much more tightly-knit city than it is now. The daily press was always forced to recognize the reality. Unemployment was heavier here than any other place in the country, and since they were thinking of circulation, they couldn't attack *Waiting For Lefty* as openly as Mayor McGeer had tried at first. After all, this production had come to something, it had won a lot of support.

"At the same time, they weren't happy that here was an unknown group, working with foreign-born, largely despised citizens. So, it was a mixed reaction.

"The opposition was stunned by the DDF adjudicator's rave about the performance. They had to accommodate themselves to the fact that *Waiting For Lefty* was superbly done. Garfield King and his co-director, Guy Glover, were both very talented. Glover was young at the time and had a great feel for theatre.

"The press reacted to the adjudicator's remarks by acknowledging them. They could hardly be ignored. There was a certain out-of-joint feeling, especially among the Vancouver Little Theatre crowd, who were the elite. They weren't at all happy about it. They had to be graceful, but I know that behind the scenes a lot of muttering went on.

"Vancouver City Council, forced by public opinion, granted a tag-day for March 28 to raise money to make it possible for the cast to go to Ottawa for the DDF finals."

Hal paused, smiling, as he recalled those exhilarating days. "Here is an item from the April 3 issue of the *B.C. Workers' News:*

"'In response to insistent demands, the PAC Players will present once again their dynamic production of *Waiting For Lefty* at the Empress Theatre on Tuesday, April 7. With *Lefty*, on this occasion, will also appear the three-act wordless play with music, *Pierrot the Prodigal*, which was presented with such signal success a few weeks ago by the Vancouver Little Theatre Association at the Stanley Theatre, and which the press praised in the most lavish terms. *Pierrot the Prodigal* is the first full-length example of the pantomime play to be seen in Vancouver and is a novel dramatic production of great beauty and sound, written by Michelle Karflis, with music by Andre Wornser, produced by Vivien Ramsay who, besides directing it, designed and executed the costumes, which add so much to its success. In the cast are Taylor, Anne Ferguson, Johnstone, Guy Glover (who is also in *Waiting For Lefty*), Randolph Gardiner and Joan Lindsay. Music is interpreted by Edna Disney, distinguished Vancouver pianist.' That program played to a packed house."

Vancouver's Progressive Arts Players, like so many others, began its activities at a particular time in a particular social climate. Denny Kristiansen, a Dane who came to Vancouver in 1930, recalled this social climate when I visited him and his wife in their apartment nearly 50 years later.

Denny is a slender, quiet-spoken man. One could see the handsome, fine-featured face that would get him the role of Syd, the young taxi-driver of *Waiting For Lefty*.

His wife recalled the bitter longshoremen's strike that lasted the whole summer of 1935. A Citizen's League was organized by the Chief of Police, Col. W.W. Foster. Members of this vigilante league patrolled the waterfront in groups of five or six, carrying baseball bats, always at the ready for action. Their bulletin, virulently anti-communist, was used to redbait and scare the men on strike. At the same time the single unemployed men, who were in Vancouver in very large numbers, called a demonstration for more relief. It was a massive gathering and the event became known as "Bloody Sunday" after Mayor McGeer read the Riot Act.

Denny showed me an old clipping in which police are seen attacking demonstrators. It was with these major battles as a background that *Waiting For Lefty*, a play about a taxi drivers' strike and its effects on the individual workers and their families, was produced. The reality of what was happening outside gave special meaning to the action on stage and audiences responded enthusiastically.

"I remember standing on a downtown street corner with this sign, *Waiting For Lefty*, across my chest," said Kristiansen. "I'd call out, 'Send *Lefty* to Ottawa!' And fellows would say, 'Who the hell is Lefty? Why can't he ride the rods like the rest of us?' Despite the cracks, we raised $600 to send the cast of 20.

"In Ottawa we were wined and dined. R.B. Bennett, leader of the Opposition (and former Tory Prime Minister), gave a luncheon for us at the Chateau Laurier. J.S. Woodsworth (leader of the CCF) took us to lunch in the parliamentary dining room.

"We didn't get the Bessborough Trophy (top award for best play) but we did get one for the best play in English. There was another award for best in French."

The winning play overall in 1936 was *Twenty-Five Cents* by Canadian writer Eric Harris — another depression-day tale of a woman who spent her last 25 cents for escape at the movies.

"I think the most amazing thing, which Bennett and the adjudicator both mentioned, was the prolonged applause of this well-to-do audience in Ottawa. We had gone down to the dressing rooms. They wouldn't stop applauding and we had to come up again.

"Lady Tupper (Margaret, wife of lawyer Sir Charles Tupper and a powerhouse in the Manitoba Drama League) walked up and down in front saying, 'The God-damned hypocrites, the God-damned hypocrites.' She meant the audience. Sir Robert Borden (one time Tory Prime Minister who died in 1937) was there. So was Lord Tweedsmuir.

"We were twice to tea at Government House. And here I was, still on relief. It was interesting for them and us. I was interested in meeting these people and seeing their reaction to the play. We had the most terrific press in Canada. *Waiting For Lefty* revitalized the whole Dominion Drama Festival. . . ."

Theodore (Ted) Boresky played Dr. Barnes in *Waiting For Lefty*. He is the son of a Ukrainian immigrant who arrived in Canada with his family in 1898, settling in Gimli, Manitoba. At the age of thirteen he left Gimli to attend school in Winnipeg. There he quickly learned his second language, English. It was in the progressive Ukrainian organization in Winnipeg, however, with its Labor Temple and the many cultural activities around it, that Ted really flowered.

He became an active participant in the theatre section of the Ukrainian Labor-Farmer Temple Association, doing plays in Ukrainian about the hard, oppressive lives of peasants and workers kept down by landlords and factory owners. As he moved into a position of leadership in the theatre, he began to think about the younger generation of Ukrainians who found the plays about the old country too far removed from their lives. Ted began to search for dramatic material which would more closely reflect the thinking of the younger generation, who were now Canadians.

He discovered a new Ukrainian writer of a more modern anti-war play, *Family of Brushmakers*. It was written in Ukrainian and Ted undertook the translation into English. He found this task very difficult since he had little experience, nor did he feel familiar enough with English. But it was so important to him to attract young people that he persisted and finished the job. *Family of Brushmakers* dealt with World War I and was anti-war in its outlook. The play was produced and well-attended by the youth Ted wanted to reach. He felt it was an important step in winning this new audience to the stage, both as onlookers and participants.

By now Ted had a family and his wife found the weather in Winnipeg too severe. They moved to Vancouver, where he continued his activities around the Ukrainian Labor Temple. His daily work was laying hardwood floors, but in 1930 all jobs collapsed and he and his family found themselves on relief.

In 1935, Garfield King and Guy Glover, who were the co-directors of *Waiting For Lefty,* came to the Ukrainian Labor Temple to ask for help in casting and finding space to rehearse the play. Boresky recalls there was immediate agreement to give what help they could, and a number of players were cast from the Ukrainian organization, among them people who had had some experience in theatre. Ted and Edward Lauk were senior members of the cast and were impressed with this timely, innovative play. It was enthusiastically received by the audiences of the younger generation of Ukrainians, who responded to the living reality of the times.

Ted had not known King or Glover before this, but he found them both very enthusiastic, talented and with a positive outlook on the human condition.

Ted felt winning the top award in the regional drama festival had not been expected by the cast. Vancouver's stormy political climate and the play's subject matter would not go over too well in the drama festival, they had thought, but they were excited and proud of winning and being chosen to go on to Ottawa to represent British Columbia in the DDF.

For Ted, going to Ottawa presented some problems. While his wife was enthusiastic and encouraged him to remain in the play, he had to make some special arrangements to have his relief continued so his family would not go hungry during his absence.

The *Waiting For Lefty* troupe traveled by CPR colonist car to Ottawa, playing in the larger centres as they made their way across the country. Performances in each place consisted of *The Bear,* by Chekhov; a small orchestra made up of members of the cast (Ted played violin) presented some musical numbers, followed by *Waiting For Lefty*. This made up a full evening's entertainment.

In Winnipeg, they played at the Walker Theatre.

Was *Lefty* really that good? Certainly a report in the *Vancouver Province* on Feb. 1, 1936 indicated that it was. The English adjudicator, Allan Wade, termed it ". . . a magnificent piece of work in production and acting." Personally, reported the *Province*, his taste did not go to propaganda plays in a theatre, but this was treated in such a way as to compel his admiration. It was extraordinarily smooth. "I don't think it could have been done better," said Mr. Wade. He singled out Joe and Edna for perfect presentation of their home scene as a sort of backdrop to the labor hall meeting, Dr. Benjamin, victim of racial antagonism in a New York hospital, and Agate

Keller, who powerfully swings the scenes into a tense climax. Every single character, more than a score of them, played beautifully in this swift-moving drama.

The *Vancouver Sun* reported that "Mr. Wade said 'the presentation was the nearest approach to professional standard I have ever witnessed by a group of amateurs. It was magnificent and I have no more superlatives to add to my statement on Friday night that it could not have been better performed. It was in a class by itself. There was reality, sincerity and power. *Waiting For Lefty* ... is one of several plays, lately written, that will help to make the theatre, what in its great day it always was — a school, a forum, a communal institution, an instrument in the hands of the people for fashioning a sound society. The play is full of power with its mass meeting scenes, its flash-backs from the homes of taxi drivers, its acting whirling stage to orchestra and back to stage again.' "

One of the youngest cast members was Harry Hoshowsky who was only 16 years old when he played the labor spy in *Lefty*. Now concert master of the North Vancouver Symphony Orchestra, he recollected his experiences as a member of the cast of *Waiting For Lefty*.

"As a teen-ager I was going to school and I helped my father after school in a small business he had. I was a member of the Ukrainian organization, at that time known as ULFTA. As a child I belonged to the music groups there. My parents were involved as well, being working-class people.

"I can't really remember how I got to know about the PAC theatre. I think it was because I had been in a couple of youth club plays. Mike Kunka and myself, we were in a dance group, and I played the mandolin, as did Bill, Mike's brother. Maybe somebody saw the possibility of using us as an interlude between plays. This is actually what happened later on, when we were touring across Canada.

"I recall the first audience we played for. A full house and the response was near to becoming a riot in one of the scenes. We placed some actors in the audience to prompt people in that vicinity to either applaud or laugh, with comments directed at the actors on stage, with a view to getting sympathy from the people around them, or do the opposite, antagonize the spectators. This is how the excitement was being generated to such a peak.

"I believe it was in the spy episode where we had to run on to the stage. I ran up first and Mike Kunka, who was also in the scene, was going to contradict the statements I was making to the executive on stage. He was already making preposterous asides in the audience. The people were almost sure they were at a meeting. They tried to contain him and it was pretty rough. He was a little afraid that he wasn't going to get up to the stage. There were a couple of times later on, he was late, missed his cue and we were ad-libbing until he could tear himself away from the audience. We had others spotted around at later performances to ensure that he could get away.

"We didn't mind the play-acting and the excitement in the audience, but we were kind of fearful for him. He would get up on the stage eventually. It wasn't a surprise to the audience, it was as if it was a natural movement of the evening's proceedings as they tried to contain the actor — protesting against what was happening and standing up and threatening. When he decided to move down the aisle, people moved right out of their seats and bodily tried to contain him."

Harry told me how excited they were to win in the local festival. Then came the problem of getting the group to Ottawa. The Vancouver group had the distinction of being the only ones to win the city's consent to have a tag day in which hundreds of people helped to collect money.

He referred to the train trip to Ottawa as a "beautiful experience. We had a railway car to ourselves."

Harry recalls the group's arrival at the theatre in Ottawa to play for an audience in full dress coming to see the play, representing a society he'd never been associated with. "We were apprehensive. At the same time, we were rarin' to get out there and do our best performance." Which they did.

"We were an ensemble. We were by then professionals. I've never looked at it that way, but we had to be in order to captivate the people we did.

"When we came back from Ottawa, we put the play on again, quite a few times. We also did a parody on *Waiting For Lefty* for cast and friends. But we now had to search for other works. It's pretty hard to get excited all over again. I think there was a period when we were doing an awful lot, very rapidly. Come to think of it, that shows the progress of the people in the PAC. Already in that short period, three months, there must have been the other nine months that the club had done many, many plays. For two, maybe three years afterwards they were involved in a number of productions. I don't think we were searching for another *Waiting For Lefty.* I think we were now making up our own minds as to whether we were going to continue in the field of acting. I never thought of being a professional actor. I didn't think what I did was good enough, except I really have to feel proud of what we accomplished. I knew I had to be part of it.

"I must recall for you a couple of adventures Mike and I had in Ottawa, outside of performing. We were the youngest members of the cast and for us everything was new and exciting. Mike and I saw the museum in Ottawa, we saw the mint, we saw the Parliament Buildings. We were guests of Percival Price, who at that time was the carilloneur.

"Both Mike and I were involved in music. I think Price saw the performance we did after the Festival. (We had provided musical entertainment between plays). He invited us to the Peace Tower, which was very impressive, through the Memorial Chamber and then up to the suite of the carilloneur. Just fantastic! Then we went up into the control room to watch him play the bells. He sat in a Tyrolean leather outfit — short pants with a halter and cross-braced both front and back, short-sleeved shirt, soft boots. The program could be heard ten miles away.

"He later got called up on the mat for playing *The Workers' Flag Is Deepest Red.* Ten miles in every direction and maybe further! PAC was in Ottawa and the world knew we were there. Ostensibly he had played *My Maryland* set to the same music. But there was no doubt Percival Price had arranged that program especially for the PAC.

"The Governor-General entertained us. This brings out the problem that Mike and I had. We were poor. We had no money. When we got to Ottawa and were honored at Rideau Hall, we had to go downstairs to the washroom. That washroom was something I never dreamed existed. We went back up to the assembly. Mike and I were inseparable. After tea, we looked around. All around the room were high-backed chairs and little tables, with silver boxes on them. We discovered the silver boxes contained cigarettes — not one, two or ten, but lots of cigarettes. We didn't smoke very much, but we did smoke. So, we filled our pockets from the silver boxes. I feel a little ashamed about that, but it was a natural reaction for us at that time.

"I remember one of our boys coming up to Lord Tweedsmuir. I didn't know he had bodyguards around him. The Governor-General had a cigarette offered him by one of his aides. He took that cigarette and he was waiting for a light. Our chap came over. He had a pocketful of household wooden matches. He lit one by striking the match on the back of his pants and along his thigh. The match ignited and he brought his hand up to light the cigarette. He was pushed away by two guards. I don't know who was more shocked, the Governor-General or Fred, who was trying to do the nice thing.

"We attended a reception by R.B. Bennett at the Chateau Laurier. I remember Mike and I sitting at the table, about twenty people away from the head table. We thought the waiters were in costume because they had knickerbockers on, some kind of funny-looking shoes with buckles and straps, and jackets with ruffles, almost like the costumes of a ball in the 17th Century.

"There were three or four glasses of different sizes in front of us. The cutlery — we had never seen that much — from forks, maybe four or five knives. We were just totally confused. Here were two kids who had been eating oranges in the vestibule of the train sitting in the Chateau Laurier hotel, with this array of glasses. Well, one of them was water, we knew it was water. The other one looked like water, but we didn't want to try it because one glass of water is enough. The other two had nothing in them.

"We decided to try the second glass. We didn't know it, but it was wine. We drank it like we were told to drink milk — down rapidly. We had no sooner done that when these waiters took a bottle out of the ice, unwrapped it and filled the glasses again. After about the fourth time, people began to look at us. They couldn't tell us we were doing anything wrong. After all, most of us were not used to this kind of dining. We were very good boys. We left three clean knives and three clean forks.

"As a matter of fact, we had been served squab, but it was set on a nest of dried spaghetti or something, on huge silver platters. There were a couple of silver spoons lying on the platter. Well, I used one spoon and that poor bird was all over the place — into the other birds. I finally got the eye of one of the boys who was nodding his head in the direction of the other spoon. I guess they were forbidden to speak. So I got the message. I used both spoons and put the pigeon down on my plate and put the spoons back. He was clearing his throat. Aha, I thought, that's why he couldn't speak, he has a throat problem. But he was trying to draw my attention to the fact that I had neglected to take the nest. Well, I couldn't. It was like passing someone on the street and you don't know which side to pass him on. There didn't seem to be any room on my plate. I decided to put the pigeon back up on its nest. I got the pigeon up, put it on the nest. By this time, I was getting pretty vexed. Everything got very quiet, not only at our table, but at the head table. Here was the former leader of Canada, sitting here absolutely stunned. I finally got the bird and the nest onto my plate.

"Mike and I must have consumed six glasses of wine. We could hardly talk to each other. Still, we were waiting for dessert. Dessert was on a five-tiered plate of some sort, and we weren't too sure what it was. We took these bonbons. We took most of them. We didn't know they were supposed to be passed.

"Then we figured they wanted us to sober up because they brought a bowl of water with lemons in it, without any spoons or anything. You know what's coming, eh? Already the table is becoming tense. They can see we are in a quandary. We're not talking — but communicating. Mike motioned, possibly by throwing his head back, that it was supposed to go down the throat. I gingerly gripped the bowl in both hands, got it to the point where I was able to rest my elbows on the table (and Mike was doing the same thing), when I was hit so violently in the ribs, I thought I was going to lose not only the pigeon but everything I had had before and after. The bowl was jarred and splashed on its way down the table. I think it was Stevie who hit me in the ribs and whispered in my ear, 'You wash your hands in there.' That's when my voice came back and I said, in a voice louder than usual, 'My hands!' That broke the ice. People were laughing. I realized that in our innocence, we had created one of the greatest comedies that had ever taken place in the Chateau Laurier.

"One of the other interesting things I remember about Ottawa was that they had flashing electric bulletin-boards for the news on some of the buildings. There were huge crowds of people watching; it was in French. We went for a haircut, they spoke French. Everywhere we went they spoke

French. There had been a serious mine disaster and people were concerned. At that time, with the strife in the world, and communication coming more into its own, people were becoming more aware and concerned about their fellow-men in other countries.

"I can't help recalling with fondness the women in our company. In the musical interludes of which we were a part, Stevie sang. At that time the popular songs were *The Rebel Girl, Hold The Fort, Solidarity Forever* — union songs; very dynamic songs like *Brother, Can You Spare A Dime.* I wish I could remember more. The women of our group were just beautiful. I don't know which one I liked better. They were all so good. They weren't mothers, they were sisters, just exceptionally good friends and good-looking and well-mannered. They took over a lot of the chores that we sixteen-year-olds didn't think necessary — laundry, food, etc. I think we helped to clean up."

It is interesting to read some of the reactions to the production of *Waiting For Lefty* as reflected in the community and press of Vancouver.

Here is what A.M. Stephen, Canadian poet, thought: "A revolutionary play — red-hot and sizzling with trenchant truths! A drama of the class struggle that lifts an audience out of their seats by the sheer cumulative force of its climax! Art that is propaganda and propaganda that is art! Such is *Waiting For Lefty*, as produced by the Progressive Arts Club and recently presented at the Labor Theatre, 805 Pender East. . . .

"The Progressive Arts Club must be congratulated. It has made history in the Canadian theatre. Its work marks the beginning, we hope, of even greater achievements. By laying the foundations of proletarian art in this Dominion, it is truly creating 'the nucleus of a New Social Order within the shell of the old.'"

And just to indicate the community spirit behind this effort, the following appeared in the *Vancouver Sun*, April 11, 1936:

STREET CARS TO
'WAIT FOR LEFTY'

"In order to accommodate those attending the special performance of the Progressive Arts Club production, *Waiting For Lefty* in the Orpheum Theatre, opening at midnight Sunday, the B.C. Electric Railway Company will run special street cars to all districts following the performance.

"The special cars will be located on Granville Street, near the theatre, at the conclusion of the show."

(If there is an occasion anywhere in Canada where street cars were put on at midnight to accommodate a theatrical performance, I would like to hear about it. In any event, in 1936, in Canada I am sure it must have been a first.)

From a column in the *Vancouver Province* of Nov. 22, 1935, when *Waiting For Lefty* was banned after its first performance:

"An organization called the 'Progressive Arts Club' recently did a powerful play called *Waiting For Lefty* and produced it in the Ukrainian Labor Temple on Pender Street. The play was directed by Mr. Garfield King, who has been actively connected with the Little Theatre since its inception.

"The play contains here and there a few strong sentences and expletives and concerns labor troubles. It has been produced with tremendous popular success in England and New York and has not only interested the people but has also thrilled those who are included in the higher artistic thought.

"I now have before me a copy of a letter sent to the chief of police by Mr. Garfield King and which reveals by indirection that the police have taken quite a hand in the matter of that play, to such an extent that they communicated with a certain Mr. Urquhart, who is the licensing inspector of the city. . . .

"There has never been a play of Shakespeare's censored in British territory as far as I know. There are far more stout and ribald words in Shakespeare's plays than there are in *Lefty*. In Shakespeare, also, there are quite low and libidinous ideas expressed in covered language. There are not in *Lefty*. There is no word in this play that is not in the Bible and there are a good many words in the Bible that are not in *Lefty*, I mean foul words.

"The whole trouble with this play and the touchy authorities is that it has a labor angle. It does not incite to riot, neither does it provoke revolution. It merely states a case and states it not quite so strongly as it should be stated.

"Art is concerned with showing things as they are on the one hand, and things as they might be on the other. It does not express or force opinions. It is descriptive."

VIII

Guy Glover

GUY GLOVER, CO-DIRECTOR OF *Waiting For Lefty* and who also played the leading role of Agate in the production, began his stage activities in the Vancouver Little Theatre and, after working with the PAC Players, went to England and became very busy in the theatre there. He returned to Canada to begin his association with the National Film Board and John Grierson, the man who made Canadian film documentaries world-renowned.

Glover, now retired from the NFB, is a slender, intense man who still radiates the passion and energy of the creative artist. He seemed to relive the period of the thirties as he spoke eagerly to me about those times and that theatre:

"I graduated from university in 1931, where I specialized in zoology or biology. I found, of course, that there was no work. Somebody got me interested, thought I'd be suitable for a small part in a play being done by the Vancouver Little Theatre. Between 1932 and 1935 I did a great deal of work in and around Vancouver in amateur theatre. Really, that's all there was. Vancouver was a pretty good theatre town. There had been, in the late twenties, a professional repertory theatre. I think it had a pretty good public. Certainly the little theatre had a great, faithful following and the productions they did were quite interesting. That was really my school. I was not what you would call a leading-man type, but I could do character, all kinds of parts. I also started to direct and I did Chekhov's *Uncle Vanya* for the Vancouver Little Theatre. I wasn't really a kid. By 1935 I was in my mid-twenties.

"Anyway, I got to know Garfield King through my little theatre work and when he discussed with me the idea of doing Odets' *Waiting For Lefty* I thought it was a great play, and a marvellous idea. By that time I had read the play. It had been published in a magazine, in New York, *New Theatre*. It also coincided with a lot of my political views at that time. I was a young man and most young men who had had roughly the same kind of academic background were interested in left-wing views. At the same time I was doing all kinds of other plays.

"Garfield King was really the moving spirit. He was a mature man, a lawyer, well-educated, interested in progressive views. I think he was fed-up with the conventional theatre and he wanted to try something different.

He said, 'Wouldn't it be marvellous to do this play with real working class people, unemployed people. I know one or two.' That's how it started.

"Garfield and I approached the Ukrainian Labor Temple for help with cast and rehearsal space. I would say that two-thirds of the players were Ukrainians. There were a couple of Yugoslavs. People of English background were in the minority. I was one, one of the girls was one, and maybe one of the other older men. We just cast to type, you know, we didn't have anybody put false moustaches on or wigs. We looked for characters as much as possible who, we thought, coincided with the author's description.

"We weren't interested in whether they'd had any previous experience. We said we could train people to give a realistic performance and that's what we tried to do. They had to be taught to speak up, to learn their lines, to project. Certainly there were no microphones or any of that nonsense.

"It occurs to me that we couldn't have happened on a better year to search for people. The Ukrainian Labor Temple were the left-wing side of the Ukrainian immigrants. When we took *Waiting For Lefty* across Canada, in prairie towns and cities, we performed in the Ukrainian Labor Temples. It was a flat-floored hall. It had a stage. It had scenery that was very often in place when you came there, usually a Ukrainian rural exterior scene with wings of birch trees. Sometimes it was the interior of a farmhouse parlor. But this was a living theatre tradition. They did operettas and 19th century plays. There was nothing like it in Canada. All of their young kids, and some of them were very young that we had in our play, had performed. They knew how to dance. They could sing and play instruments and were quite accustomed to performing during the winter at the Temple.

"They knew how to deal with an audience perfectly well, probably better than we did. I look back on that now as a very interesting glimpse that most Canadians really don't know about — that whole kind of 19th century Eastern European theatrical tradition, transplanted into Canada. Really, looking back into the roots of Canadian culture, to try to dig out some of that kind of thing, I think it would be quite amazing. I didn't really see it as I see it now, on reflection. We knew we were plugging in to an older theatre tradition with the very latest theatre, which was an imported play we got from the States. It wasn't Canadian, but it was North American theatre, socially-committed theatre which had a decade of life. What is interesting is that it never really survived the war. Odets and all those other playwrights of the 1930s, what happened to them?

"I'm not quite sure how long we rehearsed *Lefty*. It was a fairly long period. We worked evenings, but because most of the cast was unemployed and I was unemployed (Garfield was employed), we could do some rehearsals in the afternoons, and we would have sectional scene rehearsals without doing the whole play. We would do the whole play in the evening with Garfield King there. Then we started to try it out in public.

"We knew very soon we could move an audience and get them very excited. We knew we would shock some people, because it was a disturbing play to some people. Middle class audiences found it a bit disturbing, and it was meant to be so. The audience participation in the play was quite shocking. It broke down the curtain between the audience and the stage. All I know is that with that play, as distinct from other plays that I did, you knew you were getting some kind of involvement from the audience that was unusual. When you did conventional plays, you didn't get that, except when you were doing comedy.

"About the trip to Ottawa, well, it was an adventure. We were young people for the most part. Most of them had not traveled thousands of miles by train before. From that point of view everyone was terribly excited. I had been to one previous drama festival in Ottawa, so it wasn't so novel for me as it was for 99 percent of the cast. For them it was a terrific adventure. They didn't really know what they were coming into — the Governor-General and the social activities.

"All of it was an education. That whole experience was part of my education. I don't mean drama education. It was part of my political education, a kind of cultural education in the very broadest sense. Although I wasn't a kid exactly, it was invaluable to me. I'm sure for all of the cast it was a marvellous experience, something they would never have gotten in any other way at all.

"By the time we played it in Ottawa, we had a great ensemble feeling. The staging was really nothing, but it had to have very knife-edge lighting cues and that was all done by the crew backstage and on stage. Everybody did everything. Not only could they play the parts, but they knew how to work the show.

"For the festival finals, we agreed all we could do was do it extra well. We didn't know we were going to win, but on the other hand, we knew we had a good vehicle and an experienced cast and we weren't at all bashful about presenting it. We weren't quite sure how that audience would react. They really warmed to it quite well. It was a pretty stuffy audience, upper levels of embassies and that kind of thing. *Lefty* really got its effect even in that unlikely place.

"I'm sure the adjudicator, Harley Granville-Barker, as a dramatist himself, was aware of the currents in contemporary drama, including what was happening in America. He was an extremely knowledgeable man. He himself had written plays that were critical of society. He was interested in social drama and when he saw a real fire-breathing example of North American social drama being presented in this kind of place, he was very generous, I must say. We did come away with the award for the best play in English.

"I had a rather interesting experience while I was in Ottawa. I met Yousuf Karsh, the photographer, there. He was struggling in Ottawa, lived with his wife in the studio which had a European look, advanced-looking, had cushions on the floor, red paint on the walls, things like that. He was terribly excited by *Lefty* and was the official photographer for the festival. He photographed a scene from *Waiting For Lefty.* I remember the picture. I also remember being invited to his studio. He was very impressed with our production. He didn't think Canada had this kind of theatre. Our production reminded him of European theatre.

"I recall that in the production of *Waiting For Lefty* we set a very high standard for our work. There were no problems about turning up for rehearsals. We could really give the actors hell and they would take it. Nowadays you couldn't get that kind of discipline with a group of amateurs. We had total discipline. The cast knew the play had political implications, they were 100 per cent behind it, from that point of view. They were dedicated to it and we were ruthless in the way we worked. If anybody didn't work out, we let them go. We made tremendous demands and we really did get the best we could manage. We worked for that. We knew what we were doing. I had some experience; and so did Garfield.

"You might be interested in my production of *Paradise Lost* in England. It just happened that when I started to rehearse *Paradise Lost,* Stella Adler and Harold Clurman, both founding members of the Group Theatre in New York, came to London. They came to see rehearsals and gave me some very good pointers, including a prompt copy of the Group Theatre *Paradise Lost* with, I might say, an ending which was never used, which was suppressed by Odets himself.

"How would I summarize the period that I spent with that social theatre in the 1930s? Well, it was a decade of discovery for a whole lot of people and not just in the theatre — political discovery, social discovery. Think of the things in Canada that trace their roots back to the thirties — a political party, all kinds of notions of social progress, social legislation. The thirties was a time of breaking new ground, as it were, for all sorts of things. They may have been lost years to some people who are inattentive to the recent past. All over the world, it was a lively decade and, fortunately, Canada shared in that.

"It was more difficult in Canada. Communications were not as good then as they are now. We travelled by train and not by plane. There were no great things like television going on. It was much more broken up. But even then — witness *Waiting For Lefty* and the Drama Festival. There was something happening on a nation-wide scale, even in so unlikely a place as Canada.

"It was difficult, not much money around, so anything that got done had to get done on a marginal economic level. It was tough, but it was certainly lively. I spent half of it in Canada, a little over half, but what I experienced just made me into a human being, that's all."

To my mind, it was a most fitting sign of the times that the *Ottawa Journal* should devote its lead editorial on April 28, 1936, to the two top awards at the Dominion Drama Festival finals. It is true that newspapers in the past carried news reports of the drama festivals and what awards were made. To my knowledge, I can't recall a lead editorial being written to sum up what the two awards at that particular drama festival signified. The head is: "Awards Went to Plays that Deal with Vital Truths." It goes on to say:

"Concluding his task as adjudicator in the Dominion Drama Festival, Mr. Harley Granville-Barker said that Canada had 'the material for a real national drama.' Achievement of that end will be helped, we think, by study of the character of the plays which, in the festival just concluded, received first and second honors. These plays — *Twenty-Five Cents* and *Waiting For Lefty* — dealt with real life. No pale echoes of the production of authors who wrote of contemporary times in their own lands, they shunned the trivial, dealt with the stark realities of our day, with the sorrows, tragedies, deeper truths and implications of the existence of thousands in our midst.

"That, the challenging of emotion, and its use, to make men see life in all its circumstances, and not merely its froth and superficialities, is the true mission of the drama. It is art at its highest and best, just as it is literature at its best. 'Literature,' said one of the greatest of writers and philosophers, 'literature is life.'

"What we have in mind was brought out strikingly by Mr. Granville-Barker in his comments on *The Old Trouper*, presented by the Theatre Guild of St. John. Acted excellently, the play itself was divorced from reality, or from reality that matters, and Mr. Granville-Barker said of it: 'It is a futile and clumsy play. The actors are wasting their time and yours when they produce such a play. It is not like anything in heaven or on earth.'

"In *Twenty-Five Cents*, Mr. Eric Harris, a Canadian business man, made us see a truth which, alas, is too much on earth. Too many of us are apt to think of the depression, of the story of these years in terms of cold economics. Mr. Harris presented it in terms of flesh and blood, in terms of human values, in its consequences for human souls. Tragedy, grief, pain, pity, the 'clutch of circumstances' which bring unutterable sorrow to thousands, were depicted with a restraint which only added to their terror, to the moving quality of their appeal. Indeed, it was this quality of Mr. Harris' play — its restraint — which made it a more impressive preachment than its rival for highest honors, *Waiting For Lefty*.

"Mr. Clifford Odets is a professional author and playwright, whose chief work is for the theatre of the Left. The weakness of his work in *Waiting For Lefty* was in the violence of his protest. Using the same material as *Twenty-Five Cents*, he used it with more of exaggeration, lost something in consequence of that inarticulate hopelessness which is the soul of tragedy at its greatest. . . .

"But the main thing — the lesson for our playwrights and our actors — is that both plays dealt with life's true values, with its realities and implications. When more of our dramatists grasp the significance of that, and more of our authors, then the Canadian drama and Canadian literature will be on their way to greatness. Mr. Granville-Barker, in his fine judgments and keen comments, has done us a high service."

The award-winning group repeated their performance in Ottawa, and went on to play in Sudbury, Winnipeg, Calgary, Edmonton and Penticton on their return trip to Vancouver.

I would like to add one personal impression to that Ottawa performance. I was one of the five or six members of the Toronto Theatre of Action who traveled to Ottawa by car to meet our successful colleagues from Vancouver and to see that production. We must have been nearly as excited as members of the company. It was, after all, the first social theatre in Canada to present a strong working-class play which had succeeded to such an extent. We were most anxious to cheer them on.

We sat in the audience and enjoyed the sincere, passionate and honest performance. We were excited by the confidence of the ensemble acting on stage and the intensity created in the audience by this real and innovative play. It was a thrilling experience. All these feelings were vindicated when the adjudicator spoke so glowingly about the acting and directing he had seen.

It was a great moment for the Vancouver PAC Players and I recall how proud we were of our colleagues from the West. We shared their excitement because we were part of this social theatre movement which, even at its beginnings, and in the face of so many difficulties, so successfully made its presence felt nationally.

IX

After *Lefty*

THE PAC PLAYERS DID NOT cease activity after their long and happy association with *Waiting For Lefty*, though, admittedly, it was a difficult act to follow.

Hal Griffin, who was active in the PAC Players, continues the story of the group and its further activities as he recalls them with the help of reports in the *B.C. Workers' News:*

"After *Waiting For Lefty*, the Progressive Arts Players presented *Private Hicks* and *Devil Among the Skins.* Then came Irwin Shaw's spectacular anti-war drama, *Bury The Dead.* The director was Harry Louis.

"On March 6, the *News* reported, 'A public reading of the play (*Bury The Dead*) to which have been invited trade unions, church, peace and women's and other representatives will be given at the Orange Hall. *Bury The Dead* has already played with success by new theatre groups in Montreal, Toronto and Winnipeg. It is playing in Seattle at the present time to capacity houses. Intimation is also given by the Progressive Arts Players that it does not plan to enter the Drama Festival this year. Tickets at 75¢ and 50¢ are reserved and are now on sale. There are also unreserved seats at 25¢.'

"In the March 19 issue: 'On Monday, April 5th, 1937, the Progressive Arts Players will give a special benefit performance of *Bury The Dead* for the League Against War and Fascism . . . Included in the large cast are: Bill Turner, Bill Palmer, Harry Howshowsky, Malcolm Finlayson, George Ossipov, Max Osovsky, Jerry Delaney, Bill Schaffer, Dave Rankin, Ellen Nikula, Rosie Prokopchuk, Edna Braverman, Valerie Woodside, Ethel Smith, Dave Braverman, Norman Pelman, Vernon Sanvidge, Mike Kunka, Aser Rothstein, Cliff Hunter, Una Bligh, Muriel Hepburn, and Katherine Bruce . . . Prof. S. McKay of Washington University will personally supervise orchestral accompaniment of Friday's performance of *Bury The Dead.* Provision of a musical background for a play of this type is believed to be an innovation in Vancouver amateur productions.'

"I was in *Bury The Dead.* I was one of the soldiers who refused to be buried. It was one of the minor parts. It was quite a successful production, although there was some criticism that we had given the play a metaphysical rather than a realistic interpretation.

"I felt the anti-war theme of the play was put across very well. My father was killed in the First World War about three miles from the battle of the Somme. That's one thing I grew up with and you can imagine that when I took part in an anti-war play, I really meant it. We were all conscious of what war meant and also that we were all prospective cannon-fodder.

"That was the last of the major productions. I suppose you can only hold a large group together for a certain length of time. They were coming and going. The young population was shifting constantly. Somebody got a job up the coast, for instance. Dave Rankin organized a band and went up coast on a boat with a small band to play at logging camps, that were literally starved for entertainment.

"August 6, 1937: 'The PAP production of three one-act plays in a special performance in memory of Patrick O'Neil, a member of the group, killed recently while serving with the Mackenzie-Papineau Battalion in Spain, planned for Saturday, Aug. 7, has been postponed to Saturday, Aug. 21 ... This Sunday, Aug. 8, PAP is producing Hal Griffin's one-act play on the Spanish war, *Hostage at White Rock*.'

"August 20, 1937, we have two items: 'Three one-act plays will be presented by PAP of Vancouver at their club rooms, 1273 Granville Street this Saturday, August 21, special memorial performance honoring Paddy O'Neil, PAP member who had played in *Lefty* and was killed while serving in the Mac-Paps. Plays to be presented are: *Hostage* by Harold Griffin (PAP Chairman), *Gentlemen Be Seated,* directed by Sophie Shaffer, and *Blocks,* directed by Harry Louis. In addition there will be concert numbers. Admission 25¢. Half of the proceeds will be donated to the Friends of the Mac-Pap Battalion. The other half to the PAP maintenance fund.'

"In the same issue it says: 'First of the PAP new mobile productions to go on tour, *Hostage,* Harold Griffin's one-act play on the Spanish war, is meeting with a favorable response. Presented at White Rock two weeks ago, under the auspices of the Friends of the Mac-Pap Battalion, it is scheduled for presentation at Victoria, also under the auspices of the same organization. Performances are also scheduled for other places on Vancouver Island and on the lower mainland.'

"From the August 20, 1937 issue of *People's Advocate* comes a piece I wrote. By this time, the name of the group was changed to Theatre of Action because it better expressed the program of mobile theatre. I was director of the organization at the time and interviewed Sophie Shaffer on the plans for the group:

"'After the great success of *Waiting For Lefty* and the tremendous publicity we gained from it, we thought we were sitting on top of the world. But we found that we had the biggest job ahead of us, that of building a solid organization. On the strength of *Waiting For Lefty* we produced *Bury The Dead* this Spring. It's true that more than 2,000 people came to see it, but it crippled us financially and occupied all our efforts.

"'Consequently, we decided to turn to short, mobile productions. The audience isn't yet sufficiently interested in what we are doing to come to us, then we will go to the audience and prove that we really have something to offer.

"'We now have six plays either already produced, or in the course of production. Most of them, naturally, deal with social problems. Every other Saturday, we hold a social evening here to try out our productions. If they click, then we send them off to the various organizations, to concerts and the like, for the cost of transportation. The criticism helps us and enables us to improve our standards. Right now we are trying to interest the trade unions in whatever we are doing.'

"I asked Sophie Shaffer if PAP planned any full-length productions for the coming season. She shrugged. 'It all depends on the progress we make and the support we get. Full-length productions require a lot of money and we feel that we should build our organization on a solid footing first. Henryk Berg, our technical director, and Ethel Smith are holding weekly classes in theatrical work with a view to training and developing our members, so that we can aid other dramatic groups and assist in the formation of new groups. In this way we shall interest an ever larger audience to a point where we can put on big productions profitably.'

"So it became the Vancouver Theatre of Action in November, 1937.

"December 17, 1937, *People's Advocate*: 'Most of Vancouver's dramatic groups were well represented at the symposium held Sunday in the Italian Room of the Hotel Vancouver, under the auspices of the educational department of Vancouver Theatre of Action, when Mrs. Yvonne Perkins, Vancouver Little Theatre Association, Miss Dorothy Somerset, University Players, Ben Golden, New Theatre League (New York), discussed the purpose of theatre. Garfield King, prominent in city dramatic circles, was chairman.'

"I should explain that Garfield King was spending more and more time in civil liberties affairs. The group needed some expert direction and, frankly, we didn't possess it, nor did we feel we could acquire it except through long experience.

"Through Seattle we had heard of a young director down there named Ben Golden. We brought him up here. His wife, as I recall, was a school teacher who had some sort of professional job. I think we agreed to pay him either $10 or $20 a month. So he came up week-ends to direct rehearsals. During the week, of course, we would conduct our own rehearsals. He would whip the production into shape. He was quite talented and introduced innovative techniques to Theatre of Action which were different from any we had done before.

"*People's Advocate*, Feb. 4, 1938 — Report on outcome of the Dominion Drama Festival (Regional) eliminations here the previous Friday: 'Vancouver Theatre of Action's Jewish social drama, *Return At Sunset*, did not meet with the approval of the adjudicator, Capt. A.N.D. Fairbairn, who revealed a distinct anti-Jewish bias in his criticism of the play. The play, a one-act drama written by A.D. Shiffrin, deals with everyday incidents in the life of a Jewish family living in a New York tenement, and is a convincing attempt to prove that the life of the Jewish working class is little different from the life of the American working class people or any other nationality. Despite the fact that all but two of the players were cast from among Jewish members of the Theatre of Action, and the Jewish community here were consulted on the play, Capt. Fairbairn held that the actors were not "Jewish enough" and that the play failed to give a "Jewish atmosphere." On only one player, cast in an exaggerated role, did the adjudicator comment that he gave the impression of being "a real Jew," leaving the impression that he had expected to see the Jewish people caricatured. Again, Capt. Fairbairn stated that the make-up was not "Jewish," although it had been done by H. Osovsky, who had specialized in Jewish make-up for years. The play was directed by Harry Louis.'

"That play, apparently, was the last that the group put into any competitive festival. We couldn't continue to bring in a director. We didn't have the money. Even though we had Jack Newman who, compared to the rest of us, was wealthy and I know subsidized us very generously, it was too heavy a load.

"February 11, 1938: 'The Vancouver Theatre of Action has been invited by the CBC to participate in a radio drama festival, Jack Newman, acting executive director of the group, announces. Among plays being considered as suitable festival material, Newman states, is Archibald MacLeish's *Fall Of The City*, and the group is going into rehearsal immediately with several short mobile plays, including *Embargo*, a new sketch by Harold Griffin, centred around British Columbia's position on the Pacific. Rehearsals of *Class of '29*, which were curtailed during production of *Return At Sunset* for the drama festival, are being increased and the Theatre of Action also plans to revive *Blocks*, a one-act peace play with which it had considerable success last Fall.'

"April 14, 1938, which seems to be the last mention of any theatre groups: 'Progressive Arts Players of Victoria are planning to enter two plays in the provincial drama festival this year — John Galsworthy's *Defeat* and *Hostage* by Harold Griffin. The latter play was presented here recently with great success. Last year the Victoria group presented *Voice From The Living*.'

"The group did not formally dissolve itself, people just drifted away. It carried on, to the best of my recollection, into 1939, but its membership dwindled to the point where it was not really capable of presenting anything more than a local night in its own headquarters.

"I would say, looking back, the depression offered only the tail-end of a culture that was passe, which ceased to have any broad appeal, or any connection with people's lives. It dealt with the romantic past, and the progressive theatre, in consequence, took up themes that people would relate to. The largely unemployed people watching *Waiting For Lefty* turned to organize their first mass unions, or any unions other than the craft unions; it was a mirror of their own experience, but being drama, of course, it had point and focus.

"The same thing with *Bury The Dead.* In a period when everybody realized that the world was headed for war, except the people who were busy with their heads in the sand, it too focussed on the danger and on the hatred of war, because the First World War vets had been very shabbily treated and that constituted a substantial part of the population.

"Our intellectual life here really started in 1921. The university was still a small university and the only one in the province. We had an art gallery starved for funds. We had a museum confined to a collection of Indian artifacts and various mementos handed down, not catalogued, which occupied the top floor and didn't even have a proper curator. The boom for culture was not there. It wasn't part of people's lives.

"Now, we have the Art Gallery, if you like modern art. We have an Aquarium. We do have the attributes of a metropolis. In those days it was a city just barely removed from the frontier, in which people were too busy struggling for a living ever to see the stars."

Forty-five years after the beginnings of the social theatre in Vancouver, I asked Harry Hoshowsky, a teen-ager in those days, what did he think this theatre had contributed to those times?

"Personally, I am convinced that whatever you sing about, whatever you act about, whatever kind of dialogue you present in concert with others, will pass a message over that's indelible.

"A play, like a song, influences people, it helps them face up to the strain of difficult times.

"The trek to Ottawa, the riots in Regina when the police attacked a peaceful assembly, alerted, educated and united people.

"I don't say, for instance, that *Waiting For Lefty* or the PAC did it, but I think all the people across Canada in one way or another — the balladeers, the singers, the dancers, the actors, trade union men — I think these people are all part of the scene. The plays we produced happened to be an extra shot in the arm for everybody.

"I'd like to think of it that way."

X

Winnipeg — City Of Immigrant Culture

MY FIRST TRIP TO WINNIPEG was in 1933. I was going there with my husband, who was to edit a new labor weekly. I was to assist him as secretary and office manager. We had made our trip in the early winter then, when the landscape looked hard and forbidding. Trees and bushes were bare. They looked so vulnerable against the strong wind. Lake Superior was vast, mysterious, grey and very threatening under a cold sky — much like the familiar paintings of Lawren Harris.

In the day coach (pretty luxurious by Depression standards) as the train made its way west, my excitement had mounted. Trying to sleep sitting up for two nights didn't matter much. All I could think of was that I was travelling across the country I had read about and I was going to the city of the most important event in Canadian labor history — the Winnipeg General Strike. I was looking forward to this new environment.

When we arrived, I could hardly wait to step onto the street. It was a cold, windy day. I remember thinking how wide Main Street was — lots of room for the wind to sweep around. I would, in fact, nominate the corner of Portage and Main as the coldest, windiest corner in the whole world. I had been told that in Winnipeg you don't feel the cold as much as you would in Toronto because it was "a very dry cold." Having spent a Winnipeg winter with temperatures dipping to thirty below (added to the violent wind) I have to disagree. I have never been so painfully cold anywhere, dry air or not.

I suppose if you have the proper clothes and get around by car, perhaps you don't feel it so much. But if your winter clothes consist of the barest minimum, as they did for me in the thirties, and you have to wait for streetcars and buses on that bitter corner, it is an experience never forgotten.

The people on the streets looked all curled up in themselves, as though desperate to hang on to what little bit of warmth the body provided. My first impression, too, was of people and buildings and streets beaten down by those difficult, grim times.

Our own financial situation was also precarious, which meant we ate poorly. It was a very tough job we undertook — to start a new labor paper at the height of the Depression. It was certainly needed in that city of rich labor history, but trying to find financing for it was rough going indeed.

We spent close to a year in Winnipeg and made some good, warm friendships. We also joined the Progressive Arts Club there — my husband as part of the Writers' Group and I as part of the theatre section. Unfortunately we were not able to give as much time as we would have wanted.

One thing we learned quickly was that Winnipeg's division into the North End and the South End is more than a geographical separation.

Max Golden, one of the early members of PAC there, told me that it was in the North End (north of the CPR tracks) where all the immigrants were — the Ukrainians, the Germans, the Jews, the Poles, the Roumanians, the Hungarians, the Slovaks. These people were all first-generation immigrants and, by and large, they brought with them left-wing socialist ideas.

"If we don't talk about theatre in these organizations," said Max, "then we are not talking about theatre at all here. Drama was an important activity in Europe and they brought it here. The Ukrainians certainly had a very active theatre, one which dealt mainly with transitional problems of immigration. There was always Jewish theatre in Winnipeg too. At one time it was in the Queens Theatre and the man who ran it was named Sverdlov. There was a Polish theatre doing plays as well. They were quite nostalgic for the country they had left. But their theatre also dealt with the hard times and the oppression they had suffered in the Old Country they had fled."

The South End of Winnipeg — the centre of the city — is that area which the original pioneers settled. They were a mixture of poor Scottish and English.

"During the Depression," Max recalled, "they suffered the least. If someone was to be laid off, the immigrants were the first to go. By and large, people in the South End during that period, were placid and they developed a very placid, English type of socialism. The real action was in the North End.

"The Progressive Arts Club really came as an oasis from the terrible load of the Depression and the feeling of not being wanted — of being excess baggage in this world," said Max. "The PAC flourished in many arts areas, especially theatre. My own story was fairly typical. I was cut off from university. Went down to Toronto at eighteen. Got on the cattle train at the CPR yards in the middle of the night. Went to Toronto, walked the streets hungry, found no work there, came back to Winnipeg. And then, through people who belonged, wandered in to the PAC. I got involved in the labor movement, as did everybody else I knew, because we were looking for an answer, for a way out. I was interested in writing and wanted to get into any group that could influence and motivate expression in this town. My wife Sophie and I were part of PAC for more than 10 years. It gave people hope and focus. We had speakers, we wrote articles. It was a really important place for a lot of people."

Another PAC worker at the time was Fred Narvey. He was a student up to the age of sixteen, when his father died. Several weeks later he got a job working for an ice cream company. When he joined PAC and its theatre, he admits, he knew very little about acting, or art generally. But it is this association that educated him. In particular, it was his contact with Joe Zuken, a magnetic personality. "When Joe Zuken spoke," said Fred, "you listened. He really inspired us to the idea that the theatre could be a weapon in the class struggle. It was a terrible time of crisis and this was one way of expressing our frustration, our indignation and our disgust with living conditions at that time. This is what brought most of us into the progressive theatre movement.

"At that time we were searching for a new dramatic expression. You know how it is when you're young and new to a movement, you look for different ways to do things. One form we used a lot was the mass chant. What we lacked in training we made up for in sincerity and volume. I remember one mass chant we did called *Troopen (Troops).* This was an anti-war chant. We must have had fifty people on stage. We borrowed military costumes and we put it on in Yiddish. Most of us couldn't speak Yiddish very well. Fortunately, Joe knew everybody's lines, so if anyone slipped up, Joe would fill in. It was very dramatic in its rhythm. It was all about workers fighting against each other. We put it on for any organization that invited us.

"One evening we performed *Troopen* at a Ukrainian concert. No one spoke Yiddish but we got a good round of applause and were told it was very effective. I guess, the intensity and rhythm got through to the audience, even if the words didn't. That was one performance I remember very distinctly.

"In about 1936, there was a transition from PAC's Workers' Theatre to what we called the New Theatre. The change indicated more ambitious productions which would, in turn, extend and broaden our audiences. At that point we hired a director (who didn't get paid very regularly) and had classes where we studied the Stanislavski method of acting."

Fred recalled that many of their problems were related to inexperience; others to a lack of money. While he can now laugh about some of the incidents, what is interesting is how he learned to cope with the unexpected.

On one occasion he was in a short play. At several points he had to look out a window which was painted on brown paper and tacked to a wall. Fred recalled peering out of this "window" and saying his lines when the whole thing came loose and fell off the wall. He spent the rest of the performance holding it up with his hands.

Another incident describes a situation all too familiar to actors.

"In 1936," said Fred, "we put on a play in support of democratic forces in Spain. It was called *Waiting At Madrid* and was written by John Loftus. It was also entered in the DDF regionals. At one point I was supposed to shoot a fascist. We had borrowed a gun from the Police Department. We told them it was for a play and they gave us a gun with blanks. When it came to shoot, though, the damn thing wouldn't go off. I could hear whispering from the wings. Suddenly, I ran over to the fascist and hit him on the head with it. I ran off calling the key line: 'I'll be waiting at Madrid!' I couldn't believe I actually got away with it."

The people in New Theatre were exceptionally dedicated. The group's members were committed and self-disciplined. They gave enormous amounts of time to evening rehearsals.

"Often," said Fred, "I'd come to rehearsal so tired I could hardly keep my eyes open. I was working twelve hours a day for $40 a month. One week I'd work from noon till midnight, the next week from midnight to noon. I was always tired. But I never missed a rehearsal and I never failed to study my lines. This was the first theatre company any of us were ever in. The beauty of it was its spirit. It all came from the heart, was very sincere."

New Theatre, he told me, also produced a number of *Beer and Skits** evenings. This was their way of raising money for the group, as well as having some fun. A hall was rented. The audience sat at little tables and the whole theatre company doubled as waiters. These evenings, I am told, attracted many people who never before had come to performances. The skits took an amusing look at the group's own work, but also commented satirically on contemporary happenings.

"We called it a sign of maturity to be able to laugh at ourselves," Fred recalls. "I remember one skit where Frances Goffman came out completely wrapped up in a long cape. She took her time, then dropped the cape to reveal herself dressed in a bikini, and said, 'Workers of the world — tonight!'

A verse of one song from one of the evenings (with lyrics by Reuben Ship) may give some sense of the work. The song came from a revue called *We Beg To Differ* produced by Montreal New Theatre:

A wonderful friend of the Czar was I
A very close friend of the great Nikolai,
We practically slept in the same double bed,
He at the foot and me at the head.
But all that seems distant, all that seems far,
Those wonderful nights in the palace of the Czar.

**See* Appendix B *for examples.*

Chorus:

When I went shootin'
With Rasputin
Ate farina with Czarina,
Blintzes with the Princess
And the Czar — ai, ai, ai.

"Perhaps it is not great art, but with appropriate acting and movement, it was fun and quite pointed."

Imbert (Bob) Orchard came to New Theatre as their professional director in 1941. The product of English public school and university, when he completed his education he stayed on in England and met many interesting literary and theatre people. Like them, he became part of the pre-war intellectual community that participated in progressive causes such as the Spanish Civil War.

For a time he was associated with Unity Theatre in London — a workers' group of the thirties with its own small theatre built by union workers in various trades who donated their labor. It was there he saw Paul Robeson in a one-act play, *Plant in the Sun*. The theatre held four or five hundred.

In the fall of the Munich crisis, Orchard went to Russia where he briefly met Meyerhold, spent some time at the Vakhtangov Theatre and saw the Moscow Art Theatre. When war started in 1939, he was in New York teaching at the New Theatre School. He spent nine months there. It was shortly after that he heard New Theatre in Winnipeg was looking for a director.

"When I arrived in Winnipeg," he told me, "New Theatre had a studio on Main Street. The first thing I did was to immediately set up classes, which were essential for the group. I'm not sure exactly what I was paid, but I know it wasn't much. When there was a deficit, it was made up by Joe Zuken or Sol Cherniak. Later on, I also had children's classes, which were most successful.

"Some people in New Theatre did have a little experience. But most of them needed training. The Little Theatre still had a strong influence in Winnipeg and some people connected with them began to be associated with New Theatre. I think they recognized that something new was happening."

It was Orchard who discovered *Six Men of Dorset*, a play about the Tolpuddle martyrs, written by Miles Malleson and H. Brooks. He recommended this play and it was agreed by the group that it should be done. This was the first production he directed for New Theatre; he also designed the sets and played the lead.

"The important point is that everywhere — in England or the States or here — members of social theatres felt an obligation over and above theatre.

It was an obligation to society. You put yourself out. You folded programs, distributed leaflets, worked backstage because you were part of a collective effort. And within limits we set pretty high standards theatrically. I had the feeling then, as I have now, that the actor is the core of a play. The setting, the creating of space, can be relatively simple. The actor counted. He could act anywhere — on the street corner or in a small office. As it was, we had a little stage about a foot high. Actors and audience came in the same door. We could string a few lights around and we had a screen which we changed, and we added a few odds and ends. Another thing we did was to study the play — the background, the history, your characters, etc. It was part of our understanding of Stanislavski's approach to theatre and acting."

Orchard recalls that *Six Men of Dorset* was well received. It got very good reviews in the Winnipeg *Free Press.* As a matter of fact, the editor himself came one night to see the show. The audiences for the production came, for the most part, from the North End of the city.

He recalled the *Beer and Skits* evening as being "very successful, so long as we kept them in the studio. But once we got over-confident and thought we would do a big revue in the Dominion Theatre. Ben Lepkin wrote something called *Pay the Piper* and I worked with him, supplying lyrics. We were not experienced or slick enough and there were long waits between skits. There was a lot of talent, but it just didn't jell in that big theatre.

"The second year I was there, we moved into much larger premises on Smith Street. We built a stage that left some room for a backstage area. We did two productions there, as well as classes. One of the outstanding plays we did was *Professor Mamlock,* by the well-known German anti-Nazi playwright, Friedrich Wolf. It was a great success. We had a marvellous cast. The lead was played by a Jewish refugee named Louis Bassman. He was one of those tremendous players who could achieve depth of character and pathos. We performed this play for quite a while because of audience response to its strong anti-fascist theme.

"New Theatre continued during the war. I can remember the period of the conscription referendum. We did an agit-prop play on that. I wrote some things about voting Yes. We took this around to various groups that were having meetings and would put on songs for them. We were part of society. We reacted to what was going on.

"Another thing we did at that time was a *living newspaper* about China and the war against the Japanese. This form was being developed by the Federal Theatre Project in the States and excited me very much."

In the thirties not many of the "little" theatres invited press reaction to their work. The social theatres, on the other hand, felt they had something new and different to present and did go out of their way to invite drama critics. The responses varied. In some cities they resulted in harsh treatment of the shows, mainly because they disliked the subject matter. In other instances, the productions were completely ignored. In Winnipeg, unfortunately, only one or two of the people I saw had kept scrapbooks of clippings. I did manage to come up with a few, though. It's always interesting, in looking back at theatres of the past, to read about the reaction to their work.

The *Winnipeg Tribune* of March 2, 1942 reported:

Bassman Stars in Professor Mamlock

> A remarkable performance by Louis Bassman, newcomer to Winnipeg amateur dramatic circles, made *Professor Mamlock*, the play presented by Winnipeg New Theatre last week, worth seeing.
>
> Bassman, playing the title role, gave it meaning and dignity. . . . With a good voice and excellent stage presence, he created a character that rose far above the mediocre play.
>
> Another newcomer, Mary Gordon, was excellent as Mamlock's wife, giving her part that maturity so often lacking in adult roles on the stage. . . . The play was directed by Robert Orchard.
>
> — B.L.

The *Winnipeg Free Press* of February 2, 1942 wrote:

New Theatre Presentation Is Vital Play

> A dramatic picture of the festering hatreds that broke out in Germany with the coming of nazism, was given by the Winnipeg New Theatre Saturday night at its studio, in the presentation of *Professor Mamlock*, by Friedrich Wolf, a thought-provoking and vital play.
>
> The New Theatre production was given an unusual and strikingly effective setting, bringing the actors almost into the laps of the spectators . . . The sets were designed by Robert Orchard, director, and Ruth Scott.
>
> There was a fine sincerity about the acting Saturday night. It is a difficult play to do, since it relies for long stretches on the ability of the actors to color and shape their speeches. . . .
>
> The title role fell on the shoulders of Louis Bassman. He played with a deep appreciation of the humanities of the part, bringing a fine voice and heartening sincerity. Mary Gordon as his wife and Ben Chud and Ruth Popeski as his children, were excellent. There was also good work from a number of others, Mary Madden, as an intern torn between nazism and decent impulses being particularly convincing.
>
> *Professor Mamlock* can be ranked as one of the finest efforts

by the New Theatre. It proves that a propaganda play doesn't need to be blind in one eye. — F.A.M.

And the *Winnipeg Free Press* on another occasion reported:

Winnipeg New Theatre took a stride forward in its enterprising career, when it presented a modern adaptation of Ben Jonson's *Volpone*. . . .

The production had a glitter, bite and a very real understanding of the robust treatment that Jonson's comedy needs . . . and director Max Glandbard . . . has pointed up the action with satirical zest and has seen to it that characterizations are given with bold strokes. . . .

Joe Zuken played Volpone to the hilt, underscoring his venomous cunning. As Mosca, Saul Cherniak gave a virtuoso account of himself. He has a real feeling for the stage.

The simple stage settings proved very effective and costuming was excellent. . . . F.A.M.

And from Brandon on March 16:

Some 500 civilians and as many men in uniform witnessed the Winnipeg New Theatre's production of *Professor Mamlock* from the spacious new stage of No. 2 Manning Depot, Saturday night, sponsored by the Brandon Rotary Club.

The most striking dramatic features were: the use of the three-level ramp, the few sticks of suggestive stage properties, the amber light shafts on the darkened stage, the actors' backs to the footlights and the hand-in-pockets naturalness. . . . K.R.

Another newspaper clipping says:

Under the auspices of the Winnipeg Council for Allied Victory the play, *Professor Mamlock*, was staged in the concert hall of the Winnipeg Auditorium Wednesday evening.

Produced by the New Theatre group and directed by Robert Orchard, the presentation was in aid of a Red Cross Fund to provide comforts for prisoners of war in Hong Kong. More than 600 persons attended.

During the intermission Mrs. Laura Goodman Salverson briefly outlined the aims of the organization in presenting the play . . . H. Whyatt told of the work of the Council since November in raising $12,000 for Russian relief.

Included in the cast were: Louis Bassman, Leon Mitchell, Soli Jackson, Howard Madden, Mary Madden, Ruth McEwen, Elin Johnston, Morris Goldin, Roland Penner, Mary Gordon, Ben Chud, Ruth Popeski, Abe Roytenberg, Tommy Bredin, Oscar Antel. . . .

Fred Narvey spoke of Joe Zuken as a "magnetic personality" who inspired and led the Workers' Theatre in Winnipeg. Zuken is truly magnetic. He is an articulate spokesman for those times and their theatrical expression in Winnipeg.

As a young man Joe was a student at the University of Winnipeg. His parents supported labor causes, so he came quite naturally to be personally involved from an early age. He gained some of his theatre experience in university dramatic work. He also took part in Yiddish plays produced at the time. These two elements in his youth led him to membership in the Progressive Arts Club and to the formation of a workers' theatre. Joe also lived (and still does) in the North End of Winnipeg, a location where a great deal of the social action was taking place, and radicalism had strong roots. A lot of the immigrants who settled there had some experience in the radical movements in Europe. It says a great deal about Joe Zuken and his deep roots in the community to know that he has been the labor representative for that area on the school board and City Council for 37 consecutive years.

"During the Depression," Joe told me, "the North End became a pressure cooker. The young people came out of university with their diplomas and nothing happened except that they had their degrees and no place to use their knowledge. Many of these young people became involved in the labor movement, including the theatre. A lot of demonstrations and meetings took place at the Market Square, which became an institution, Winnipeg's Hyde Park. People of the North End were very active and participated in all these activities.

"The Workers' Theatre was the initial stage of expression and the concentration was on mass recitations and agit-prop work, which was closely allied to the labor movement," Joe recalled. "I remember that Workers' Theatre as such didn't put on performances uptown. We played working class halls. I remember one performance we had in the Patricia Hotel on the Main Street strip. There was a labor meeting going on and we were asked to participate in the program. So we began as part of a program for working class audiences in working class halls.

"Our plays dealt with unemployment, a war that seemed imminent, and so on. There was a punch to it. We didn't have a director as such. We used a collective approach. I was prominent in it, but I wouldn't say I was the only one. At the beginning it was more like the whole group got together and said, 'Let's do this.' It was alive, it was strong, it was new, and used new techniques to express the ideas. I think it was generally well-received by working class audiences.

"We attracted mainly younger people to participate. They were pro-labor in background and were intrigued by the new techniques we were employing. It was only later as it evolved into New Theatre that the representation broadened and people who were not necessarily working people or students were attracted to the kind of work being done.

"Workers' Theatre had no headquarters. We went from one working class hall to another for rehearsals, as well as performances. We didn't have a formal membership and there was very little money required for our work. We used whatever platform was available, and that was it.

"In the thirties there was a lot of theatre going on in the ethnic groups. The Ukrainian Labor Temple had very large audiences for their very strong and capable dance groups and choirs. They attracted a tremendous response from people. There was some theatre going on intermittently in the Jewish community. Of course, they brought in prominent theatre groups from the States, professionals, outstanding people like Jacob Ben-Ami, Maurice Schwartz, and so on. There must have been some activity going on in the other ethnic halls as well. They all did mostly classical work in their own languages, but there was very little in terms of immediate contact with audiences on basic issues of the day.

"So far as Winnipeg is concerned, there was the 'little' theatre but that was *la-di-da* stuff. It was pretty sterile drawing room comedy. The average person didn't relate to it, and they catered mainly to the upper middle classes.

"The people who gathered around the Progressive Arts Club and, later, the New Theatre, began to ask themselves, is this what theatre is all about? Or, is there something that must be said and should be said on the stage that is meaningful to them and to their lives? What PAC tried to do (and later New Theatre) was innovative, it was challenging and it filled a vacuum and a need."

Joe was eager to tell a story that involved them with the question of censorship of *Eight Men Speak* in Winnipeg.

"The production of that play in Toronto became national news. We heard about the tremendous first performance there in the Standard Theatre, the ovation given and so on. Someone suggested we get hold of the script. We got it from Toronto. But after that, our experience was quite different.

"After the play was banned in Toronto, the police here were apparently alerted. When we got the script, we rented the Walker Theatre. Rehearsals began. Then the police banned it, without even allowing a first performance. They intimidated C.P. Walker, the owner and manager of the theatre, and he was very much on the defensive.

"He informed me that the play could not go on, although we had made an arrangement for rental of the theatre. The police threatened that if the performance were to proceed, Walker's license would be cancelled.

"I was called before the deputy chief of police, McIver was his name, and I was told that he wanted to see the script and would then decide whether the play could proceed. Obviously, that was an impossible request and we refused to give him the script. The performance didn't take place.

"All hell broke loose. The *Winnipeg Free Press* took up the cudgels on the civil liberties aspect — the police arbitrarily banning a performance before a play is even shown. The pretext was that it was obscene. How ridiculous! The only thing obscene was the action of the police. They were frightened. I have no doubt they were also acting in conjunction with the police in Toronto and the Bennett government in Ottawa.

"Later, the ban was broken. We showed excerpts of *Eight Men Speak* in working class halls. The police didn't dare to interfere. Later, other parts of the play were produced in a labor hall.

"The ban didn't really work. I remember a huge mass meeting in the Market Square. There must have been 1,500 to 2,000 people present to protest the ban. Later a resolution was introduced at City Council which failed by one vote to condemn the actions of the police and called for the right of *Eight Men* to *Speak*.

"Later on the PAC, for the first time, had a home," Joe went on. "It was in a basement on Burrows Avenue in the North End. It grew because it attracted all sorts of people who were interested in expressing themselves. One of them was Professor Phelps, a very eminent teacher of literature. He gave a talk, *Is There a Canadian Culture?* People who wanted to participate, who were not politically involved in other things, got involved in one or another aspect of PAC. It became a gathering place, a second home for people — working people, unemployed, some intellectuals — others who were beginning to search for answers about the role of the performing arts in the context of the 1930s. There was a strong popular movement concentrated around PAC.

"PAC never really had a repertoire of plays. We just started putting on performances for our own group. Later, when it became the New Theatre, there were professional directors who came to that theatre. Max Glandbard came down from New York and worked for a while. There were Bernard Latham, Mercer McLeod and Bob Orchard. Then performances began to emerge, classes in acting were begun, major plays were produced.

"These directors were paid when New Theatre could afford it. I think $10 or $15 a week for Max Glandbard, when we had the money. I believe Latham was on a more permanent basis of pay, so was Mercer McLeod, who was active doing radio work. He was a professional.

"New Theatre eventually rented a studio at 460 Main Street, outside the North End. We wanted to attract larger and broader audiences for our productions there. After war broke out, we went on to produce *Rehearsal*, which was very successful. This play had a labor theme, but what was powerful about it was that there was no barrier between those who were performing and the audience. It involved the spectators and gripped them. *Rehearsal* took top spot in the Manitoba Regional Drama Festival and was then selected to go on to the Dominion finals in London, Ontario.

"At that time, though, we didn't have money to get the group to London. John Queen was the Independent Labor Party mayor of the City of

Winnipeg then, and somehow we got some money from the city to make the trip possible. At the Dominion Drama Festival, *Rehearsal* won the award for the best play in English.

"Later, we outgrew the studio on Main Street and new studio quarters were rented on Smith Street, uptown in Winnipeg. Some of the numbers for our *Beer and Skits* evenings were adapted by Bob Orchard, who added some new original material. We did these in a revue called *Off the Record.* It attracted young performers who came to us because this was the vehicle. There was so little else available in the way of meaningful theatre. We had by then quite a group. We were attracting talented people who had something to offer a theatre such as ours."

I asked Joe about the various attitudes to New Theatre. "Theatre critics and the daily press generally recognized that something new and special was happening," he said. "They didn't look upon it with disdain; there were some who might have said, 'Well, this is propaganda, but it's well done.' But on the whole, they had a very positive approach to our work. They recognized not only *what* was being done, but *the way* it was being done.

"The Workers' Theatre, primitive as it was, did try to bridge the gap between the performing stage and the audience. Our blackout techniques were new, we used a stage that wasn't pretentious, we tried direct communication with the audience. These were innovations at the time. Although they were not always done in a polished way, what was done was, nevertheless, meaningful.

"The people who had looked upon us as 'just a radical group' and who came to see what we were doing were impressed by the involvement of the audiences. Maybe they had never seen such reactions before. I think this timely theatre captured the emotions and the feelings of the spectators. They felt, 'Look, they're talking about us, we're on stage too!' There was this feeling of identification. In this sense, both Workers' Theatre and New Theatre played a positive role.

"Of course there was criticism of some of the performances. But I think these theatres won their credentials, because in their day this was the theatre that meant something, that was saying something that had to be said and was getting audience response. Needless to say, admission to New Theatre shows was popularly priced.

"I think our standard of work grew with experience and training. Remember, we were not professional theatre people. Later I did some professional work with John Holden at the Dominion Theatre in a couple of plays. All of us grew artistically as we studied, gained experience and worked with professional directors. They all contributed to our artistic growth.

"Those revue evenings were also pretty special. Audiences responded. People came. I remember Tommy Tweed visiting them from time to time.

He was attracted to our kind of work. There was great interplay between him and the actors. This added so much. It certainly wasn't grim. The theatre began to laugh. It had its own sense of humor. That was seen as we grew in confidence and realized that we could do a take-off and laugh at ourselves in some ways.

"New Theatre also gave young people a chance to try their talents and I think that experience had some meaning later. New Theatre was a home of activity, very intense activity. Everyone connected with it, no matter which way they went later, whether in the theatre or something else, I think they felt it was an experience they wouldn't have missed.

"The strength of that theatre was that it took place during what Harold Clurman, speaking of the American experience, called 'the fervent years.' The strength was the dedication. The strength was the fact that we were actively engaged in something which was in the context of the times we were living in. If it was protest, well, we were part of that protest; if it was bringing some enlightenment to some of the issues of the day, like the rise of fascism, we felt we were doing something to help people understand what was happening. That was the strength.

"I would say the weakness was that while we were contributing to the understanding of our times and had attracted people of talent, we needed to learn a lot, to develop our artistic abilities both on stage and off. That was achieved to a greater extent once we hired people like Latham, McLeod and Orchard. Our standards of production were rising just as the war cut it all off.

"People came to New Theatre for different reasons — those who were more active on the political scene had their viewpoint; others came because they wanted to perform; others because they were unemployed and were searching for an anchor, a compass. In Winnipeg we didn't have a tightly structured organization. Nevertheless, people who joined us recognized that there was a contribution to be made in the theatre at that time by the content of what we performed.

"Perhaps the most important thing about New Theatre was that it said something that was important in dramatic terms at a time when it was badly needed. Without exaggerating, we helped to pioneer some of the positive things now taking place on the Canadian theatrical scene."

XI

Montreal — The New Theatre Group

FOR ME, MONTREAL HAS BEEN almost a second home. My husband was born there and, difficult as the thirties were, we somehow managed to scrape together the $5 each for a week-end excursion there from time to time. In those days the train left Toronto about 11:30 in the evening and we would arrive in Montreal about 7 the next morning. One of our real treats was to stop off after arriving — it really was too early for a family reunion — for a full breakfast at Murray's, where you could also sit and drink as much additional complimentary coffee as you could hold. Thus fortified, we would be ready to meet Oscar's family and spend our weekend with them.

Mother, sister, aunt and cousins greeted us warmly. Together they were a happy, hospitable and considerate lot, even though their own situation, due to the lack of jobs, was pretty gloomy.

It was on these visits that I realized just how inadequate my high school French was. What a grave injustice to my generation of students in this bilingual country!

I did enjoy the sights though: the distinctive houses with their outside stairways; the streets running uphill and down; the mountain dominating everything; elegant Sherbrooke street; the busy night life of this old, historic city on the St. Lawrence. At that time there was also the colorful Bonsecours market near the waterfront and many ships sitting in the harbor from all parts of the world. One could almost feel the city's history — such a contrast to Toronto!

After each visit, I realized why my own city was called "Toronto the Good." At night and on Sundays, it seemed to be a city shut down. Montreal, by contrast, was bustling all the time, with much to do and see. The distinction was particularly sharp in its attitude to drinking. You could have a drink with your meal in a restaurant, or you could go to the grocery store and buy a bottle or two of beer to take home. There was no signing of legal forms, nor was it necessary to buy large quantities at one time, as in Toronto. There was an openness about this — you didn't have to rush home with your bottle and hide the fact that you might like a drink.

Later in the thirties, however, Premier Maurice Duplessis and his Padlock Law, sweeping in its application, tried to repress social and political activities which were said to endanger his government and province. It was then that some of the open spirit of the city changed — though not for long.

Personal reasons aside, there were other magnets which drew me to Montreal as well. For some time, from the early thirties on, we in the Progressive Arts Club of Toronto had heard stories about ground-breaking experiments in Montreal. Some of us had met Montrealers visiting Toronto and some of us had received correspondence. Still others of us had heard rumors of a Montreal movement similar to our own, a movement motivated by similar social and artistic aims.

A recently-formed Montreal stage organization, New Theatre Group, was presenting two productions, *Private Hicks* and *Waiting For Lefty*, on May 19, 1936 at Victoria Hall. It was their first show in a large auditorium. In their program, under a heading which read, *We Introduce Our Group to the Public*, they declared:

> The New Theatre Group believes that the study of good plays and their production has always represented one of the mainsprings of culture in any community. We believe that the play — in other words, the idea which is projected from the stage — is the basic art motif of the theatre. That acting, stagecraft, etc., represent the secondary art. Therefore we do not aim to develop outstanding performers — people who can take 'star' parts. We wish to develop a permanent, closely integrated company of competent actors and technicians, capable of doing justice to a fine play written by a master playwright.
>
> For this purpose, some one system of acting must prevail throughout all the work of the company if a cohesive and unified performance is to be given. Our group bases all its work on the Stanislavski method of acting — realism, with dynamic projection.
>
> Starting with a membership of seven people, all of whom wished to make an intensive study of the drama, our group has grown in one year to a membership of one hundred and twenty-five.
>
> The programme of this group for next year is one in which study plays the largest role, but three productions will be undertaken during the season. . . .

Rose Kashtan was one of the early members of New Theatre in Montreal. A striking, tall woman with strong, handsome features, dark hair and large brown eyes, she was eager to share her memories of that theatre. As with so many, both her parents were in the labor movement and were also very interested in their own Jewish background and culture. Yiddish was her first language and she learned to speak English when she entered kindergarten. Born in Toronto, she received her first taste of theatre from her parents who sent her to a progressive English-speaking organization on Sundays, where she was in her first play, one produced at the Labor Temple on Church Street in Toronto.

When she was fifteen or sixteen years old, her father suffered a fatal heart attack. The idea that she would be a lawyer evaporated. Why law? Her father had wanted her to be able to defend people like Sacco and Vanzetti.

In the summer of 1933, she met some people from Montreal and went there to work as director of a children's camp. Married in 1933, she lived and worked in Montreal until the summer of 1938.

"My life centred around the progressive political movement," she recalled. "I arrived with high school French, which I thought I could speak. My first effort to go shopping using what French I knew was a complete disaster. It was of no use in everyday living.

"There was an organization known as the Progressive Arts Club in Montreal at the time and I found my way to it. This organization would appear at rallies doing mass chants. The theatre section of PAC was the only active group I knew about. My own interest was in theatre and not long afterwards I found myself directing some of the chants. We played wherever we were invited. We were asked to places like Prince Arthur Hall, for organizations that wanted entertainment at mass meetings. Some of us, though, had a terrific desire to do something a little more interesting than mass chants. We wanted very much to do plays. At that time, there was the well-established English-language Montreal Repertory Theatre, headed by Martha Allan. We went to see the plays they produced, and while we had no desire to act in *those* plays, we did want to act.

"A friend, Sylvia Mendelssohn, told us she had an aunt, Lilian, who might be interested in coming to direct and maybe help us establish a theatre, an alternate theatre which would do different kinds of plays. For family reasons, Sylvia suggested that I get in touch with her. So I phoned Lilian Mendelssohn and she agreed to see me and gave me an address in Westmount. It was now 1934.

"I arrived at about seven o'clock in the evening at this very imposing home. I knocked at the door and a very petite woman who, it seemed to me, was in a nightdress, answered the knock. After a weak hello I said something like, 'I'm not late, I hope.' I had never seen anyone in an 'at home' gown. I understood about this kind of dress for a formal evening. But in one's own home, such a gown could mean only bed to me. It was very funny. That was my introduction to Lilian Mendelssohn. She became the first director and generally the guiding spirit of Montreal's New Theatre Group.

"At the time we met and established a relationship, Lilian was an active member in the Saturday Night Club of Montreal. Among other things, this liberal-progressive organization sponsored lectures and open forums on contemporary topics featuring well-known literary and or political personalities such as John Strachey.

"Lilian had a deep and abiding interest in literature — English and French — the written word was a passion with her. She was ready for our group of eager young people who wanted to act. The play form was of particular interest to her. In fact, she already had a play which she wanted to produce — *A Day in a Soviet Court.*

"I remember it very well," recalled Rose. "There was a Soviet judge, a woman, and two assistants. I played the judge. The trial was about a woman with a child who complained that the father had refused to pay support. I talked for an hour and-a-half. That was the play.

"After that first effort, we met and decided to call ourselves New Theatre Group. We found we had a similar approach to theatre. We wanted to do 'theatre with a purpose' and we wanted to do it well. We wanted to study, we wanted to learn, and it was Lilian who set about showing us how. The setting up of a studio she saw as a necessity and she plunged into the work of obtaining financial support for it, encouraging us to create a 'Friends of New Theatre' body. Many of Lilian's friends in the Saturday Night Club became 'friends' of our theatre.

"This petite woman with the large, expressive hazel-to-green eyes, who tossed her head like a lioness, who chain-smoked through a self-designed holder (a stem of silver with a circle on top for the cigarette and two circles at the bottom for her fingers) proceeded to cast the play. This was the only 'closed' casting I can recall. For the other endeavors under Lilian's guidance, we called open casting evenings and this was how our theatre attracted people from other 'little theatre' groups in Montreal — from Martha Allan's MRT, from the YM and YWHA, from McGill.

"Lilian had a great deal of patience, yet would brook no nonsense. She took part in discussions on the play and, as director, often led them. Interpretation and method of presentation were discussed with everyone. When we had an approach and a method agreed upon, then it was Lilian who was to have the final word. And this was where there was to be no nonsense.

"She certainly worked with an actor to get the agreed-upon interpretation. She would urge the actor to try anything that would work to that end. From the beginning, she used improvisation. She had imparted to us her understanding of the Stanislavski method. She worked hard to help the actor get at the truth of a characterization.

"She also never let us forget the need to study. Once, she arranged for a member of New Theatre to get a scholarship with New Theatre School in New York. The idea was for this member to come back and teach everything — voice control, body movement, history of the theatre, play analysis. Lilian was the one who urged us to import a director-teacher from New York. To the best of my knowledge, the first theatre school in English in Montreal was the summer school organized by Montreal's New Theatre Group. Albert Lipton was our first import. Then came Paul Mann.

"It was never Lilian's ambition to become *the* director for New Theatre Group, but it was her ambition that we should create a place for ourselves by hard work, choose plays that mattered, and strive constantly to raise the quality of productions. She could accept constructive criticism; in fact, she sought it out. She invited people she knew in the theatre milieu to rehearsals for just this purpose. Sometimes they became friends of our theatre. She also urged us into and prepared us for regional drama festivals.

"Lilian Mendelssohn was, at the time she began her association with New Theatre, easily twice the age of most of us, and it didn't matter a damn. Her rapport with 'the kids' was complete. She was a woman of means, with a gracious home in Westmount which she offered for fund-raising purposes. Her approach was direct, forthright. One could feel the steel in her backbone, and the warmth in her heart. She had a ready sense of humor and a zest for life. Whatever the task at hand, she gave it a truly remarkable effort. She was an inspiration to all of us who were fortunate to work with her.

"One of the first things we decided was to find a studio where we could work until we were ready to go out to the community.

"We heard that the Millinery Workers' Union had renovated a second floor in a building at Bleury and Dorchester and it was going to be their meeting hall. Somehow we got together and arranged to share the hall. First, we built a stage with a grey flannel curtain. Eventually, we began to give Sunday night performances in the studio and invited discussion from the audience.

"The Soviet play I mentioned was our first offering. I think the next one was *Waiting For Lefty*. We really plunged. But, as you recall, that play had mostly two-person scenes. It was not too difficult to put together. So we dared this and, I think, after five or six performances, we invited the press. At that stage, in the first press reviews, the production was praised, as I recall. It was a new and exciting play and we got a positive response. Some people who came to see it had played with Martha Allan. There was Jim Mellor and his brother John, for instance. The next thing we knew, Martha Allan wanted to put on *Waiting For Lefty*. A serious request came to us: would we lend her several of our actors? We had discussions about it and decided yes, we would do it.

"Martha Allan had a lovely little theatre and that's where *Waiting For Lefty* was produced. Of course, some of us went to see it. The first shock was to see Edna, wife of the striking taxi driver, dressed in a beautiful English tweed skirt and a very lovely pure silk blouse. I remember it to this day. In this outfit she was speaking bitterly to her husband about their poverty! It was with great difficulty that we kept straight faces. It was incredible to see this production and hear Odets' down-to-earth lines spoken in deliberately-cultivated English accents.

"We played *Lefty* — I can't count the performances. We took it all over the city, to the outlying suburbs, to workers on strike. Always, always the response was tremendous.

"The social and political climate in Montreal was grim, of course. Unemployment was rife. The hold of the Catholic church on the vast majority of the population was just about total. Any struggle in terms of demands for any kind of relief was viciously put down. It was the time of evictions, times of trying to organize the youth, the young unemployed who were totally dispossessed. For them there was absolutely nothing. This preceded the twenty-cents-a-day camps by a number of years. It was a very repressive time, and yet protest still took place.

"I was a member of the New Theatre executive as well as an actor. Most people in our group were expected to contribute their talents in all aspects of theatre, because we were completely amateur, in the best sense. Nobody was paid, not at that time. Our struggle was to pay the rent every month. We performed Sundays. There may have been a silver collection, I don't even remember that. We paid dues, all of us. These dues, plus silver collections at performances, and the tickets we sold when we played in other halls, were our sources of income. We did have fund-raising affairs as well. After a while we also tried to enlist patrons for our theatre. Lilian played a big role there.

"I think the first attempt to pay someone must have been in late 1937, when I was to have become the executive secretary. But I left Montreal just then. By that time, we had organized our school, which also helped financially.

"It was in the summer of 1935 or 1936 that the group asked me to go to New Theatre School in New York for a summer of study. I was there from late May to the beginning of September and I was to come back and teach whatever I had learned. I did try. We had acting classes, history-of-theatre classes. I think we even tried a little bit of voice and movement. Whatever I was taught, I tried to share with the others.

"After that, we had requests for teachers. I gave acting classes at the YWCA in Montreal. It became very evident to me that we needed something better than a teacher with three months' study under her belt. So we decided to bring in a director. Albert Lipton came to New Theatre after our production of *Bury The Dead*."

I asked Rose how the group chose its plays. "Scripts were first read by a playreading committee, which reported to the executive. When the executive had a recommendation to make, there would be play-reading evenings for the entire membership. There we would discuss and decide which play to do.

"The director would often introduce a play and state the reasons for his or her preference, if any, and then the membership as a whole made its decision. We had a fairly large membership. The acting classes had done that for us.

"People would come to us from various places. There was a fine English-language theatre at the YMHA, and some of its people joined us. That's how Ada Span came to us.

"We rehearsed major productions for roughly two months, about three nights a week, and Sundays, of course, mostly mornings. Sometimes we had classes on Sunday morning and rehearsals in the afternoon. Sunday was busy. There was a fine *esprit de corps*, a wonderful group feeling. People were responsible and exercised a fine self-discipline. Lilian was quite a disciplinarian. Everyone soon learned that they had better come on time. If you didn't, you had to answer to Lilian. It wasn't a joke; it was very hard and serious work.

"Lilian directed *Bury The Dead*, the play that followed *Lefty*. We played it for about a week. We got good houses. Some of the Montreal press branded *Bury The Dead* as propaganda. That was the first attack. I recall a letter Lilian wrote in response to the criticism. Audiences were terrific. I was in the cast again."

I later looked up the *Montreal Star's* issue of Oct. 17, 1936. Under a heading which read, "Erratic Anti-War Play Is Strikingly Produced," it declared:

> A commentary on the New Theatre Group's production of Irwin Shaw's *Bury The Dead* at Victoria Hall last evening must of necessity be divided into two distinct parts. Here is a case in which presentation is one thing and the play quite another. . . .
>
> Shaw, said to be only twenty-three years of age, obviously believes what he has to say in this drama, and says it with all the fiery vehemence of a youth seized with the gross insanity of modern warfare. But he is inexperienced in the technique of dramatic writing.
>
> *Bury The Dead* is a *jejune* anti-war thesis distinctly Communistic in flavor, rather than a moving anti-war piece of theatre. In it soldiers shot and killed at the front in "the war that is to begin tomorrow" arise from the grave to shout their condemnation of the policy of war and all the tragedy, spiritual and physical, which follows in its wake. . . .
>
> Lilian W. Mendelssohn and her band of workers staged the play most effectively. . . .
>
> It must suffice to note that a difficult production was carried through without a single hiatus; that the actors played for all they were worth; that the women in the cast outshone the men consistently and gave consistently sound performances; and

> that the mechanics of the production bespoke careful forethought and painstaking preparation.
>
> If New Theatre Group will drop Communistic propaganda and get hold of a good play, then things may be mighty interesting.

The review was signed by the late S. Morgan-Powell, Montreal's outstanding cultural taste-maker.

Shortly thereafter, the Mendelssohn letter appeared in the *Star's* Letter Box, under the heading, "More on *Bury The Dead*":

> Sir — my group of players ask the privilege of commenting, through your columns, on certain remarks contained in your review of our production of *Bury The Dead*.
>
> Certainly we appreciate the serious and constructive attitude you have taken toward our work. It signifies on your part a real desire to foster local theatrical enterprises.
>
> Your opinion as to the dramatic worth of Mr. Shaw's play is interesting. It is your duty and privilege to evaluate a play from your own angle and the public is likewise privileged to accept or reject that opinion.
>
> What we regard as inaccurate and even provocative is your concluding paragraph. You say: "If the New Theatre Group will drop Communistic propaganda and get hold of a good play, then things may be mighty interesting." And in another article you say: "When a group of young people . . . deem it their duty to present plays which contain undesirable propaganda . . . it is a legitimate part of criticism to draw attention to the fact."
>
> To take the last sentence first, to whom is anti-war propaganda undesirable? . . . We venture to say that anti-war propaganda, from whatever quarter it emanates, and however violent it may be, is not undesirable to the youth of the world, whose blood will flow into the seas, and whose remains will clutter up the highways and biways of civilization in the very near future, if their elders have their way. To whom, then, is it undesirable? . . .
>
> What do you mean by "communist" propaganda? . . . Do you mean that only communists are agitating against war? To almost every line in that play any pacifist will agree. There are a few lines in the play that are socialist by implication . . . and our local CCF would most likely agree heartily with the point of view advanced. I challenge anyone to pick out one line in the play with which only a communist could agree. . . .
>
> *Bury The Dead* is a militant peace play and in our opinion no good is served by putting wrong labels on literary articles.

> . . . But it is quite true that we shall shun using our stage to root for war and the *status quo.* Our group is allied on the side of progress and on the side of truth. It believes that art that is worthwhile in any period has always been allied to the forces of progress . . . We would like to develop a people's theatre in which every point of view relating to the progress of the masses would be represented.
>
> If the theatre can help to make people struggle against war, in our opinion, that is a higher art function than attempting to rest the weary nerves and tickle the sensibilities of the public.

The above review, and the letter replying to it, give some idea of how the work of New Theatre Group was received at that time. Another critic, Walter O'Hearn, referred to *Bury The Dead* as a play that "makes you stop and think" and estimated the standard of production and the play itself in a much more objective fashion.

"We were young people," recalled Rose. "We worked hard, but we also socialized together outside the theatre. We had a lot of fun. There was singing and dancing and horsing around. Some of our cabaret evenings were a source of great pleasure. One skit I remember came right out of *New Theatre* magazine which came from New York. Those evenings were staged in our studio. None of us had had much experience with song and dance, but we had a marvellous time trying it. We also helped create a dance group which we could call on for cabarets. It was not part of the theatre, but many of us participated in it on Sunday nights. We didn't serve refreshments, nor were the audiences seated at tables. They came to see a show which they thoroughly enjoyed. It was also a way of raising money, mostly by silver collection.

"The summer I left to return to Toronto, New Theatre Group did produce a terrific musical, *We Beg To Differ.* That was in 1938. It was by Reuben Ship (lyrics) and Mel Tolkin (music). They were very bright boys from McGill and they had done some daring stuff about the padlock law on the doorstep of the university. They brought this material to the theatre and we just went out of our heads, it was so wonderful. Lilian was full of plans — she was going to get the book published.

"When the revue was staged it was a tremendous success. Victoria Hall sold right out. Reuben and Mel went to New York at the end of the run and took this work with them. You may recall that Reuben Ship was creator of *The Investigator,* heard on radio during the McCarthy period. He was very talented and it is unfortunate that he died quite young. As for Mel Tolkin, I'm sure you've seen his name on television. We feel very proud that both of these talented people were successfully introduced by our group."

Rose became thoughtful for a moment and then smiled. "I can still recall some of the words of the theme song:

We beg to differ
With everything that's bigoted
And rotten and wrong.

"I remember another one even better:

We will raise our fist in the sky,
We will raise our banner up high.
If we all unite,
If we all agree to fight,
Who'll resist our fist in the sky?
The battle's calling us, the fight has just begun,
We've both might and right in our hand,
All the world is ours to command.
So join in parade with us and victory is nigh,
Raise on high, the people cry,
For none can resist our fist in the sky,
Fist in the sky.

"I had promised I'd come back to opening night of *We Beg To Differ,* and I did. What a moment! It was fantastic! There was an S.R.O. sign up at the theatre. I lived to see that in Victoria Hall.

"By that time the Padlock Law was in force. We did everything we could to support the struggle against it. After I left Montreal some of the theatre's performances were affected."

She admitted that it was difficult leaving the city, especially New Theatre and all its people with whom she had had many links, but it was unavoidable. Fortunately, Toronto was not too far away and she kept in close touch with the activities of the Montreal theatre and went to visit as often as possible.

In Toronto, she joined us at Theatre of Action. "I didn't find any difference in purpose," she told me, "but there was a difference in atmosphere. I seem to remember an ambivalence towards me. I didn't sense an open-arms acceptance.

"When I think about it now, there was no crying need for me; the theatre was getting on very well. That perhaps explains it best of all. There were people who were established in the group and doing their jobs. I expected it to be different. I didn't know most of the people in Theatre of Action and it was a bit difficult to get to know people.

"The first play I was in was *It Can't Happen Here* which was directed by Danny Mann. I played Lorinda Pike. I had been in that play in Montreal, but played a different role there. I found the general approach to the play and the acting very similar.

"I also participated in *Life And Death Of An American,* a most unusual documentary type drama with music. It was a great experience for actors who had to play a variety of roles in the course of the evening. After that production, my activities with Theatre of Action dropped off.

"When I reflect now on the thirties and the social theatres of that period, I can't help feeling that they laid a foundation for theatre in Canada. They were theatres which had standards, which insisted on standards, both in material produced and in production, which strove to develop people, which strove to treat theatre as a craft to be learned and through which a contribution could be made to contemporary life.

"The people who were in those theatres felt that they had a rare opportunity to be part of their times in a way that gave them personal satisfaction. It was worth the struggle. Those were ten of the best years of my life.

"We could be considered to have been *ahead* of our times, but also definitely *of* our times. How else can you consider a playwright like Clifford Odets who wrote of his time? Because Odets was so much a part of the thirties, I think his material will live. It was so welcome because it was part of the life that people knew.

"As for weaknesses, well, those were theatres that depended for their existence on the efforts of all members and on how well they carried out their responsibilities. To the extent that the groups were able to involve a broader community, they were absolutely self-supporting. It was a tremendous struggle. Nobody in those times dared to think that theatre would or should be supported by the state. Sure, we thought of it, but how do you go about it? Certainly, those groups have to be considered pioneers in Canadian theatre. Certainly respect should be paid."

Joe Golland, another actor with New Theatre Group at the time, followed his early stage ambitions and has continued to this day as a professional actor. He too recalls Lilian.

"I remember my first impression of her. She came in, a small woman, wearing long earrings, and she was dressed in a kind of heavy tweed suit, certainly well-dressed. When you're seventeen, someone in their forties seems old. I wondered what this 'old' lady was going to do for us? Well, I tell you, she was determined to make a theatre company of us. If any of us thought we were conscientious about theatre, she was doubly so. She was a tyrant about work. Rehearsals went on and on and on and we learned as we went along.

"If you didn't come to a rehearsal and you didn't have a good excuse, you were out. This we learned very quickly. I learned about discipline in theatre very early from Lilian. I can't remember all the plays we did. One I remember specifically, of course, and it was played right across this country — *Waiting For Lefty.*

"There are two things I remember about *Lefty*. One was the fact that we played it quite a few times. We played on weekends because we were sharing space in a union hall and the only time we could get it was on weekends. Before we started, Lilian would always ask whether everyone had eaten, because there were so many of us who were unemployed. Now, depending on what money we had, you either got twenty-five cents or fifty cents to go downstairs, where for two bits you could get a fair full-course meal. We'd come in the afternoon and re-rehearse the play and then play at night.

"At the end of each performance we came on stage, opened the curtain, and asked the audience for criticism. At that time, we didn't send tickets to critics. Surprisingly, a number of critics did come and gave their criticism from the audience. We looked forward to that. It was open criticism and we felt the spectators should say what they felt about the performance, ask any questions they liked from the performers.

"I remember one critic — I can't recall his name — got up with copious notes, which surprised us. He criticized a number of the characters. He thought the play had a point to make. I think he felt there was much too much 'propaganda' about it. He liked the intimate individual scenes.

"There is one other experience that has remained with me from that production of *Waiting For Lefty*. I don't remember which hall we were playing. At the back of the hall, I saw a man in a greyish turtleneck sweater. He told us he was having a group of doctors and nurses at a sort of garden party where they would have a meeting. I think at that time they were discussing the question of medicare which, in the thirties, was a dirty word. He asked us if we would come to the party and perform. We accepted gladly.

"It turned out to be Norman Bethune and we met at his home on Beaver Hall Hill. The door was open and he greeted us by telling us there was beer in the fridge and to eat anything we wanted there. The room I especially remember was the bathroom because all his certificates, all his degrees, were hung on the walls. Eventually we got into this little car of Bethune's. I recall getting into the rumble seat. He drove like a bat out of hell, and on Montreal streets that can be pretty frightening. We finally arrived at this party and it seemed to be miles and miles away. 'Okay,' Bethune says, 'the actors are here.'

"We quickly got ready to do a couple of scenes from *Lefty*. We got out on a sort of balcony and the audience was down below in the garden. After the performance, Bethune gave us $10, which was like a million dollars to us. That was a very special performance. He asked if we would do it again and we assured him that we were ready at any time."

I asked Joe about other groups in relation to New Theatre.

"At that time, there was no professional theatre as such in Montreal. There was only one other English company. The most exciting theatre was the French group, Les Compagnons, which formed the base for Théâtre du Nouveau Monde. It was the training ground for Jean Gascon, Jean-Louis Roux and others. Les Compagnons — like our group — played anonymously. Programs carried only the names of the characters, not the names of the players. Later on, when we entered drama festivals, when they wanted to name the actor they had to call the name of the character. We were so pure that we felt no one person should feel they were a 'star,' or any better than the other.

"In one show you might play a little nothing of a role, or you might help in the box office, or the next time play the leading role. We all did everything. It was a period when we built our own sets, made our own lights. It was a great day when we finally got someone who was studying to be an electrical engineer at McGill and asked him to build us a dimmer. He told us he would not only build us a dimmer but a switchboard as well. How we treasured that switchboard! The dimmer was like a dream. For the first time we could bring our lights up and down. We carried this equipment just about everywhere. We had it on top of our car when we toured to Toronto.

"Flats were something else. Flats came in every way, shape and size. People raided homes for props. We just knew if someone said I want your couch, you gave it because that was the only way we could ever get it.

"We seldom had much money. Our headquarters changed, depending on how much money we had. We had a very good scheme. We built our stage on horses. If someone had a big shed, that's where we kept our stuff. As soon as we got a hall we ran and put the platforms up and produced right then and there. Our lights were always available. We made our lights from cans. There were sheds all over the city with our stuff in them.

"There's one story about our production of *Bury The Dead* which, I am sure, is unique. If you recall the play, there is this big scene where the soldiers who are dead refuse to lie down and the general staff come in and decide to shoot them down. Well, what we needed was a machine-gun, which was not easy to come by.

"One of our members found, though, in a dump somewhere, an old World War I gun. It was scrap, rusty, none of the mechanism worked, but it looked great. We cleaned up this rusty gun, attached a toy sparkler on the side. Then, offstage, we had a wheel that turned and you had the sound of bullets going off.

"We had rented the United Jewish People's Order hall for a performance. They had a gorgeous, brand-new building. Now, whatever the politics were at that time, in relation to Duplessis and the UJPO, I don't know, but obviously there was no love between them. We performed one night and when we came back the following day for the next performance, we found a padlock on the door and were told we couldn't get in.

"That day in the newspapers there was a nice, big banner headline, 'Arms Cache Found.' We were interested in only one thing, we wanted our gun, our broken-down gun, and we wanted our sets, our entire investment, our switchboard, lights. I don't know who pulled the strings. Lilian or someone must have done that. We were allowed to go in and bring out our belongings, which we did. But where's the gun? No gun. That gun was missing. They had taken our 'arms cache'!

"Actually we came up against Duplessis in more ways than one. Once we did a play — I think Len Peterson was the writer — which called for a number of songs. One was *Down By The Riverside* and the refrain was 'Ain't gonna study war no more.'

"We entered this play in the Regional Drama Festival. We were told the song would not be allowed, that it was a religious song and we were changing it, and that was sacrilege. All this happened prior to the adjudication. An official of the Festival Committee spoke out against the play and that kind of song. He suggested that there should not even be an adjudication. There wasn't.

"There was a furore in the audience. Obvious plainclothesmen (they must have been Duplessis' people) came up on stage. When we came out for the adjudication we saw what was going on. I don't remember where the performance took place. It was in some church. I think there was some indication that if we played in this church, something bad was going to take place. Those were the incidents and conditions under which we operated. It must have been very important for the police to keep an eye on us.

"I remember a speech class at our school. One day, the door opened and three big men — really big men — came in. Now, as far as the teacher was concerned, these people were new students and she said to them, 'Please, don't stand at the door, take seats at the back of the class.' The men slowly went to the back, carrying out the teacher's instructions. We were doing vowels. The teacher was calling out, 'Everybody!' and the three men sheepishly crept out of the class.

"These characters would appear in the most unlikely places and actually got to know us very well. As a matter of fact, there was a time when we did a revue and we dedicated one of the numbers to them. It was called *The Padlock Blues.* It was a beautiful number about three hulking big men singing the blues because they had no place to padlock that day.

"There had been an enormous renaissance in theatre in the United States at that time. It spilled over into Canada. For example, at that time we did a play by Sinclair Lewis, *It Can't Happen Here.* That play opened simultaneously in sixteen theatres in the United States and Canada. We were receiving material from Hallie Flanagan, who was in charge of the U.S. Federal Theatre Project of the WPA. I still remember receiving early one-act plays by Arthur Miller.

"We brought in one of the directors of the Federal Theatre Project, a man by the name of Peter Huen, who also gave us classes. We felt we could never learn enough. Another person we brought in to teach acting during the summer was Paul Mann. He came for a couple of seasons. We had at least 150 people in those classes.

"I also recall that we received a number of awards in the festivals. When we did *The Flame Within,* which was an adaptation of Albert Maltz's novel, *The Cross And The Arrow,* we won the best actor award. *The Flame Within* actually had an interesting background.

"We must have rehearsed that play at least a year, because one of our own members adapted it. Since this was going to be a Canadian entry in English (the only other Canadian entries at that time were those from the French companies), we were very anxious that it should be an especially good performance.

"We had arranged to do the play in the Jesu Theatre, which Les Compagnons used. It was in the basement of a big Jesuit church. We had a very fine relationship with the Jesuits. We would come on Sunday mornings, knock at the door, and we'd get in downstairs, while the services were going on upstairs. Our only restriction was that we were not to be too noisy.

"*The Flame Within* told the story of an anti-fascist German who lit up a field of hay or corn, cut a cross and lit it up to guide the Allied bombers. For some special reason, known only to Duplessis himself, he didn't like the idea of an anti-fascist play and he tried to tell the Jesuit brothers that it should not be allowed on stage. They replied that they had read the play, it was about man's inhumanity to man, and they could see no reason why this play should not go on. When we did our plays the authorities always sent people to 'supervise.' Perhaps to be sure the play actually went on, or to intimidate the spectators. The opening night of that play was no exception. At the back were the usual plainclothesmen in attendance.

"We also played *The Flame Within* in Toronto. It was a very big event at that time. We were only worried that we would lose our flats, which we had brought in a couple of cars. We were received very well."

I asked Joe about the Montreal Rep Theatre's production of *Lefty.*

"MRT was a very select group. They were doing Noel Coward and the kind of theatre which we had not attempted in any way. After Martha Allan and Cecil West, who were then in charge of MRT, came to see our production of *Waiting For Lefty,* they wrote us saying they were considering doing a production of the play and asked for a number of our actors, which we thought strange.

"We had a very cohesive group and no one would go anywhere without getting permission. So we met together and we finally agreed that some of our actors should play with MRT — on one condition: that the group be recognized. When you saw the program of *Lefty* at MRT, after the names of three or four actors appeared the caption, 'With permission of New Theatre Group.'

"It seemed obvious that some members of MRT and their patrons didn't like the idea of doing a play about a strike of New York workers and their problems in the Depression. This was obvious because every night before curtain time Martha Allan came out and said, 'We are not doing this play because it is propaganda; we are doing this play because it is good theatre.' That's how *Lefty* was justified.

"Now — *their* production was quite different. In the Joe and Edna scene, for instance, the taxi driver comes home after hacking all day and his wife tells him they've taken the furniture away and the kids never saw a grapefruit. At MRT (we could hardly believe it) the husband came in dressed in a nice clean shirt and suit and she had on a lovely little apron and her hair was made up — and it just didn't sound right. Agate, a workingman, speaks to the union members, after they learn that their leader, Lefty, has been killed, in very strong and tough language. He appears wearing a white ascot. This interpretation was based on what Martha Allan thought workers were like, but it was very startling to us. (I should add that much later I came to MRT and played with them and had a great time.)

"You know, Clifford Odets came to Montreal. We had done his *Awake And Sing* and *Paradise Lost,* in addition to *Lefty*. He was then finishing the last act of *Rocket To The Moon*. We met him and showed him around the city. We ended up at the top of Mount Royal. He looked out and saw the Victoria Bridge and said, 'What a beautiful string of pearls.' After his visit, he sent us a donation of $50."

Montreal's New Theatre Group was active up to 1939 and the start of the war. Afterwards, there were attempts to revive it under the name Drama Playhouse. It continued on up to 1952.

"The breakup of Drama Playhouse," Joe recalled, "occurred as radio was flourishing, television was coming up, Reuben Ship had left, a number of actors had gone to the States, others had left town for Toronto. There was about $25 left in the group's treasury. At that time there was talk of a new theatre being formed in Stratford, Ontario. We sent our last $25 as our donation to what we hoped would be an exciting Canadian theatre.

"I went on to professional theatre. I don't know why, but I stayed on. Of the Montrealers who survived, I was the lone wolf going into professional theatre. To me, the theatre was a profession 'way, 'way back. I always wanted to be an actor."

There is one final story I must tell which underscores Joe Golland's dedication to Canadian theatre and the kind of love he learned in the New Theatre Group. When John Drainie died, Joe felt very deeply that we had lost one of Canada's finest actors. He considered how best to create a fitting memorial. Through the actors' union, he started a fund to plant a tree in Vancouver's Stanley Park. Beside the tree today stands a plaque inscribed to the memory of Drainie and his considerable contribution to the theatre of this country. I saw this vibrant, green tree and the plaque in Stanley Park on a visit to Vancouver some years ago and was deeply moved by the thoughtfulness of Golland's effort to keep green the memory of a fellow actor. It may be unique in Canada.

The inscription? Drainie's own statement and one which still touches me: "The actor is the custodian of the spoken word."

One of my evenings in Montreal was spent with three members of New Theatre: Rosalind McCutcheon, who was secretary of the group for a short time; Erna Allet, actress; and Malcolm Samuels, who was business manager.

Malcolm first wanted to put the New Theatre in its time and place and the climate that prevailed in Montreal. The situation was so repressive that even a theatre producing unconventional new works was suspect and worthy of harassment. He referred to a building New Theatre shared with Jehovah's Witnesses, located one floor down. This organization was also being watched by police.

"Our studio was on Crescent Street in 1939-'40. It was easy for the boys in the Red Squad — one guy would do the work done by two before.

"We also had a young man who was a member of the RCMP. He worked from within the group and was a *provocateur,* in the real sense of the word. He joined the theatre and became very active. I remember saying to him to take it easy, we're in the province of Quebec, there's a Padlock Law. At the start of the war we had the Defense of Canada Regulations. He roared: no one was going to tell him!

"He was also in other organizations. We used to wonder how the hell can a guy spend so much time in these different organizations. He was unemployed, but had money. Afterwards, when we found out, we wondered how we could have been such fools, he was so obvious."

Malcolm continued. "My main responsibility in the group was in a business and executive capacity — selling tickets, working out budgets.

"I'd like to talk a bit about the many benefit performances we gave. I remember we played *Plant In The Sun* for a union on St. Lawrence. We did scenes from our major productions for many organizations. We'd go to people's homes, halls, meetings.

"To me being in New Theatre was part of being in the larger left wing movement and, in the main, I have very good memories of that movement."

Rosalind was for a time secretary of New Theatre, but did a number of jobs around the group, particularly when their studio was in the Millinery Workers' Hall. She did see all their productions and I asked her to tell me what she can recall about performances she saw and the response of audiences.

"The performers, while inexperienced for the most part, nevertheless acted with conviction and with a full knowledge of what the plays were saying. It gave the performances great punch.

"Audiences responded enthusiastically. The standard of work presented was high, often innovative and technically excellent. We were operating on a shoestring, but productions never looked shoddy or threadbare.

"I think those of us who became involved in one way or another with the progressive movement began to see a real purpose in our lives. We had a real belief that what we were doing was going to change the world. New Theatre contributed to that optimism."

"My participation in New Theatre," Erna recalled, "was strictly on stage. I acted in most of the productions." While her work was favorably received, she remembered that the plays themselves and some of the other acting received negative criticism. "We were going against the stream and were subjected to condescension, if not outright criticism."

At the end of our conversation, Erna looked very thoughtful and when I asked what she was thinking, she replied: "When you work hard together, as you do in a theatre, something establishes itself which just continues. What it does to people depends on what they brought to it initially. It would amplify and enrich whatever was there. It may be the first experience with a creative art form which enriches them. New Theatre group did that for me."

One of the early members of Montreal's New Theatre group was Irving (Jerome) Myers. I spoke with him as well and he described Montreal in the early thirties as very similar to the rest of Canada and the States — those coming out of school were coming into a world that didn't want them.

"Somebody making $10 a week," Irving recalled, "was rich and probably supported two or three friends with pin money. It was difficult. You were unwanted. You were part of an entire generation that was trying to flex its muscles and do something, but really had no place to go. You were looking for something that was real, that had some meaning, on which you could vent your feelings, express yourself.

"My association with New Theatre began when I saw some of the performances, the agit-prop work at the time, and I was attracted by that form of theatre, the meaning it suddenly imparted to theatre, the added dimension it gave. Instead of plays like *Frannie And The Servant Problem,* suddenly there were people doing plays that dealt with realities.

"There were students and there were workers in the Group. It was a mix. I think the workers' theatres — except for the early ones like ARTEF, or the theatres that specifically dealt with the needle trades or fur workers — had quite a mix of people. There were businessmen, old-time socialists, intellectuals, kids who came from socialist families. You had people looking for some form of social acceptance, some form of social interaction in a very, very tight kind of world. You couldn't go through the normal forms because nobody had any money, so you were looking for new forms of interaction.

"And money was not an important thing in these groups. People could mix, people could see each other and could be accepted. That acceptance was absolutely essential to the majority of young people of that period. Maybe that's true of any period.

"Lilian Mendelssohn was a great lady. A very fine lady. She was an intellectual with a fairly good knowledge of theatre in the objective sense. Her leadership, certainly at the beginning, was invaluable. As time went on, she recognized the need for further training and development of the group. She brought in people from outside, at that time from the States. She brought in teachers and directors whose theatrical experience was greater than hers. Lilian's contribution to New Theatre Group was just immense on so many levels. I think she was a really marvellous person in her intellectual grasp of things. She made a contribution that you just can't overestimate.

"She was dynamic, very strong. I think she was very much aware of the things I'm talking about. That's the beauty of her character. She didn't become destructive. She didn't clutch and hang on. She saw the group going as she had prepared it to go and she let it go. That was a great thing on her part. Lilian always kept a close relationship, but not as Mama holding on.

"My main work in New Theatre was as an actor. I played in many of the productions. To some degree I was also involved organizationally. We all did that. In the late thirties I began to branch out.

"Raising money for New Theatre was not the most difficult thing in the world. There were many people who were interested. There were means of raising money for our needs. We always spent more than we raised. It was devising the means by which people could get it to you which, to my mind in fund-raising, has always been a problem. Devising the means by which people can give it to you properly, so that it will have some meaning.

"In our theatre we weren't playing to make money. We'd cover expenses. The purpose of our group was to get our message across, that was the main thing. Even if we lost money, it had to be raised to cover the loss. You leaned on everybody who had a car, who had a business, you got as much help as you could from them.

"We played to good houses, probably the best houses of anybody. We were the envy of all. Don't forget we had a whole labor movement to draw from, who were supportive to one degree or another. Objectively, if you want to look back, you can pick a lot of flaws in the lack of awareness on the part of many union leaders who didn't see the value of what we were offering. But, at the same time, those who did understand it, and were ready to use it, supported us.

"We played on picket-lines and in strike situations. To some degree we became part of the movements that were going on. I don't want to overdramatize that here, but in essence the theatre played a supportive role, I think in a good sense.

"On the other hand, I think our theatre should have been more eclectic and less dogmatic and narrow in its choice of plays. It needed variety, it needed change, needed experience in other means and other forms. You couldn't apply agit-prop to every single production you were doing. And every single production couldn't answer the problems of the whole world. What we were producing always led in a certain direction and always had a bit of the quality of agit-prop. Now, I'm not saying that was necessarily bad, because I do that today. I still work on a play because I want to get its message across. But I'm not prepared to say the message needs to be that clear-cut. I think we were a little narrow in what we were producing. I remember we did an Ibsen play, which turned out to be a fine production. I was thrilled. But there weren't that many Ibsens produced. Many people didn't like our doing it. That's my point. A theatre has to try many things and we didn't do enough of that.

"I remember I wanted to produce Lorca's *Yerma* and the group thought it would not be understood. Sure a lot of women had broken away from it and there were women at that time who didn't necessarily live those lives and had options. But there were a hell of a lot of women who didn't. The fact that many thousands of women don't live that way, doesn't invalidate Lorca's play. My feeling is if we had done that play in the thirties, people would have understood it very well and it would have advanced theatre that much more."

Irving stopped to think for a moment when I asked him whether the political climate in Quebec at that time affected the work of New Theatre. He told me — as so many had before — that it did.

"New Theatre was under police surveillance all the time. Plainclothesmen sat in cars across the street from our rehearsal halls, watching people, sometimes following people home. They attended our performances and there were several incidents in which they actually attempted to stop performances. That happened when we entered the Regional Festival with a play I directed. The controversy around that was classic.

"We took a CBC radio play called *Who Killed Cock Robin?* and built it into a three-act play, with the author's permission. We produced it and entered it in the festival. During the performance, we didn't know it, but they had the whole Red Squad at the theatre. They came backstage prepared to stop us. At the end of the performance, the fellow in charge of the festival jumped up on the stage and attacked the group as being left-wing. The police tried to provoke us into a fight. I saw it coming and I cooled everybody down, appealed to them not to respond. The police kept egging us on. Finally, the members of our group left. Then started a letter-writing controversy in the press. There were letters back and forth. They kept attacking us. It was a constant political battle for expression by New Theatre Group.

"The other incident I recall was with *The Flame Within.* All of us helped rewrite it. It was good theatre and very timely.

"Well, two nights before performance, the Jesuits called to tell us they were cancelling our use of their hall. We asked why. They told us the provincial police had come and told them we were a communist group, a red group, and they shouldn't let us perform there. We had a very long discussion with them that lasted through the night and through the next day. The brothers were caught in a quandary. They didn't particularly want to cancel our performances but, at the same time, they felt they had to. The police had threatened to close the theatre and everything that went with it.

"While we were trying to convince the brothers, we got a lot of people involved in organizing a whole series of telegrams and calls soliciting support, including support from the Lieutenant-Governor of the Province of Quebec for a Canadian play, adapted by a Canadian and performed by a Canadian theatre. He sent a message of support which we took to the Jesuits, pointing out that though this was a group which may have had some left-wingers in it, it also had other people as well and this was a play by Canadians.

"After a long, long session, they agreed to let us play. By the night before the performance, tickets had been sold out. The police were, of course, furious. They stood inside the theatre and watched everybody who walked in. We performed the play and received an ovation. In the Regional Festival, our lead in the play won an award for best actor.

"This was the kind of climate we were operating in. They were constantly harassing and digging at us. They did frighten some people, but most stayed. We took the position: what are we going to do, knuckle under to the authorities? So we did our thing, the best way we could. It was as simple as that. It worked.

"In addition to our productions, we started a regular summer school. In the first of these I became a first teacher who, in an organized fashion, taught classes in acting, speech, body movement. We subsequently brought up teachers like Paul Mann, Albert Lipton — some very good people who had a very profound effect on our approach to theatre, certainly to mine. These schools helped to raise the standard of our work. Their input became the galvanizing force for a better theatre."

I knew that Irving had researched and documented a history of theatre in Quebec. One can hardly talk about any dramatic activities in Montreal without at least some mention of French theatre. Irving pointed out that "the French used theatre in a revolutionary sense from the early 19th century. They even used the writings of Voltaire to get the message across against the English who monitored their shows, often arresting them, breaking up their performances. As for French-language theatre in the late 1930s, there was really only Gratien Gelinas working as a social satirist."

I asked Irving about New Theatre *after* the war when it had become the Drama Playhouse. He recalled it as "an attempt to continue a social theatre that would broaden and develop along the lines of New Theatre. I was asked to direct and teach. At the Drama Playhouse, we produced such plays as *Born Yesterday, The Flame Within, Le Bourgeois Gentilhomme.* The nucleus was some of the people who had worked with New Theatre. It was a group with a left-wing orientation to social problems. What we were trying to do, certainly I was, was to get beyond agit-prop, even though I had no disrespect for that form. I directed *Rehearsal* and some of the other one-acters into a series of programs which we did. I wanted to do more, to broaden it out, to do Moliere for instance. By the fifties, it had become a bit easier at that time. (We're into the late fifties.)

"I left Drama Playhouse finally to work on a cultural exchange program between Canada and other countries, including the Soviet Union. The group continued for three or four years after I left. It sort of faded out. I think it was partly because it didn't have a school, and partly because of not having really consistent leadership.

"I think the important thing in looking back is not to surround social theatre with any aura. There is a tendency for us to do that. It was a period in which socially-minded people were attempting to express ideas that had to be expressed through theatre. Perhaps many of them who should have made a further contribution didn't do so because they turned to other forms of expression.

"I am now at the point where I can look back at New Theatre Group and Drama Playhouse and say: the theatre I was part of at that time was not the ultimate. It was inept in many places, it was gauche, it was young, it was awkward sometimes. But it had a dynamic and it had a goal that was absolutely right, in spite of the fact that it may not have achieved it all. The fact is that the impact of those social theatres on the Canadian scene was far, far stronger than people know, or appreciate. This is something one has to understand. It mattered a great deal.

"The things we were fighting against absolutely had to be fought against. We fought and yelled and screamed and 'agit-propped' and did whatever we had to do. Those social goals are today accepted facts of life in Canada — social security, unemployment insurance, medicare — all of those things that we expressed and advocated in our own groping way."

Part Three:

THEATRE OF ACTION

XII

Toronto

TO TALK ABOUT WHAT HAPPENED IN TORONTO — the beginnings of Theatre of Action — we now have to go back in time a bit — to 1935. That year, both Jim Watts and I returned to Toronto at more or less the same time — she from her studies in New York and I from Winnipeg. We wanted to start a theatre and had already agreed on the kind we were aiming for, the kind we felt essential. In short order, Jim rented a small office at 989 Bay Street, which gave us an address to work from and a phone to set in motion our activities.

Jim was the first one who had come into contact with *Waiting For Lefty*. She had read it in New York and brought a script back with her to Toronto. We both felt this play would make a fine debut for our theatre, as it had already done for so many theatres in the United States.

Waiting For Lefty was given its first performances in Toronto on February 27-29, 1936, under the auspices of Theatre of Action and the Students' League at the University of Toronto. Jim was a member of both these organizations and cast the play from the membership of both. It was directed by Jim and Martin Loeb, who wrote theatre reviews for *Varsity*, the University of Toronto student newspaper. Theatre of Action produced the play again in May of that year under its own auspices with some of the student players replaced by members of the theatre.

As for my own participation, it was confined in the main to administrative work in the office, this to allow Jim to work on *Lefty*. It was important at the time for me to undertake this responsibility. I did, however, also look forward keenly to my own participation as an actor on stage.

Throughout this beginning period I also worked at a part-time job which helped to pay the rent for a furnished room where we could do a bit of cooking as well. But it was my work with the theatre that was all-consuming and which made the more mundane struggles of life seem unimportant.

Art and Lillian Messinger were also early members of Theatre of Action, as well as of the Students' League at U. of T. Art recalled being first contacted by the Progressive Arts Club after having done *The Bearded King Of England*, which was written by Johnny Myers and Kip Kaplansky. It was a comic show using the music of Gilbert and Sullivan. As a result of that production, members of the Students' League were asked to join forces with Theatre of Action to put on *Lefty*.

Another early member and in the cast of *Lefty* was Jack Kaell who had come to Toronto from Winnipeg. He was 18 years old and had never done any acting at all. He was cast in *Private Hicks* (written by Albert Maltz) which was the curtain-raiser for *Lefty*. It dealt with the U.S. National Guard and a strike.

Syd Banks, now a veteran television producer, had a job washing dishes during the early thirties and another job delivering on a bicycle. He was sixteen and worked both shifts.

He heard about Theatre of Action from an American magazine, *New Theatre*. As he tells it, he "happened to pick it up one day, and saw the name in a story. That's where I got the first indication there was such a thing. I went up to an office on Bay Street and Jim Watts was there. She didn't tell me much. In fact, she didn't tell me anything. She said, 'You're interested, well, come on in.' And that was about as much information as I got. My first role was as Sid in *Lefty*."

Though *Lefty* was a huge success, *we* knew that we needed more training and that we had to improve our skills. We also needed new members. Because of Jim's contacts with New Theatre League in New York, we wrote and asked them to recommend a teacher for our summer school, and to suggest scripts they might have available.

It will probably be difficult for today's Canadian theatre people to understand Theatre of Action's reliance on scripts from the States. During the period I am writing about, only the Canadian "little" theatres were doing plays in a regular way. Without an indigenous professional theatre in Canada, there were not too many playwrights writing about Canada. Those few who were producing scripts did not write about the issues of the time which were so important to the majority of people in this country. Thus, for a theatre such as ours, committed and socially aware and looking for scripts to dramatize the themes of our day, virtually no one was writing.

I have always felt this lack in the history of our social theatre movement, but at the time we could do little to change the basic situation in Canada regarding playwrights and the kind of plays needed. In the States there was a great flowering of the socially-oriented theatre. Many writers, especially the younger ones, were tackling in imaginative dramatic form the major themes of our time. Not all their scripts were great, but it was possible to give them good productions. They were universal and relevant enough to be done in Canada and to be understood by ordinary people facing similar situations here.

David Pressman was the teacher recommended to us and we got to work publicizing our summer school. We attracted quite a large group of people who were eager to study, especially since our fees were so modest.

We were fortunate to locate a coach house on Grenville Street, just east of

Bay. It belonged to the painter Tom Greene. He was not going to be using it and he offered it to us for our school as well as a rehearsal hall for our fall production. I can't recall now whether we paid anything or not. If we did, it must have been a very small amount. He was sympathetic to our plans and made his generous offer, which gave us a start in a convenient location.

David Pressman was (and is) a handsome man with a warm smile and personality. It was easy to like him immediately. He appeared confident, yet modest — none of the trappings of the brash "American director." He impressed us with his interest in Canada by asking lots of questions. He wanted to know about theatre here, about the situation in Toronto and in the rest of the country. He seemed sincerely interested in helping Theatre of Action grow.

He was a very good teacher. He was able to impart clearly his approach to acting. There was ample opportunity for all students to participate actively. For those just beginning their study of acting, there was always constructive criticism, never a "put-down". As a result, his classes were thoroughly enjoyable as well as enlightening. Students came eagerly during the summer to all the sessions.

In fact, by the end of the summer school the majority of the students had decided to stay on as members of Theatre of Action. We were so delighted with this enthusiasm that we felt justified in asking David to stay on as director of our group. It took a lot of courage to take this step — he was our first paid official. Youth is always optimistic and daring. We were no exception.

David Pressman remained director of Theatre of Action for two years — the crucial two years of our growth. He recalled the period for me recently and his own impressions:

"In 1934, money was impossible. We were on home relief. The Federal Theatre wasn't in existence yet, but it was talked about. But I wanted to be in theatre and I wound up at the Neighborhood Playhouse. It was there I got a really good grounding in all aspects of theatre. At the Playhouse we had an outstanding faculty. For instance, in 1934 Martha Graham came twice a week for two years to teach movement. In speech, we had a woman who is now dead, Laura Elliot. She was, at that time, private coach to Katharine Cornell and Judith Anderson and people like that. She herself had been a Wagnerian singer.

"The acting teacher at that time was Mary Tarcai. She gave us what was then the Stanislavski method. Subsequently, as I began to teach myself and learned more, I realized everything we got from her was terribly wrong, but it was terribly exciting. I couldn't wait to come to class in the morning. We spent months feeling sand on the ground and heat on our faces, and then, after four months we had a script to do and we didn't know what to do with it. I remember specifically Mary said to do the scene from *Tobacco Road,* which was then a hit. I looked at the scene and didn't know what to do. But she was an exciting person, time would fly by.

"We also had Louis Horst. His class was extraordinary. He was Martha Graham's pianist and composer and he taught a very special class in choreography. It was for dancers really, but for me, who was already interested in directing at that time, I got more out of the sessions than others. He gave us the theory of artistic form which had to with choreography, but had to do with any art, especially theatre art. He imparted the whole sense of how to begin, how to do the middle, how to end and he did it with music. When I was in Canada I used so much of what I learned from Louis Horst in some of the scenes which required moving large numbers of people.

"I graduated in 1936 and I was looking for a job. It was a terrible time to graduate. I had studied for two years — now what do I do? Well, the New Theatre League had classes and schools. I knew it was politically oriented (at that time, what wasn't?). If you were not political, you were an idiot. If you were not concerned with the left or right of the scene you were a vegetable.

"At the same time, there were exciting developments in theatre going on. The Group Theatre was formed and Odets was writing. Theatre Union was producing new plays that were reflecting the times. I decided to go to New Theatre League and find out what was doing. There I met Alice Evans and we talked. They told me they had a letter from Toronto saying they were looking for a director. Subsequently, I met some other person there and told him I had graduated from the Playhouse. He asked if I would like to go to Toronto and teach a summer school there. Canada was in the wild woods, so far as I was concerned. But I wrote and was accepted.

"For me, going to Toronto was a whole new experience. For my mother it seemed a very frightening break. I was, after all, her youngest. I remember going to the bus. It was pouring rain. My mother came with me to see me off. My brother accompanied me to Buffalo, I think. I arrived in Toronto in the summer of 1936.

"I had never taught anything before. It was all off the top of my head. I could only repeat what I'd done at the Playhouse and that meant a lot of what I thought was Stanislavski. I realized later, it was often just misunderstood Stanislavski. This came about, I think, because when he first came here in 1923 with the Moscow Art Theatre, he talked about what they were doing in Moscow. His own explorations were not finished yet. There was also the difficulty of language. I think Americans got a lot of wrong impressions, as well as a lot of good ones. The good ones were: here is a group of actors working from the inside and trying to get at the emotions. I think a lot of misunderstanding at that time came semantically. For instance, American actors like to use the word 'beat.' There is no such word in the Russian language, not in anything I've ever read. My conjecture is that they were talking about doing sections, rehearsing things in bits, chunks, hunks, and in Russian there is a word which means a piece of something. Stanislavski later described how in rehearsal, the idea was to rehearse a dramatic section by itself, and used the word bit. But, with a Russian accent, the word came out 'beet.' This was translated to mean beat.

"Take, for instance, the expression 'sense memory.' It does not exist in the Russian language. They talk about doing exercises with non-existent objects, but that's just an exercise. The use that was made of it by Lee Strasberg and others is 'way beyond what Stanislavski had in mind. He was looking for a conscious technique to get to actors' emotions. You can't really teach acting, you can only train talented people and the reason the word 'method' came along is that Stanislavski was looking for a method of work in training talented people.

"The American approach to Stanislavski also promoted the idea that he did not worry too much about speech or movement. I should point out that in the theatre in which Stanislavski worked, the actors knew how to do all those things to begin with. They took those things for granted, the famous Russian actors of the later Moscow Art period, like Schukin, for instance. He was a marvelous actor and in an interview with him he said he worked on his voice two hours a day.

"Take, for instance, the title of Stanislavski's well-known book, *An Actor Prepares.* I have the original Russian book. It's twice as long. In Russian the book is called *Work Of The Actor On Himself.* That's a hell of a lot more specific. What does it mean, 'An Actor Prepares'? For what?

"All of this confusion was an American development, which was unfortunate, I think. But it also became a bit of a joke in acting circles and prevented actors from seriously exploring an approach that would enhance their work as actors.

"I'm sure that in the first summer school in Toronto I brought a lot of these mistaken ideas with me. But I think I also brought excitement, because I myself was excited about teaching.

"My salary was $5 a week and I was promised that my room and board would be looked after. I must say people were very gracious about inviting me for meals. I remember that the entire group was very concerned. But especially you and Jim Watts and Art Messinger and Ray Harris were always making sure that I had some place to stay and that I was eating well. This friendship impressed me tremendously.

"At the end of the summer sessions, there was a meeting held at Jim Watts' place, where I was staying. The gathering was discussing the future and it was there I was asked if I would consider staying on to direct the first production in the fall. I remember my feeling was, 'When are they going to ask me?' I was so anxious to do it.

"By that time, I must say, I had really fallen in love with directing. It wasn't that I was ready to abandon acting, but directing offered really much bigger scope. Since I had a feeling for music and choreography and the total picture of a production, it really became something I wanted to do very much. So I accepted gladly."

XIII

Bury The Dead

EVEN BEFORE THE SCHOOL SESSIONS WERE OVER we had the script of *Bury The Dead,* by Irwin Shaw. In fact, it had appeared in *New Theatre* magazine. We decided to start our season with this unusual, timely anti-war play. We now had a large group of people to fill the numbers the play called for. We consulted with David and he agreed with the decision.

Because we had a new play and a new director, we decided to introduce them both by holding a public reading of the script. From the start, the Toronto press showed a good deal of interest in this new theatre and helped to draw attention to the reading by interviewing David. He spoke about Theatre of Action, the new play, and our future plans.

As a result, we had a good turnout for the reading and were able to found Friends of Theatre of Action, which would help to attract audiences and support for our group. With this backing, we felt we were on our way.

This was as David recalled, his first major directorial job — a full-length play, large cast, setting and lighting. "It felt scary," he told me so many years later, "really scary. I really didn't know much about lighting. It was mostly instinctive. All I knew was that I was excited by the play. I knew I had to lead a group to be disciplined, that people would have to listen to me. I think my love for the theatre, my love for the art of acting, was so enormous that it was possible for me to work in a comradely, but firm way. In this sense, my studies had prepared me well.

"In a way, it was great working with people who had not developed any bad habits as actors. To some extent, I was teaching while directing, but everyone was so eager to learn, and enjoyed it, and there was a good feeling at rehearsals. I have always believed that everybody has a little bit of an impulse to act, to perform, to pretend, and that I could bring it out. Somewhere in my attitude was the thought that everybody was talented and that I could enhance it.

"I remember the people reading for parts in *Bury The Dead.* I would listen to their voices, the quality, the personality — and that had a lot to do with my instinctive feeling about casting. The fact that the theatre didn't have much money didn't hamper things, but it certainly wasn't easy. Why should anything be easy? I remember thinking we should get a subsidy. Something radical like that. But I also remember Max Bloom unable to come to rehearsal one night because he had to work overtime. Other guys saying, 'I got to make deliveries.' Everybody had jobs if they could find them, but they all broke their backs to get to rehearsals.

"Everyone in the play understood what Irwin Shaw was saying with his play, and we did have some very interesting discussions as rehearsals proceeded. I felt, in that first production, that the group was beginning to respond, there was a collective spirit.

"I also designed the set. I had seen the production in New York and I hadn't liked the way it was done. I thought there should be a ramp. I remember sitting in my little rented room and making little models out of cardboard. I was not a designer, but I made lights and all those things. The boys in the group looked at it and got to work. They got wood from somewhere and scrounged burlap. It was a home-made set, but it worked.

"As for the curtain-raiser, in discussions we had during summer school and later, we talked about wanting to be a theatre that would be broad in its approach, to appeal to large numbers of people. I think I brought up, at some meeting, the idea of doing a Moliere one-act play with *Bury The Dead.* There were some smirks. I said I'd like to do it, and why shouldn't we show that face, that image to our audiences. A lot of people agreed and we chose *The Affected Young Ladies.* I think I also had the gall to teach History of the Theatre that summer. I knew a little on the subject, but went to the library and did a lot of research. I recalled that Moliere was a great social satirist.

"It seemed a difficult job for us to undertake, but I remember saying to someone at the time, that's one of the problems of the Group Theatre. It was probably one of the causes of the failure of that theatre. They didn't dare to do Moliere or Chekhov because many of the actors were limited in the art of acting. Their understanding of the Stanislavski method did not include voice work or speech, movement, dance, all those other things which they did not go into. They never really got out of that bad New York speech. Morris Carnovsky was the exception. He eventually moved on to play Shakespeare, as he did many times later on.

"I took one of the parts in *The Affected Young Ladies,* as well as directing it. I loved it. I remember doing terrible things on stage, like taking laughs away from other people. I was criticized for it by one of the reviews. In fact, I was scolded severely for it. But it was my inexperience. I really didn't know what I was doing. As I look back, I thought I was being very funny and spontaneous.

"For the run of *Bury The Dead,* I stood on the bridge and gave all the cues. I was also stage manager, even though we had one, but I really didn't feel that I could teach or trust anyone to give the cues properly. It was a very complicated play where the lighting was concerned.

"I must confess that I didn't know anything about Canada. In our schools we learned nothing about the country. But I soon learned about

1837. I learned that there was a CCF. I learned about the parliament. All this from my colleagues in the theatre. I got to know about the West, what Manitoba was like, what Vancouver was like, and having seen the players from those places, I saw what an enormous amount of talent there was.

"We all talked a great deal, at our meetings, about the fact that there were as yet so few playwrights in Canada. As a matter of fact, we instituted a contest for one-act plays later on. All this new information about theatre and politics in Canada was stimulating for me.

"It's interesting that the press in Toronto was very enthusiastic about the quality of the production, the acting and so on of *Bury The Dead* and the Moliere play. I thought we would be automatically flogged. The enthusiasm, plus the talent, were impressive. It wasn't just my work. I couldn't do it without the talent involved. You can't have a good conductor without a good orchestra. The reviewers looked at it as a serious group. They couldn't help but say, 'This is a hell of a good show!' "

Bury The Dead was entered in the Regional Festival, took the award and went on to the finals in Ottawa. David thought the whole idea of these festivals in Canada was unique because they didn't have too much of it in the United States.

"As for the people around the festivals," David said, "I think they were fearful of groups like Theatre of Action, not knowing what they really were about. At a reception, after we got the first prize at Hart House, I was standing with a bunch of the kids from our play, champagne glass in hand. Some little old lady came over to us, shook our hands. Then she said to one of our players, 'When the time comes, please don't kill us.' We all stood there like absolute idiots. Then the humor of it struck us and we laughed. She really believed all the propaganda she had read and related it to us."

Art Messinger was business manager for Theatre of Action. His job had special import — and difficulties.

"I don't recall how I became business manager. I would say that since I was in the business world and had a degree in Commerce and Finance, it was assumed I would be able to look after the financial problems of the theatre. I had a committee working with me. Our main source of income was the associate memberships. We offered, in return for a sum of money, a year's membership, free tickets to all plays, and to the parties afterwards, invitations to studio productions, readings, and advance material on our activities. I think we may have charged something like $100 for the year.

"Another way of making money was by giving discounts to organizations when they bought tickets for productions, especially unions. The Fur Workers' Union was approached, I remember, and they took a benefit night. They would get a batch of tickets at a lower rate. I would go out and speak to different unions. They would buy maybe 100 tickets at a discount.

"Unfortunately, I don't now remember what we paid in rentals. I know that we once tried to rent Eaton Auditorium and that was quite expensive. Margaret Eaton Hall was much less expensive, but I can't recall exactly what it cost. I think in certain cases, like 490 Yonge Street, maybe something like $40 a month comes to mind.

"I know we got the upstairs of the Hudson Tennis Club free, just to mind the place over the winter. I think the Children's School classes were held there and that was a money-maker for the theatre.

"There were other events to raise money. We had a big garden party at Chudleigh House and a cabaret at Knights of Pythias on College Street. *New Advance* magazine sponsored a production of *Bury The Dead* in Hamilton. At our studio on Yonge Street we had Sunday evening entertainments that helped financially. Generally, I would say we had our problems raising money, but that didn't deter us from carrying out our programs."

Theatre of Action attracted many kinds of members. There were students still at school and those who couldn't find jobs. Some members had jobs of a sort. A few others worked in industry. One of these last was Philip Knibbs. He was a handsome young man, very tall, with a good, deep speaking voice. Philip had a job at General Electric and understood the need for trade unions. He became actively involved with the CIO (Committee for Industrial Organization), which was then just starting. He undertook to organize a union — the United Electrical Workers — in his shop.

"I stuck my neck out and promptly got fired. We fought back but it was pretty hopeless. We didn't have an agreement or anything. One night I went down with my girl friend (I think it was to the YWCA on McGill Street) and saw a production of *Waiting For Lefty*. I was absolutely taken with it. When I came out into the lobby, someone handed me a prospectus advertising this summer school in theatre. After this beautiful production I had just seen, which was so stirring, I went down and saw Jim Watts. I think Jim was puzzled. I was rather tall. I was definitely from the establishment. I don't know whether she thought I wanted to join for some other reason.

"I paid my fee and went to the summer school. I looked forward to that. When it began I was very much a stranger, but I wasn't a stranger for long. I met an awfully nice group of people, what I mean is, warm and friendly people. David Pressman was teaching, as well as others. He was a wonderful teacher.

"I'd done school plays and things like that. This was really a chance to find out what acting was all about. David went rather deeply into the technique. He placed great emphasis on Stanislavski and *An Actor Prepares*. It stayed with me. I haven't been able to shake it.

"I remember David, in trying to get true feeling, would say, 'Try doing it with a broken arm,' and 'remember your arm is paining.' That approach helped immensely. Well, with me it helped. Somebody else it might just roll off their backs, but he managed to get me actually feeling the part I was playing.

"When we wound up in Ottawa with *Bury The Dead*, I was conscious that I was a worker in Acme Screw and Gear and I was glad we didn't *have* to go and sit in John Buchan's living-room with everybody elegant and all that. I didn't go because I felt out of place in those surroundings. I had a tremendous respect for John Buchan and his novels. I read every one of them. But Lord Tweedsmuir, the Governor-General, was a different kettle of fish.

"I realize now that Theatre of Action was a very special kind of group where everyone did everything that was necessary for the operation of the theatre. I've been associated with one or two little theatre companies, community theatre we call it now. We do have far, far too much of a separation between the people who work as actors, but who won't sweep or sew or hammer a nail or anything. What impressed me most about Theatre of Action was the co-operative spirit that prevailed. The girls grabbed paint brushes and hammers and worked right alongside the men in building sets — and heavy sets: 2 x 4 lumber and 2 x 6 boards for planking, enormous things. Everybody did everything that was asked of them.

"There were always plenty of bodies to go up and tackle the job. Somebody had to go out and hand out leaflets, somebody had to go out and sell tickets, and there wasn't anyone that I can think of offhand who didn't do their share of the backstage and building work of the theatre. Every single performer did everything they could to help the group.

"It was pounded into us, and in our formative stage, when we first came in to learn about theatre. David made a great point of the fact that theatre was communal — the lighting, the scenery, the costumes, the general appearance, the condition of the house — all these elements come together to make a stage production for an audience. Your bit on stage is just the frosting on the cake, that's the finish. Audiences come to see the playwright's script performed — let's give them the best we can. David would make as much fuss about a well-done piece of scenery, as he did about a well-done acting job.

"My association with Theatre of Action was very important to me. The beautiful production of *Waiting For Lefty* that I had seen said things I'd never heard in the theatre before. *Springtime For Henry* and all those jaded London comedies coming to the Royal Alex, they were enjoyable, frothy and so on. But *Lefty* was really down to earth. It had a special meaning for me. I wanted to be part of a theatre which spoke for workers and unions.

"One point I must make — we worked hard in that group, but it was great fun too. We were broke. We were poor people. How we had so much fun when we were so poor, I don't know. Somebody would bring in a box of bagels or something and we'd have a feast. I don't know that young people now would see it the same way we saw it then. We enjoyed each other and the chance to exchange jokes and ideas. We had lots of wild ideas. If anybody had a couple of bucks we'd spent it on coffee for everybody, or something like that. We even enjoyed working, there were always gags going.

"We got different people to see our plays and we changed some of them. W.S. Milne for one. I seem to remember his articles in *Saturday Night*. There was a man who reviewed theatre and he must have been sick to death of the stuff he was being fed. Then, all of a sudden, he sees something like *Bury The Dead* and he sits up. I think there must have been many people like Mr. Milne, who came there because it was their job to come, and found themselves sitting on the edge of their seats, seeing something different and exciting."

Ben Lennick, another early Theatre of Action member, also recalled the time:

"I was present one of the nights *Bury The Dead* was done at Hart House. You could hear a pin drop in that theatre. I thought it was fantastic — live theatre, actors on that stage working in groups, in different areas on that stage, the lighting effects — quite, quite brilliant.

"At the end of the play, the soldiers start moving out of the trench. It was a very, very moving moment. I remember that as the curtain fell, the audience began to applaud. Then they rose. It was like, I suppose, the first time the *Hallelujah Chorus* had been played and everyone rose, still applauding. That was the first time I was ever present at a 'standing ovation.' It was a fantastic moment in theatre. To me this was pure, complete theatre. The ringing cries of 'bravo, bravo' were echoed and re-echoed and I thought, my God, this is theatre, this is what it's all about. I've got to be involved. My orientation as an artist took second place to my wanting to get involved in theatre.

"I recall speaking to someone in the office and telling them I'd like to study with David, if that were possible. I didn't know what the fees were. All I knew was that I didn't have any money for the fees. But I had a lot of enthusiasm and dedication and was quite willing to spend the summer studying.

"It was suggested that I meet with David and let him make whatever recommendation he wanted. I sat down and spoke to him. He asked me what my thoughts about theatre were, what I thought I'd like to achieve, how I felt about what Theatre of Action was doing. I gather, on the basis of our interview, that he recommended I be given a scholarship to take the classes.

"That was like manna from heaven — great, beautiful. So I got involved in the classes. Of course, most of my theatre was going to movies. I thought I brought a fairly critical assessment to my viewing of performances on screen. I very quickly learned that what I thought I knew was nil because David, in his very gentle way, disabused me and everyone else in a class of fifteen or eighteen or twenty people.

"I think Theatre of Action at that time was on St. Nicholas Street in a loft. There were posts, it seemed, everywhere. We had to move and set our class in between those pillars, but to me that was a fantastic summer, because I really learned a lot! David held forth in long sessions where we just sat and listened. He spoke about theory, on what he felt the actor should be thinking, how he has to prepare before even taking a script and working on it. He talked about the esthetics of theatre and how he felt that beauty was most important. He coupled beauty with truth and I always wondered about that coupling. To me, quite often truth was ugly, not beautiful. His idea was that when you are delving for the truth and you have to decide what is true for you within a situation, you still must make what emerges beautiful. That remained with me.

"There was a lot of give and take in those sessions. He was full of marvellous stories about what he'd seen of the Group Theatre and other productions, and when he'd worked at the Neighborhood Playhouse with Sandy Meisner.

"At any rate, we got to do scenes. One scene we did was from *Three-Cornered Moon*. We chose our scenes, worked them out, showed them at class, and David gave his criticism. It was a very good learning time.

"About that time, *Waiting For Lefty* was being readied for presentation again. We started to rehearse while the classes were going on, I think, and then we started to take it out on bookings.

"On one occasion we played it on the back of a truck, of all places, in the park off King Street near Niagara. We were doing it at lunch-hour while some Massey-Harris workers were either contemplating strike action, or were already on strike. We played out in the open on a summer day. We had a fair audience. It was a real agit-prop sort of thing and I recall, after the performance, someone said George Gershwin died. That's how I relate that particular occasion.

"Another time we were taking *Lefty* to Oshawa. That was about the time of the sit-in strikes at General Motors. Tremendous things were happening there. I remember Arthur Roebuck and David Croll resigning from the Ontario Cabinet over Premier Hepburn's policies in that strike.

"We also took that play to Kitchener for the Kaufman plant workers and the rubber strikers. I don't know where we played it — it may have been in an auditorium or union hall in Kitchener. At a very dramatic tight moment in one scene, someone in the audience yelled out, 'Hit him!' Talk about audience being involved. This was real participation.

"I do recall another incident. I think we were playing in the Foresters' Hall on College Street, just opposite Eaton's. This time Max Bloom was sitting behind his desk and he has a carafe and offers me a drink and I say, 'No, thank you.' He replies, 'You don't mind if I do?' He pours a drink and drinks it. I was watching his face. He went black and white and blue — every color in the rainbow. Someone had filled the carafe and inadvertently put turpentine in it. He stayed for the rest of the scene, then ran off the stage calling for somebody to do something. He was rushed to the hospital, where his stomach was pumped.

"We took *Waiting For Lefty* around a good deal, as I recall, and that was done in addition to whatever major production was being rehearsed. I think *Class Of '29* was the play after summer school, but I was not involved. I think I was trying to make a living at that time.

"I remember when we moved into 490 Yonge Street. We started to build a studio theatre up there. We built a stage and had seating capacity for about 100 to 120. We didn't have a raked floor, but it was fine for studio productions. We got into a play called *Plant In The Sun* by Ben Blake. I enjoyed playing in that. We played Sunday evening and drew some nice crowds for that production. It must have been 'pay what you can,' but we had packed houses. I guess there was nothing else going on in Toronto on a Sunday and we got to be a place to spend an interesting evening.

"People were enthusiastic. There were discussions after performances. David fielded some questions from the audience. That made the evening more interesting for the spectators.

"*Plant In The Sun* was about shippers in a candy factory. The characters were almost right out of *Dead End*. I remember needing a Bronx accent. I was delighted to try out an accent. I think we played with a lot of vitality and got a lot of good laughs. That was my first taste of getting laughs in a play. It was marvellous, it was great! The audience responded beautifully."

XIV

The Way It Was — A Toronto Dialogue

The Setting: *An office at the CBC.*
The Time: *A break in a hectic schedule.*
The Cast: *Frank Shuster and Johnny Wayne.*

FRANK: When we got into the University of Toronto, we both went to work for *Varsity* and we both wound up being editors.

JOHN: We were both on the *Varsity* staff and had great dreams about some day, when we graduated, getting a job for $20 a week as young reporters on the Toronto *Star*, or the then *Telegram* or the *Globe*. The result, of course, didn't work out that way, because they weren't hiring anybody when we graduated and we drifted very, very accidentally into radio, and then from radio into television.

FRANK: How did we get to know about Theatre of Action? I'll tell you how. I was still in high school. I lived on Shaw Street and around the corner lived Joe Orenstein and his younger brother, Leo. He knew I was interested in theatre. He said, "You know, there's a summer school opening up, it's called the Theatre of Action. They're bringing in a New York director and that might be interesting for you." I thought it would be marvellous. If I'm not mistaken, the fee was about $5 or $10. I didn't know whether I could handle that kind of money or not. At the university, my daily allowance was ten cents and that was it. In high school it was less. Anyway, John and I *did* go down there. And that was a revelation to us, because we never knew anything about acting, really.

JOHN: We didn't know there was a system in acting. You see, all we wanted to know was about acting. We wouldn't give you a nickel for class-consciousness, social things, alternative theatres. That's the compliment we're going to pay that theatre. Everybody had their own motivation for becoming involved. To us it was merely a chance to learn about acting, and, as we got more and more involved with David —

FRANK: — and he gave us those terribly critical exercises and worked with us —

JOHN: — it became the best training we could have for professional theatre.

FRANK: We use it to this day. And we thank him.

JOHN: Everything we learned, we use today. And we are implacable about our own performances and about the directing, as implacable as David was. You know, he had only one standard and that was professional. I don't think he made any allowances. It would have been unfair to himself to say, "Okay, these are amateurs, I'm going to go easy on them." He cuffed us around. I'll tell you a funny story. We were invited to London, after we were successful here, to appear on the BBC. Charles Laughton was on the show. We met a director, Coby Ruskin, who was directing there. He was one of those Americans who had fled during the Red Channels-McCarthy period and was teaching there. These two strangers from Toronto walked in. We were discussing something, and I suddenly said to Frank, "We've got to have sense memory here." This guy turns to us and says, "What the hell is that?" So we said, "What the hell do you mean, 'What the hell is that?' We worked with a guy called David Pressman." At which point this guy yells, "DAVID PRESSMAN!" Suddenly, he hugged us. Well, it turns out he was with Neighborhood Playhouse. He had been suspicious of these two idiots from Toronto. All of a sudden we started talking about listening and acting and working at the whole scene. Every word we said struck a note in this fellow.

FRANK: Also, as I recall, we were impressed with him. As we started to block this particular sketch and we knew what we wanted, he went right along with it. I must say one thing, a sidelight. Ever since we left Theatre of Action and worked with David and Paul and whoever we had —

JOHN: — and Danny —

FRANK: — and Danny Mann, we thought this was the way the average director worked. Then we turned professional and I must tell you we never met one director —

JOHN: — since then —

FRANK: — for years that would compare to those three. We wound up in the Canadian Army Show. Remember, they brought in someone from England. He came over and he —

JOHN: — couldn't direct his way out of an unlocked toilet. None of those guys could.

FRANK: And we'd sit there and we'd say, "Well, don't you think it would be better if it went this way?" And he'd say, "Good idea, boy." So that's what we went through all our lives with directors. We thought David was the average. We realize now, he was a genius. There are very few like him around. I think there was a vitality there. I guess it came out of the Playhouse and their approach that you just don't get usually in the average director. After the summer school with David, we were in the first production, which was *Bury The Dead.* John was the sergeant. I was one of the four soldiers digging the grave with Bert Gold, Murray Acker. I remember my first line got a marvellous laugh. We were digging and I looked up and I said, "I used to take a shower every day, can you imagine?" And then there was the laugh. All those lines were great. What was your line?

JOHN: "I'll get you a picture in the Saturday Evening Post." This was a show!

FRANK: You were engaged, you were involved in this production.

JOHN: But you see, that isn't a function merely of the so-called alternative theatre, it is the function of all theatres. All theatre's got to catch your heart.

FRANK: If it was junk, we'd say it was junk, no matter what theatre it was.

JOHN: Comedy has to have the same sort of intensity. I talk, you'd swear it was David. I turn around to some guy and say, "I don't believe you and if I don't believe you, you are not convincing me. It's not a question of converting me to a political philosophy, convert me to a sympathy for yourself and your character, you miserable son-of-a-bitch, convert me to sympathy for you." There is a certain amount of sneering going on against the so-called "method" actors. Some people cover up by saying "method" acting is mumbling. If a man's a bad actor, he's a bad actor. It's got nothing to do with the "method." To reach out and touch somebody, you just have to be human. This is strange, talking about the technique. I think that Frank and I are unique in North America for having adapted that particular training into comedy and into writing too. I sit and watch other people who play so-called sketch comedy, and there is a kind of flippancy, there is a shallowness to their characterizations. If you watch very carefully what we do in our writing and in the characterization of the comedy, we try to use that sort of depth that we learned from David, to give it a little more meaning.

FRANK: Even if some of the jokes are primitive, we try to find a little more in it.

JOHN: When we were really big on the Sullivan show, we were walking along the street in New York. I saw a bald-headed guy go by me, a little heavier, and I looked at him and I said, "David?" He turned around, came toward me. I said, "David Pressman?" Hadn't seen him for years. He said,

"You're Wayne, aren't you? I saw you on the Sullivan show. You're not a comedian, you're an actor." So I said, "David, that's the nicest thing that's ever been said to me." I told him it was his fault because he trained us to dig deeper. There's another thing we learned — transition from stage to radio to television. They are three different disciplines, like water-colors, etching and oils. Each one requires a different technical facility. You can train yourself, if you've got the persistence and realize you are going from one to the other.

FRANK: We did a series in Hollywood. We spent thirteen weeks trying to find out how you play for film.

JOHN: Here we come to the key. Frank has just mentioned what I think is the key to what we got from David and from the Theatre of Action and from the people around us who were working — the ability to get a script, look at it and ask questions. Nobody asks questions today. They just stand up and read the thing. David taught us to be analytical. First of all, you read the script. Then you say to yourself, who is this man, why does he say or do that? Now, most amateurs don't do that. Most amateurs get the impression that the script is there totally. They don't have to inject any of their own interpretive techniques. They don't have to study or anything. That's wrong. It's that wonderful business of questioning, analyzing and improving that we got from David, and it's never left us. Once we were coming from a rehearsal for our television show. I turned to the director and told him it was fun, because we found a lot of things in that rehearsal. Now, if you can't enjoy rehearsals, then get out of the business, because most of your life you're rehearsing. You only do a performance once, particularly on television. You've got to enjoy it. To get back to *Bury The Dead*. It was a hell of a production.

FRANK: Very theatrical. I don't think anyone could have picked a more dynamic play. The lines were really crackling.

JOHN: It was perfect. You know, to find a good property, that's what everybody is looking for. In today's terms — it was a hell of a property. What a wonderful springboard!

FRANK: It had guts. I must confess I had not the slightest interest in the message that was there. I was interested purely in the technical, and it was a good story, kept the audience engaged.

JOHN: I recall the festival production.

FRANK: Sure. We had to win it to get to Ottawa.

JOHN: We went to Ottawa, yeah. We were scared. In those days it was considered such an outrageous thing, an anti-war play. I think that's what militated against us. You had general so-and-so sitting in the audience, and on stage generals were being questioned for their actions. This was quite a blow to a military man to watch it.

FRANK: That wasn't why we didn't win there. They didn't think it was theatre. The reason I remember that Ottawa show so well, it was my first year at university. I had to write my first exam a day after I got back from Ottawa. I wrestled with my conscience whether I should go to Ottawa. It was a very important exam and it was French. We had a professor who didn't teach us French all year, he talked about other things. I was scared to death. I remember taking my French books with me to Ottawa. I didn't even wait for the adjudication. At the end of the show, I ran to the train and went back home.

JOHN: Talking about the festival reminds me that the arts are sort of captive of high society in this country. A real journeyman actor, a guy who works and sweats and comes up against these people, feels very strange. All of a sudden there's the Governor-General sitting there saying, "That was jolly good."

FRANK: My parents had borrowed money to put me through school. Here is my first exam ever at the university and I am off doing a show. When I come back I might fail. It was a great decision in my life. But I couldn't miss that performance.

JOHN: I know it's a long time ago I'm looking back on, but I'd say it's probably the most professional company we've ever been involved with ourselves. The dedication was there. I say it was real theatrical discipline. I used to come home four o'clock in the morning from rehearsals and theatre classes.

FRANK: By the time Danny Mann became director we were too involved with our college work.

JOHN: We got back to university and we were doing the college show.

FRANK: I went as far as Theatre of Action's *Class of '29* and *The Inspector-General.*

JOHN: And I left Theatre of Action earlier than that.

FRANK: I was upset during *Class of '29*. David asked me to play this older man. Here I am twenty years old and I've got to play a sixty-year-old man. I know David meant it as a compliment, but deep down I would have liked to have been myself on the stage. I've always hated beards and moustaches ever since. I am constantly plagued by them. When it's necessary to wear them I do, but when they put that spirit gum on me, I resent it. We've been asked, you know, to come to Stratford and do something there. I always think of the make-up and get discouraged.

XV

1937 — The Ottawa Experience

FOR ME THAT BEGINNING PERIOD was a revelation on many levels: there was the success of the school, which attracted many talented people; the response of the press in Toronto was encouraging, as they recognized the power of a new play produced by a new theatre with a new director; there was David's interesting and wholesome approach to the casting of the women in *Bury The Dead*. The six roles were double-cast and the actors alternated during the run at Hart House as well as at festival performances. It marked a good beginning.

All of these developments at the start justified our optimism about the future for Theatre of Action. We could begin to see opportunity for growth.

I played one of the women in *Bury The Dead* and, because of the alternating, I was able to see it from out front on several occasions. I can never forget the opening of the play — a lone voice singing *Swing Low, Sweet Chariot* as, very slowly, the lights come up. In the light you see a large ramp, slightly tilted forward, with soldiers holding spades. One is sitting on the ground singing. In front of the ramp, in silhouette, stand six men with their backs to the audience. As the song ends, the soldiers continue their digging and the play begins.

No matter how many times I saw the production, that opening always sent shivers down my spine. I could feel the tension each time spreading from the audience as the silence deepened. The tension, in fact, held for the whole of the play until, at the end, the audience exploded in applause and cheers. It was quite an experience out front.

On stage, it was quite different. The first challenge in playing one of the women was getting on to the slanted ramp in the dark and getting down front to your man, without making any noise. I was terrified that the heel of my shoe would catch, or I would trip, or I would end up standing in front of the wrong person. As if that were not enough, I had to start the scene as soon as the lights came up, completely in character. What made that more difficult was the type of woman I was playing — a girl who was very flighty and not too concerned with the man she came to talk to. Preparation for the scene was almost impossible, given the circumstances. As an acting experience it was invaluable, but I never felt I did my best work in that particular role.

David helped us to get offstage in the dark a bit by assigning an actor in the wings to help us as we reached the edge of the ramp. I was always in a bit of a sweat; there were so many challenges in this short scene. Even today, when I go to the theatre, and the stage lights come on and I see the actors in their places, I remember how it feels to do that quickly and quietly. It's always a miracle to me. I wonder how many spectators think of it.

As for the festivals of the "little theatres" in Canada, they were important at the time. It also seemed to us that we should be part of those yearly get-togethers. We considered ourselves part of the "little theatre" movement; more important, we wanted to contribute our particular viewpoint — through our scripts — to this showcase. The fact that the festivals were competitive simply meant that we would have some measure of our standards.

We had wanted to enter *Waiting For Lefty* but when we applied it was too late. We applied for *Bury The Dead* quite early and were pleasantly surprised when we were accepted.

We confronted a brand new audience in the regional festival performance at Hart House and, much to our delight and surprise, we were given an enthusiastic reception. The adjudicator, George de Warfaz, practically ran on to the stage to talk about the presentation he had seen. We were thrilled at his evident pleasure and the fact that *The Globe* of February 24, 1937 reported it so fully.

> '. . . If the rest of the festival proves as good as tonight, I'm afraid we'll have to work hard,' declared the adjudicator, George de Warfaz, at the close of the evening.
>
> *Bury The Dead*, by Irwin Shaw, a play 'about the war that is to begin tomorrow night,' presented by the Theatre of Action, was described by the adjudicator as 'one of the great plays of our generation, I believe.
>
> 'It is a magnificent contribution to the art of the drama. It is one of the most moving, striking, stirring plays. It is terrifying, grotesque. It gives us comedy at its best, if a bit baneful. What marvellous anti-war propaganda! It ought to be performed all over the world for the edification and illumination of dictators. I beg you to forgive my eloquence — I know I'm not in Hyde Park,' commented Mr. de Warfaz with exultation.
>
> 'I congratulate the Theatre of Action on their pluck and courage in performing it. It has been so beautifully produced that I have hardly any criticism. It was a performance that could

> hardly be bettered by any professional actors. The movement, the time and the tempo were all so good, and the technical staff did a wonderful job with the lighting,' he added.
>
> David Pressman was the very able director of *Bury The Dead*. The players were so excellent that it would be unfair to mention one and not all of the twenty-seven . . .

With this enthusiastic send-off we went on to Ottawa and the Dominion finals. Some of us went by car, other members of the cast went by train. I was included in the trip as the secretary of the theatre. This would be my first experience at a Festival final. It was an opportunity to see the work of the theatres in the rest of Canada.

Lady and Lord Tweedsmuir were present at our performance of *Bury The Dead*. There was a generally well-dressed packed house which responded enthusiastically to the performance we gave. There was no doubt they were witnessing a unique play, both theatrically and in subject matter.

In the May 8, 1937 issue of *Saturday Night*, Hector Charlesworth wrote:

> . . . The sensational event of the first half of the week was *Bury The Dead* by Irwin Shaw, presented by Theatre of Action, Toronto. I did not see it at Hart House Theatre, but it will be recalled that Mr. de Warfaz was immensely enthusiastic . . . The production at Ottawa was vital and of a nature to hit the public in the eye. No listener would drowse while it was going on . . . The stage direction of David Pressman was admirable and lighting and movement helped to sustain interest . . .

On May 7, *The Telegram* had written:

> . . . Discussing one of the Toronto entries, Mr. St. Denis warned of the danger inherent in all productions setting forth propaganda, in which 'the cause' was sometimes allowed to triumph over the theatre rather than being equal to and enhancing it . . .

And finally, the *Ottawa Journal* of April 29 wrote:

> Of *Bury The Dead*, he (Michel St. Denis) said, 'I think it is essential that we do not become confused over a play written to support an idea, and dramatic art . . . I am very impressed by the work which has been done,' he said. Sets and lighting were alright . . . He also suggested the play lacked unity . . . He thought a somewhat artificial text hindered the actors, adding the play was one of teamwork calling for silhouettes, not characters. 'I am not sure,' he said, 'that the play should not be twice more terrible. We ought to have been stopped laughing.'

A little deflating for us on one hand but very good for the ego on the other.

There were several interesting highlights at this particular final. In addition to our play, there was one called *Relief*, which was about the drought in Saskatchewan and the misery it added to the general depression; there was also Ramon Sender's *Secret*, which dealt with methods of torture employed by military police in Barcelona to get information.

The cast of *Relief* consisted of four persons — an older woman who, in addition to having written and directed the play, also acted in it; her real-life husband, who played her husband on stage; and two younger people, the son and daughter.

The *Ottawa Journal* report of April 29, 1937 explained the play's import:

> A play on an essentially Canadian subject by a Canadian authoress who was also its producer and filled one of the leading roles, was a unique feature of the Festival and opened the evening's trio of dramatic works. It was *Relief* by Minnie Evans Bicknell, a domestic tragedy of the Saskatchewan drought area, given by the Marshall Dramatic Club.
>
> 'This play is very genuine,' said Mr. St. Denis, 'and the people on the stage talk of the things they know. Both the production and acting are very close to life. I appreciate the natural quality of the work, and see that the author is also the producer and an actress.
>
> 'The acting was so genuine that at times we forget we are members of an audience, and the production is good. I say this since much of the time we do not even notice the matter of production, which is no slight tribute. There were very good and amusing moments in the scene when the mother is talking to her two children. While I appreciate the work, I cannot say that it has great size theatrically, nor that it has exceptional interest to me. . . .'
>
> (Mrs. Bicknell and her husband who act in the play have lived for 14 years on their farm near Marshall, Saskatchewan. She has intimate knowledge of the drought areas about which she has written and deep sympathy for the many people who, she declares, are in a situation such as she describes in *Relief*.)

A Canadian Press report of April 28 added information for us:

> Minnie Evans Bicknell, author of the play *Relief*, arrived here today and said: 'If writing this play should increase the understanding between the East and the West I shall feel it worthwhile.'
>
> The Marshall, Sask., farmer's wife . . . is tall and slender with blue eyes and fine white hair, curling softly. Tears stood in her eyes as she described conditions in the drought area. 'My play could be taken from the lives of hundreds of Western people — people accustomed to luxury, reduced to absolute poverty, on

relief, with only fuel enough to heat a few rooms. The climate being so severe, lovely modern homes are going to ruin, frost-coated walls with the plaster falling off.

'As in the play, men are being driven to suicide, disheartened by the terrible conditions induced by frost, drought and low prices. The young people are leaving for jobs on the West Coast.'

. . . He (Mr. Bicknell) disclaims all credit for the success of his wife's play. 'She is the sole author. All I did was read the script and offer a few suggestions and criticisms. I became interested in dramatics because my wife was so keen about it. I had to be taken in forcibly from the farm to act in my first play, some years ago,' he said . . . 'Now I am very interested and enjoy it.'

Like most of us in Theatre of Action, the cast of *Relief* felt a bit uncomfortable in the atmosphere around the festival. We did a fair bit of socializing with them out of a kindred feeling that we belonged together.

Secret, the Ramon Sender play, had in its cast Lorne Greene, who also assisted with the direction. It was David who had helped him get into the Neighborhood Playhouse, where Lorne studied for two years. During that period, he accepted an invitation to teach speech and voice at Theatre of Action's summer school.

It is, I think, of special interest that *Bury The Dead, Relief* and *Secret* all played at the Dominion Drama Festival finals in 1937. Those three plays reflected very well the desperate times in the world. Yet, at the end, both Lord Tweedsmuir and Michel St. Denis made strong pleas in their concluding remarks for more comedy and less gloom at festivals. The *Ottawa Journal* of May 3, 1937, quotes M. St. Denis as saying that "one of his reasons for choosing *The House In The Quiet Glen* (John Coulter) for a prize was that it was a comedy." One of his reasons for giving the top prize to the Toronto Masquers was that they played "a comedy and a good one . . ."

I think it's important here to deal with the official attitude to Theatre of Action in the festivals. It was made fairly obvious to those of us who attended official functions that we were intruders. I always had the feeling that if our artistic work could be faulted in any way, they would have been quite happy to reject us. But having accepted our theatrical contribution did not mean, apparently, that we were acceptable socially.

There was, for instance, one incident in Ottawa, after the plays were shown and all the groups were invited to a final ball. We discovered that Theatre of Action as a group had been left out. I could normally forgo such an invitation, but I was angry that discrimination was being shown. We discussed it and decided that David should call Colonel Osborne, the Honorary Director of the Dominion Drama Festival. When he received the call, Col. Osborne expressed great surprise and insisted it was just an oversight. He had invitations delivered to Theatre of Action's cast and crew that very day. Very few of us by then wanted to attend.

It seemed to me a rather large "oversight." In many small, as well as big ways, we were made to feel that we were intruders. As if to underline and justify this feeling, Theatre of Action was left out completely from a book which tells about the history of the Dominion Drama Festival. Called *Love and Whisky* and written by Betty Lee (Toronto: McClelland and Stewart, 1973), the title is taken from a remark by the same Col. Osborne, "If this organization becomes a success it will have been founded on love and whisky." The only mention, and that very briefly, of the social theatres of the thirties is for the Vancouver entry of *Waiting For Lefty,* which won the award for the Best Play in English.

Toronto's Theatre of Action, which entered three times in the regional festival and twice went on to the finals, is not mentioned at all. Neither is Winnipeg's New Theatre, which won the award at the finals in London, Ontario for the Best Play in English. Nor is Montreal's New Theatre and their difficulties with the local festival. It's hard to believe that all of this too is an "oversight."

Perhaps the last word on festivals of this period, and specifically the 1937 festival, should be left to David Pressman. In the *New Frontier* of June, 1937 he wrote:

> One of the major disappointments of the Festival was the lack of imagination, creativity and originality. So much imitative acting and playwriting is indulged in . . . *Bury The Dead*, presented by the Theatre of Action of Toronto, was one of the few productions which brought forth a comment from the adjudicator on 'experimentation.' 'Although not always successful,' was his qualifying remark . . .
>
> If the festival as a Canadian institution is to grow and mature into something in which the entire population of the country may be creatively interested, it will have to change some of its policies. At present, there is keen competition between the east and the west, and among the various participating groups; but the audience is almost exclusively upper class and regards the festival as a grand social affair of the year, rather than a review of the country's work in the theatre. It is remarkable to realize that outside of the Festival Committee and the competing groups themselves, very few people are really interested in the progress being made in the theatre as a cultural and educational force . . . It is encouraging to know that next year the festival will be held in Winnipeg, where a large theatre can be obtained and perhaps prices lowered, so the doors can be opened to the 'people' to participate in an art which is the most basic art a mass of people can lay claim to. The inclusion of full-length productions is an important development . . .

> A Drama Festival should be a review of the year's work in creative theatre, not an instrument for the social enjoyment of the few.

In its July issue, the magazine carried a letter from Hugh Eayrs who, at the time, was chairman of the Central Ontario Regional Drama League (CODL). He wrote in reply:

> . . . As to Mr. Pressman's remarks about the play which, in my opinion, he so soundly directed — *Bury The Dead* — I may, perhaps, now that we are some months removed from the Central Ontario play-offs, say that the admission of his play was a question considered at some length by the committee of which I have the honor to be chairman. I am quite frank to say that so far as I was concerned, whether the play was presented by a group with whose ideas a great many people might not march, and whether the play was of the stuff which a great many people in this highly chaste city of ours might not like, didn't in the slightest degree matter. My own view was that decision should only be made upon the following basis: was the play a good play? It was. Was it well directed? It was. Would the play rank with fellow entries? Undoubtedly. There was, it seems to me, no more to be said . . .
>
> Finally, may I say how heartily I agree with Mr. Pressman's remarks as to the wisdom of some policy changes. I, too, with him would take this movement — now a national movement on a really big scale — much more nearly to our people from coast to coast, and to all kinds of our people. I hope we may all of us work to that end, though as to the city in which I live I reflect that little or nothing can be done without recourse to the snob appeal. Let Mr. Pressman remember, as I do, that to go to a literary lecture in Toronto and not be part of one vast substantial shirtfront accompanied by one even vaster substantial bosom is still something almost in the nature of a crime.

This letter from Hugh Eayrs confirmed what we already knew: that for Theatre of Action only the highest standard of work as a theatre would keep us in the DDF and earn their respect. Nothing less would be acceptable.

XVI

Roar China

THE NEXT PRODUCTION WAS *ROAR CHINA*, which was David's idea. He knew about the play and wanted to do something tremendous and spectacular. China was in the news a great deal at that time, having been attacked by Japan, and it seemed a timely choice.

"I had seen photographs of the Theatre Guild production, with Lee Simonson's settings," David told me years later. "I was always fascinated with those pictures. I also knew it was a well-known Soviet play, and I had seen some photographs of the Soviet production. I knew about the playwright Tretiakov, at that time a well-known Russian writer. I had been thinking of what we could do that was big and timely and would employ everybody. So I suggested it. No one else had heard of this play.

"Once we got a copy of the script and read it everybody said, 'How can we do it?' All I said was, 'Leave it to me.' That took a lot of guts because it called for a gunboat, sampans floating in and out, a huge dock, tens of thousands of coolies. I felt it was right up my alley, that sort of spectacle.

"I can still remember the way the guys on the construction committee worked, especially Al Sandler, who built the tracks on which the sampans moved. We built the gunboat, all out of cardboard. It couldn't have lasted more than a week. There were scenes played on it. Up front, on the apron, was the dock where the Chinese coolies worked. Sampan sails were the middle curtain. They would close in and close off the gunboat.

"We couldn't have a tank of water, but we built the battleship with a platform. Then we built the sampans on tracks the guys backstage pulled by ropes on either side of the stage. We never knew who the stage-hands would be each night. I don't think I ever in my life saw such a crowded backstage as that was. How those guys crawled around in and out of those sampans to keep them moving! At the end Johnny Wayne had to be hanged underneath the cannon."

Roar China dealt with a crisis that hovered over the population of Wan Hsien in 1924, when a foreign trader was accidentally drowned during a dispute with a boatman. The coolie escapes and the captain of the battleship threatens to shell the city unless two boatmen are executed and other humiliating conditions accepted at once.

January 11, 1937 was opening night.

What remains most in David's memory were the people who made up the Theatre of Action — we were all very good friends, "a jolly bunch of young people enjoying what we were doing," as David put it. And he remembered one fellow who came and said, "We are not the same theatre anymore, doing Moliere and Chekhov and plays like that." He accepted his point of view as just that, but that man's view by 1937 was a minority. "It is sometimes difficult for dedicated people to understand that stretching a theatre creatively is very important for its growth." David said that then and repeated it to me recently.

How did Toronto respond to the idea of a Soviet play? From the *Toronto Star* of January 2, 1937, came this piece by Augustus Bridle:

> Week from Monday at Hart House we are to have a Soviet play of modern China, one of the most intensively rehearsed plays ever done on that stage . . .
>
> The China play will be the work of a strangely intensive ensemble of actors, without stars, doing plays for the power of unity in action; all local people except the director, David Pressman from New York, who came up to produce *Bury The Dead* and found such a live-wire troupe . . . and decided to stay on . . .
>
> But this group has high intensity, as may be judged from this — in their recent booklet:
>
> 'Who were the audiences during this season of 1935-36? First of all, workers' organizations of all kinds. Concerts, union meetings, mass meetings, peace clubs, cultural groups, all of these asked for entertainment. For a small sum, and the transportation of their portable lighting and stage equipment, the theatre traveled far and wide, rigging up often the barest platform to meet their needs, and overcoming almost insurmountable difficulties to bring the theatre back to the people.
>
> 'It was a common backstage sight in the season of 1935-'36 to glimpse a young member of the theatre perched precariously upon a step-ladder balancing a prompt-script in one hand and focusing a baby spotlight with the other . . .'
>
> 'We make all our own sets and costumes,' said the director. '. . . Hart House is now our theatre. Wonderful equipment it has, too! Makes us all jittery with joy in the sheer mastery of technique.'
>
> 'So you do plays that put over some phase of modern life?' suggested *The Star* . . .
>
> 'We've done a number of things that show up the anti-human aspects of modern society. That's part of our job. We react to our own age — not to that of Ibsen, or Shaw, or Barrie.'

'Political plays mainly — is that right?' 'Yes, as a criticism of what certain radical writers see to be wrong in social conditions now. The things which upset civilization are natural material. The theatre can't dodge them. It has a message which the actors must convey . . . We happen just now to realize that a certain set of upsetting ideas is uppermost, especially among thinking young people. We aim to express that. Why not?'

In the midst of rehearsals for *Roar China,* David was asked to write an article for the *Daily Clarion* on his approach to the play. He did this and it appeared on December 30, 1936:

> What makes this play timely? What creates a necessity for producing such a play at this time?
>
> Work began on recreating those fundamental elements that motivate the behavior of all characters of the play. The cast, in roundtable discussions, worked out the problem of pinning all the characters in the play to one basic motivation . . .
>
> Whether they were coolies, rich Chinese merchants, foreign naval officers, American business men, or society women — the most fundamental reason for their existence within the play was economic . . .
>
> But these basic motivations did not confine themselves to the characters of *Roar China* alone. That, in order to convey to the Canadian audience the absolute parallel lines of the Chinese coolies in their struggle against exploitation and brutality, and the struggle of the Spanish people against fascism, or the fight of the textile strikers against starvation wages and insecurity, the actors had to realize . . . those economic motivations that are inherently motivating the characters of *Roar China* are also motivating people in other plays, other situations, the actors' own country and conditions, their own peoples' struggle for liberty, freedom and security . . .
>
> They (the audience) will feel that they are in the presence of all human struggle, that they are witnesses of their own social and economic conflicts . . .

Bernard (Bunny) Cowan was fourteen years old when he came to study at Theatre of Action's summer school. He stayed on to take small roles in subsequent productions.

He was one of the coolies in *Roar China* and recalls how one actor in the play related to the coolies. "I remember we could never predict how Syd Banks, who played a newspaperman would work with us each night. I don't know whether David was aware of his surprises, but it is still vivid for me what happened in two particular instances: one, he came on stage eating an apple, took one bite, noticed all the coolies clamoring for his attention and threw his apple down on the stage. I was so caught up in the part, I picked it up and ate it ravenously."

I was especially interested in speaking to Syd about this particular bit of business. How did he feel about it?

"I think I was being pretty haughty," Syd replied. "But I felt that the play required something besides what the director had given. No actor would undertake that without the director's knowledge. I consider that behavior unforgiveable. I did not check with David. I came in every night with something new to do with the coolies.

"I do recall one actor who was thrown completely off by a piece of business I did. When he came off the stage, he took a swing at me. He was right — it was thoughtless of me. I guess I was just learning about discipline. When I look back at it, I can see it was a bad thing to do."

I was not part of the cast or crew of *Roar China,* but I did come to rehearsals in that miserably cold St. Nicholas Street studio. I was so fascinated by the really beautiful movement that David choreographed for the large number of coolies, even though the pillars of that studio hardly allowed you to see the total effect. What surprised me was this large cast loyally turning up for rehearsals in this most uncomfortable place. Even more surprising — no one got pneumonia.

I did get to see that production out front. It wasn't until we got to Hart House for dress rehearsal that I saw what a marvellous set we had, and how well David had directed his cast. As the lights came on for the opening the audience could see a gunboat looming over the dock. And the effect of the sampans moving to suggest scene changes actually worked flawlessly. The technical end of that production couldn't have been more professional. All the scenes with the coolies were performed with feeling and a great sense of ensemble. A scene near the end of the play, when the silhouette of the cabin boy hanging is projected, was a shuddering one for the audience.

In this production the people working backstage contributed immensely to the effectiveness of what the audience saw. The make-up and costumes, for the first time, required expertise, and we found that we had people willing and able to apply themselves expertly. I think it was a fine example of working both on- and off-stage as a real collective, which this production achieved so early in our development.

I should add that we were helped tremendously after seeking out and getting to know Tommy Wu of Toronto's *Shing Wah Daily News.* He gave us a great deal of technical assistance with costumes and information about the China of that period. He also enthusiastically promoted the play in the Chinese community.

The reviews, when we finally opened, were positive and revealing. Lawrence Mason of *The Globe* wrote on January 12, 1937 under the heading, *Roar China — A Bitterly Anti-Imperialist Drama:*

Roar China . . . was presented at Hart House Theatre last night . . . It was a 'Theatre Night' for the Co-operative Commonwealth Youth Movement, which is . . . a junior branch of the CCF . . .

The play . . . is not very pleasing to people who happen to be pro-British . . .

Aside from the subject matter, this production is technically one of the most intelligent that any local amateur group has given this season. The two scenic sets are a triumph of flexibility and illusion, lighting and blackout are ably used, the handling of crowds on this small stage is skilful, and the keynote of 'action', vitally energetic movement and stirring stage business is excellently sustained throughout . . . and the whole performance has evidently been rehearsed up to the hilt — a rare virtue for amateurs hereabouts.

It is a genuinely exciting presentation because it is all carried through at a vivid pace and with inspiring sincerity . . . Another first-rate achievement must be credited to Director David Pressman.

On January 12, 1937, *The Varsity* wrote:

No stronger indictment of imperialism and the exploitation that is complementary to it can be found than *Roar China,* the Theatre of Action's current production at Hart House Theatre . . .

Roar China was written by Sergei Tretiakov, who is a famous Soviet writer. He knows conditions in China, having spent some years on the staff of the University of Peking . . .

The production is amazing in its thoroughness and effectiveness. David Pressman, who came up from the States this summer to teach at a summer school, has stayed to direct two of the finest productions Toronto has had the pleasure of witnessing for many a year . . . This play is much more difficult than the previous one. It needs actors who can stand alone without the support of a mass atmosphere, it needs even in the mass scenes a presentation in terms of the individual and hence everyone, including a small child, has to perform as a person. With a lot of amateurs, and the cast consists of forty-seven characters, this is a tremendous job. Pressman has been able to do it with miraculous success . . .

The sets were extremely good. The scenes on the battleship were first-rate and as good as any set put on the Hart House stage for a long time. The expedition with which the many scenes were changed is commendable; it is a virtue not often found in amateur shows.

The acting reaches at times professional standards. Bert Gold, star of all previous Theatre of Action presentations, again shone. Lou Weingarten . . . demonstrates the same talent as a serious actor as he has shown as a comedian. Frank Shuster as the Daieen, does a good bit of character. Elizabeth Sutherland, Stuart Walton, and Donna Creed do some very difficult parts well. For sheer stage presence and acting technique Fergus Tobin was outstanding . . .

The productions of the Theatre of Action are becoming to be the big events in Toronto's dramatic world. If they go on improving in the future as they have improved in the past, they will shortly become Canada's most important and best theatre group.

XVII

Three One-Act Plays

FOLLOWING THE PRODUCTION OF *ROAR CHINA*, we discussed the lack of Canadian plays in our repertoire. It was obvious to us that we would have to find some way to stimulate the writing of plays for the social theatres. We came up with the idea of a one-act play contest.

We wrote to Montreal, Winnipeg and Vancouver theatres and received their commitment to the idea, as well as the undertaking that the first prize play would be produced by the sponsoring theatres.

We went to *New Frontier*, a left literary magazine, and suggested they join us in this project, to which they enthusiastically agreed. They undertook to publicize the contest and to find the judges. We would jointly be responsible for the prize money. Thus the following announcement appeared in *New Frontier* in the issue of January, 1936:

> The New Theatre groups of Canada — Vancouver, Winnipeg, Montreal and Toronto — announce a $150.00 prize play contest for the best one-act play dealing with the Canadian social scene, past or present. $100.00 will be given as first prize; $50 as second prize. The contest opens June 1, 1936 and closes October 30, 1936. Winners to be announced in the December issue of *New Frontier*. The judges are: Morley Callaghan, Garfield A. King and Douglas Burns Clarke, Director, Department of Drama, Sir George Williams College, Montreal.

We were heartened by the response to this announcement when sixty-six submissions were received. The eventual winner was Mary Reynolds of Vancouver with her one-acter, *And The Answer Is . . ?** No second prize was awarded, but five plays were given honorable mention.

The judges' assessment of the submissions? "Playwrights need to be further schooled in the limitations and requirements of the one-act play form. Too many attempted to make the one-act a full play in miniature. Others adopted such moving picture technique as the flashback and something approximating close-ups. One person tried to give the one-acter the

---

**Now published in* Eight Men Speak And Other Plays *(ed. by Richard Wright and Robin Endres), New Hogtown Press, Toronto, 1976.*

scope of a novel. All these things had disastrous effects upon the unity or the clarity of the work. Only once or twice were experimental techniques employed effectively."

In view of our commitment to the prize winner, we decided to do a bill of three one-acts for our next major production, which included, in addition to the winning Canadian play, an American prize-winning script, *What It Takes,* and Chekhov's *The Marriage Proposal.*

David had also not lost his desire to do some acting, and he chose to appear in the Chekhov. As luck would have it, one of his fellow-students from the Neighborhood Playhouse — a Canadian named Paul Mann — was in Toronto.

Paul, who had by this time completed his studies and was working with the Group Theatre in New York as an apprentice, was having immigration problems related to working in the States. He had come back to Toronto to straighten matters out. His difficulties were turned into Theatre of Action's advantage. He agreed to direct *The Marriage Proposal,* thereby allowing David the freedom to perform. He worked with David as well on the two other plays.

Subsequently, Paul was invited to teach at our summer school and we were delighted that he accepted our invitation. As he himself told me later, he worked as hard with our acting classes as he would have had he been working with professional actors. He certainly demanded from us very high standards. He was aware, he said, that some people responded well to this, but others felt it was asking too much from people who worked in the daytime and came to the theatre and the school in the evening. But then, it was up to the individuals really to get as much from the classes as they could. Those who were serious about their work didn't mind the heavy demands made.

The overall schedule, though, was now getting heavy. *Roar China* was produced in January. We would be launching our third production of the season with the one-act plays. And then the regional festival performance of *Bury The Dead* would take place at the end of February.

Such a program would be daunting for a full-time theatre. Yet here we were doing it — rehearsing in the evening and week-ends. Our members, though, seemed to thrive on hard work. They turned up for whatever was required and completed the scheduled program successfully.

All of this, of course, was accompanied by many meetings and long discussions at executive and membership sessions. It was there that the decisions were made.

I was a member of the cast of *And The Answer Is...?* This one-acter, in the mood the author created and the characters employed to express it, was very much in tune with the times — the fears and sickness of the depression.

The action of the play takes place in front of a war memorial in a park. The people who meet there are those who suffer most from the poverty and misery of the times: Woman with the Basket, who sells jellies on the street; Man in the Cap, a war veteran, who is very bitter, but who has some understanding of how he has been cheated and lied to; Man Under the Newspaper, who supplies the climax of the script; Hell-Fire Taffy, unemployed, driven mad and to fanaticism; Vigo, a young musician, ill and without prospects for a decent life; his girl friend, who is fighting hard to help her young man. There is a small inset scene where the upper class "do-gooders" get together to plan some charity. While they are engaged in this, they manage to destroy the hopes of the two young people. The play ends with the Man Under the Newspaper being found dead.

There is very little hope or struggle in this play, which left audiences feeling very let-down. Still, Mary Reynolds did create some very interesting characters, good dialogue which had some bite, and interesting situations. And she surely portrayed the hopelessness of the times.

I played the Woman with the Basket and enjoyed digging in and fleshing out this character who, in the course of the play, does try to give others some warmth and hope to go on. I think all the members of this cast tried to get from each other the human element which would be conveyed to the audience and move the play along. For the most part, we did succeed in doing that.

And The Answer Is. . . ? was one play with its own special mood. *What It Takes* by Philip Stevenson turned out to be a very strong play, also dealing with the effects of the depression on an individual and his family. Chekhov's *The Marriage Proposal,* a comedy, filled out what seemed an interesting evening.

Our hope was that in producing at least one Canadian play and giving it our best, we would be encouraging other playwrights to look around the country at the time and write about what they saw and felt. What we were looking for were more and better plays for our theatre.

The response was again positive. In the *Toronto Telegram* of April 2, 1937, Rose MacDonald wrote:

> That eager and considerably gifted group working under the title of the Theatre of Action presented a three-play bill last night at Margaret Eaton hall, holding in the main to its motivating purpose, which is to draw attention to, if not to solve, social problems . . .
>
> The Chekhov piece was happily done as a very fast-moving farce by a skilled trio of actors — chiefly by David Pressman (Lomov, the agitated suitor), Elizabeth Sutherland (Natalia, object of his pale affections).
>
> The piece gained in ludicrous effect by use of grotesque background and as played by the nimble three, required a quite monkeyish agility which must have sorely tried the sofa springs . . .

What It Takes covers a good deal of ground before it gets to an exact statement of its premise . . .

Here again the acting was excellent, especially Lou Epstein's. He was the automobile salesman caught on the economic wheel. His wife tries to explain him as one who whistles in the dark to keep up his courage, but the view seems over-charitable . . .

Mary Reynolds' play was much more concisely written, though done in three short scenes. The characters come together in a park on a chill evening, and alternately, in a women's club, are types rather than persons, but the main theme is poignantly given without mawkish sentimentality.

Again the cast is admirable . . . all of them know or have known hunger . . .

W.S. Milne in *Saturday Night* of April 8, 1937 wrote:

The Theatre of Action has shifted its performances from Hart House to Margaret Eaton Hall, where its latest production was presented, three one-act plays. The first, Chekhov's *Proposal* was presented in a determinedly 'different' fashion, which did not quite come off, because the players were so engrossed with their ingenious expansions of business and text that the sweep of the play as a whole suffered . . . The general effect was amusing, but one felt that the production obscured the point of the play, rather than enhanced it.

The second offering saw a magnificent piece of acting in the Edward Robinson manner by Lou Epstein, who played a poor fool of a car salesman, who loses faith in the shibboleths of his trade as he sees his family in want, and learns that his wife has seen through him all along. The play, *What It Takes,* is a somewhat confused and wordy piece . . . but Mr. Epstein's acting, ably supported by that of Jean Morgan as the wife, raised it above the commonplace.

Chief in point of interest was Mary Reynolds' *And The Answer Is. . . ?,* the prize-winning play in a contest sponsored by the New Theatre Groups of Canada. In three short scenes, depicting derelicts at the base of a war-memorial and over-stuffed clubwomen planning a Christmas entertainment for charity, Miss Reynolds has contrived to give a picture of human need and human callousness that sticks in the mind. It has little dramatic pattern, and depends for its effectiveness on the excellent characterizations of the down-and-outers. Outstanding among these were Toby Gordon and Martin Brady. Sydney Banks contributed an effective bit as a Welsh street preacher.

> Altogether the three plays furnished an evening of interest, with fine acting overcoming the obvious defects of the two last vehicles . . .

At the end of Mr. Milne's review, he aired two grievances against Theatre of Action. One, the curtain was twenty minutes late, for which his criticism is justified; the other gave him an opportunity to take a crack at us as a theatre of "social regeneration" rather than personal display, yet took too many curtain calls, he said, "consistently."

I don't recall this particular weakness. Perhaps we were guilty. But what did he mean "consistently?" We had only done four major productions, including the one he reviewed and made mention of our display. Was he suggesting unwarranted curtain calls at every performance of every play? Did he see them all? In any event, this kind of sarcastic slap at Theatre of Action tagged on to the end of a review did not enhance Mr. Milne to us as a theatre critic.

The short plays completed our season, though we still had to go to Ottawa for the finals of the festival. It also completed the first year of David's stay in Toronto as director. After we had completed plans for our summer school, which was to begin in July, David returned to New York for a well-deserved holiday.

Rose MacDonald in *The Telegram* of June 15, 1937, quotes David as saying the summer school courses would be interesting for the average theatre-goer, as well as for actors and technical people.

"Mr. Pressman and his associates go on the principle that in a well coordinated theatre movement, the audience . . . must be culturally interested in the theatre and form a sincere and critically educated group of spectators."

For the 1937 summer school, our acting teachers were David and Paul Mann while Mrs. W. Addison taught speech and Thelma Manheim, movement. A new course was also added — stagecraft, taught by Syd Newman and Nat Petroff.

The acting classes were particularly exciting, especially the advanced class, which I attended. There, in addition to the many improvisations, we also began to explore scenes from plays. It gave us all a chance to act many, many parts which we might not ordinarily get a chance to play. It broadened and deepened our understanding of how to apply the techniques of Stanislavski to actual work on scripts and parts.

One of the many I prepared and participated in that summer was a scene from Noel Coward's *Private Lives,* which Frank Shuster and I worked on together. I think we both knew that we would probably never get a chance to play these parts and so enjoyed the experience very much.

We rehearsed our scenes on our own time and brought them into class for criticism and improvement. This kind of program, added to the speech and movement classes, kept all of us very, very busy during the summer, when most people were simply trying to take time off to relax.

When some of the other actors asked for someone to help them prepare their scenes, I was happy to try. In the process, I learned how to approach a script from the director's point of view.

On the weekends, some of us got together for a trip to the Toronto islands, to enjoy a swim, sunshine and a picnic. If there was no money for that — and often there wasn't — we headed for Cherry Beach or Sunnyside.

In the fall, we knew it was important to find new quarters. Our studio on St. Nicholas Street was really getting us down. We wanted to do studio productions. For that we would have to find a space that would be warm and comfortable for our audiences. Happily, we managed to find a very large hall over a wallpaper and paint store at 490 Yonge Street. The space was marvellous, but it looked dirty and dingy. It did have many advantages, though: our Business Manager worked at Lyons' Furniture, which was next door. Margaret Eaton Hall, where we would be doing our productions, was only a few blocks away. Most important, the place was heated and had no pillars.

Everyone pitched in enthusiastically, bringing in pails, mops, soap and everything needed to clean things up. We bought whitewash for the brick walls. We set to work to clean and paint the hall, one we hoped would become a popular centre for theatre, as well as our business and rehearsal centre. We also planned to construct sets there. Once cleaned, a volunteer construction crew built a small stage at the far end of the hall. An artist (I don't remember who) painted a backdrop of a city. We managed to scrounge lights and hung them.

I was secretary at the time and was in the office during the day. Members who were not working, or had time off, would come to the studio to help build sets, do other jobs around the place, or just sit and chat about dreams, the future, the next projects of Theatre of Action.

We also had our executive committee, but we now set up a production council to work with the director in reading and choosing plays for major or studio productions. This council would also assign members to various jobs. As well, we held regular membership meetings to discuss plans and money-raising projects which would require membership participation.

One of the early projects for raising money and involving all members, plus interested outside people, was a large carnival. Our refreshments were the usual hot dogs, pop and popcorn. We decorated the hall suitably for these events. We had barkers announcing the various attractions, clowns to entertain them. There were dozens of sideshows, some political humor — all theatrically done and very funny.

I recall that Ralph "Tiny" Foster and I combined as the tallest man and the tiniest woman in the world. We were a natural couple for this attraction. We had our own barker, joined him in front of the tent so people could see us. Then the customers were invited inside to see the sideshow we had prepared and which might cost them a few cents.

It was great fun for participants and spectators alike. We attracted large numbers of people. It took a lot of phone calls, newspaper publicity and word of mouth. We were successful, though, financially and had also provided a different kind of evening of entertainment.

Generally, our studio became a popular place to spend Sunday evenings when we presented productions, an evening of Grand Guignol with an Apache dance thrown in, readings of plays, presentations of a new form called *Living Newspapers* on timely topics, improvisations done on topics suggested by the audience. These were usually followed by discussion among spectators, director and actors.

I suppose Toronto's blighted Sundays helped us. In those days nothing was open on Sunday. We had no competition. For a voluntary contribution one could spend a very interesting evening at Theatre of Action.

We attracted many different kinds of people to those studio evenings. One who attended was John MacDonnell. He had come from England and was in Toronto doing some radio plays for the CBC. The work he saw that evening impressed him very much and he invited some of our people to participate in his radio shows. Syd Banks and I were asked to join the cast of O. Henry's *Vanity And Some Sables*. I had never done radio before. You have to do your acting with your voice for an invisible audience. I found it difficult but working with Syd helped. After a few rehearsals I found I could relax and play with ease. We were told it came off well.

One of the important lessons I learned at this time was that theatre people who are not kept busy at projects which give them satisfaction are sure to begin grumbling and generally promoting discontent. Theatre of Action had some of this, no matter how we tried to involve as many people as possible. Nor was every member committed to the particular ideas of Theatre of Action. People had many reasons for joining and they were not necessarily always unselfish.

Not too many, for instance, joined the theatre to participate in the many jobs backstage. We did attract some, but most members wanted to act, even though at their initial joining they might not always be sure of what they wanted to contribute. Thus, problems were created when the membership swelled.

We struggled with that because of our awareness and our concern, but we didn't always succeed in making everyone happy. The creation of a harmonious theatre collective is a long and difficult job. I think we went a long way in involving people but it would be exaggerating to say that we achieved all that we had hoped.

Earlier I spoke of Sydney Newman who, with Nat Petroff, produced some remarkable stage settings for Theatre of Action. Nat, after a while, left for New York to study, but Syd stayed with us. He later, of course, had a distinguished career in making documentary films and went on to other creative and important jobs.

But in those days, he was a designer in his own right as well. In 1935, he and Nat left school. Syd didn't graduate because he had flunked French, arithmetic and a few other academic subjects. "Somehow or other," Syd recalled so many years later, "Petroff and I got into a business partnership, in which there was damn little business and a lot of work — a lot of fun, a lot of hot talk. We did sign painting, anything to try to make a buck. Petroff was involved with various left-wing groups and, somehow or other, I just found myself gravitating with him into what was then known as the Theatre of Action. It had just begun, because the first production I remember was *Waiting For Lefty.*

"In those days, I simply made my living by doing sign-painting, a bit of illustration for magazines, and my intentions were to be a painter. In those early years I was trying desperately to do fine painting, but then, as the years went by, it just became impossible for me to make a living. My parents were very poor.

"As for Petroff and I working as a team, I should tell you that Petroff had come to Canada when he was 12 or 13 years old. When I first met him at Central Tech, his English was very, very poor. But being very young he learned quickly, so by the time we were both about 17 or 18 years of age, when we began to be associated with Theatre of Action, his English was quite good, but he felt self-conscious about it. He seemed shy, but I think it was a language problem. He was also rather glum, gloomy, introverted, taciturn. I was always very outgoing and easy, so I guess we did make a good team.

"Petroff and I were involved with *Bury The Dead.* We helped in the building of the set. I know I was involved in that production, but not in any senior capacity. I recall that play as really my first theatrical experience. After that, we helped with other things around the studio at 490 Yonge. We helped out a lot.

"Petroff and I shared credits for the first time, for the set of *Class of '29.* It was a fairly conventional set."

Irving Hoffman recalled how he came to join Theatre of Action. "I saw *Bury The Dead.*

"I thought it was one of the most powerful things I had ever seen. It was fantastic. A whole new concept of theatre. I don't think I remember seeing anything, even to this day, that affected me so emotionally as *Bury The Dead.* That performance convinced me to join the theatre. I auditioned and was accepted.

"It opened up a whole new vista in technique, in acting, for me. I think we were all more or less obliged to take classes. I wanted to do it anyway.

"Theatre of Action gave me something special because of the times. I could dream a little and think of getting something else out of life. It gave me a purpose in life. At that particular time, if you didn't have something like that, there was nothing to look forward to. One couldn't see where one was going, so it gave me my dream."

Miriam (Levy) Hoffman was a young worker in a factory who came to Theatre of Action without any theatrical experience, or even an awareness of what she wanted or could contribute to the group. Given the opportunity to apply herself to study and the different facets of theatre activity available, she discovered a talent of which she was unaware. Theatre of Action had other members in this category.

"I think the first thing I must have done was take some classes, because I had no experience whatsoever." This was how Miriam recalled her beginnings at Theatre of Action.

"I eventually found my way into make-up. It started very simply. I would help people with the very basic kind of make-up. Then it became something I felt I could learn a lot more about. I remember going to see somebody, some man who was in that field. He gave me a lot of wonderful ideas in make-up, which I wrote down. On my own initiative, I went to the library and I sat for hours making notes and reading a lot of books. I spent a lot of time getting as much information regarding make-up as I could. I really loved it."

I reminded Miriam of what an excellent job she had done with the characters in Gogol's *The Inspector-General,* which called for more complicated make-up, and how the critics had especially praised it.

"I do feel I did accomplish something in that production. I enjoyed it very much. Of course, when you see something of your own creation that looks so real, it's bound to give you great satisfaction.

"Membership in Theatre of Action meant hard work, but it was very enjoyable work. Yes, it was difficult working all day and coming down, particularly to rehearsals when I was in a play, every single night. But I reached a point where I'd have to take a day off here and there. I enjoyed it so much that I certainly would never think it was a hardship — heavens, no!"

While rehearsals for *Class of '29* were proceeding, Theatre of Action was also preparing a repertory of three short plays, which were extremely mobile — *Waiting For Lefty* and *What It Takes,* which had been produced before, and *Kill The Bum,* a new Canadian play which was in rehearsal.

Notices were sent out to organizations in Toronto and vicinity that these plays were available for performance with two weeks' notice. We made our appeal to trade unions, labor organizations, progressive church and YMCA-YWCA groups.

This mobile theatre activity — taking our plays to the audience — was maintained for most of the life of Theatre of Action, with some plays dropped after a while and new material added.

Class of '29 rehearsals were enjoyed immensely by all of us in the cast. First, because David allowed the actors to explore and bring in many of their own ideas of the characters and how to express them. Secondly, it was a play about young people and expressed the feelings of youth about how society was cheating them. In the role of the social worker digging away with embarrassing questions, I could relate very well to the anger of the young man being interviewed. It gave me a great deal to work with.

Having said all this, I must also add that *Class of '29* was not one of our successful productions. For some reason, although it was very relevant to what was happening to students here, it was not too well attended.

I haven't been able to figure out why that happened. Perhaps we didn't get the right kind of audiences; perhaps its very relevance was too hard to take; perhaps the melodrama in the script turned people off; or perhaps we didn't do so good a job publicizing it. It could have been some or all of these.

It was, however, a good experience for the actors. This play also had a good deal of humor which our previous scripts had lacked. The technique of timing for laughs is very important for actors to learn, and in this play many of them had the opportunity to do so. In this connection, as I recall it, one of our actors, Stuart Walton, had many good, funny lines and his timing was getting to be quite expert.

Class of '29 was written for the Federal Theatre Project in the United States and was produced at the W.P.A. theatre in New York during the 1935-36 season. Our Toronto production ran at Margaret Eaton hall from November 22 to 27, 1937 and Rose MacDonald in the November 23 *Telegram* reviewed it:

> That vigorously experimental group, the Theatre of Action, is currently playing a piece called *Class of '29* at Margaret Eaton Hall, and is thereby making, more or less, a fresh experiment for them, one in following the more conventional forms of the theatre. *Class of '29* . . . is not intended as a play for the play's sake, but as a serious commentary on an economic phase not yet quite concluded. The sociological effects of unemployment are prominently and poignantly recorded . . .
>
> Tippy, graduate of Harvard, philosophically takes in washing — the spoiled canine pets of the affluent. He makes a living, helps several of his fellow alumni and keeps from going sour. Stuart Walton plays this part with good-humored ease and makes it the most consistently interesting performance of the play . . .
>
> Roy Chappelle gives a noteworthy performance . . . Sydney Banks and George Hall portray appropriately and respectively, the embittered young man who has lost his way, and a sunny-spirited self-styled revolutionist . . . Irving Hoffman was

appealing as the gentle and perturbed Bishop, and the very diverse feminine roles which fill in the pattern of the piece were well taken by Toby Gordon, Rae Harris, Jean Morgan and Donna Creed.

In the *Varsity* of the same date, C.K. Carrington wrote:

> The Theatre of Action in their current offering leave the coolie revolts of roaring China for America 1935, where the revolution is still eagerly awaited, although the *Class of '29* is rapidly losing hope.
>
> If you like plays about noble but caustic revolutionaries in Lower Depths surroundings where well-meaning but fatuous bishops bungle around, and tense young gentlemen too proud to serve as elevator boys seek death beneath the subway wheels, you may like *Class of '29*.
>
> You certainly should like the effective set of the capitalists' office in Scene 2 and will be quite won over by the much-betowelled little white dog, but you will find little in the play itself or in the acting as a whole . . .
>
> If the reports of last year's productions by this group were true, we should say they have done better work than *Class of '29*.

Even the *Jewish Standard* of December 1937 was less than enthusiastic:

> The producing company of the Theatre of Action were at Margaret Eaton Hall for one week in a play about a group of young people who graduate from college into the depression . . .
>
> The opening scene dragged along at a slow pace . . .
>
> In the second act the action was speeded up and the finest acting of the entire play was witnessed. Toby Gordon as the relief investigator brought to life the part of the steel-jawed woman government official examining the 'cavities of the relief applicant's teeth for hidden money.' Her portrayal carried conviction and understanding. George Hall and Roy Chappelle . . . enacted one of the best scenes in the play. Donna Creed . . . gave an almost perfect performance. Sydney Banks, as the only one of the group who had achieved a direction and purpose in life, while giving a good performance, did not get all that he might have out of the part and therefore was not as convincing as he should have been. Stuart Walton as the light-hearted cynic who washes dogs for a living, and Rae Harris as the owner of one of the dogs, were good . . . The direction was by David Pressman, who managed in certain scenes, and especially in act two, to make good theatre out of a play which had few possibilities for the stage . . .

By this time we were well launched into our Sunday night theatre evenings, which were going on at the same time as rehearsals for other plays. The following report in the *Daily Clarion* of February 9, 1938 reports on one such evening:

> Novel fare was provided Sunday night at Theatre of Action's second 'workshop evening' in its Yonge Street studio, Toronto.
>
> Director David Pressman and members of the group took the audience into their confidence in a demonstration of the organization's working methods. Members of the large audience were invited to suggest subjects for treatment. The first suggestion was a bookie's office near a racetrack. The players were to work out a little sketch on this idea.
>
> Deftly Mr. Pressman improvised a little plot, assigned various roles to four young men. Stage settings and props were bare essentials, picked up quickly by the players. Other props, like windows, field glasses, etc., were left to the imagination of audience and actors. Then the actors went to work, developed their characters, spoke lines invented on the spur of the moment, and the result was a cleverly-wrought, convincing sketch. The same treatment was given to a further suggestion from a member in the audience.
>
> This was no trick. Neither the actors, the director, or the audience knew what the improvisations were to be until the suggestions came from the floor. The purpose of the exercises was to demonstrate the method of this enterprising group, which bases its system on the work of the renowned Stanislavski, dean of the Russian theatre . . .
>
> Earlier in the evening the application of the method was seen in a new one-act play, *Plant In The Sun* by Ben Bengal. Here was clever direction of Mr. Pressman, fast action and (with a cast of 15) 15 separate, individual, clearly-defined characters.
>
> The play concerns itself with the shipping room of a candy factory. The young workers, unorganized, decide on a sit-down strike when one of their number is fired for union talk.
>
> The action races through to conflicts with the boss, the superintendent, a tale-telling office boy, clashes with workers in other departments, little gestures of solidarity from the rest of the factory, romance, police intervention; growing excitement until gangsters are brought in and the strikers are beaten up and taken away.
>
> By then the whole factory is in an uproar and the curtain falls on the spread of the sit-down through all departments.
>
> The play itself is one of the best one-acters of this type to be brought here. There is plenty of action, humor, drama, good

dialogue. The actors throw themselves into it with relish. Some of the dialect, however, is a bit uncertain and needs polishing up. An attempt to list one or two performers for top positions resulted in a growing list, which included most of the cast . . .

Arrangements for bookings of the play can be made through Miss Toby Gordon, the group's secretary . . .

XVIII

Steel — A Qualitative Improvement

THE CHOICE AND PRODUCTION OF *STEEL* by John Wexley at Margaret Eaton Hall, March 14-19, 1938, marked a qualitative improvement in the work of Theatre of Action, both on stage and in the organization.

"*Steel* was an enormous thing for Theatre of Action," David said later. "*Bury The Dead*, after all, required figures, expressionistic stuff, little speeches. But this was a realistic play, a three-act play, in which members of a labor family change. There were real character problems, older workers with different accents and dialects and qualities of Italian, Russian, Irish, Ukrainian, German, Polish. It's a play we would not have been able to do as well the year before, because it required three-dimensional acting and characterizations. Stanislavski once said: 'What is the purpose of theatre? To reveal the human character.' This play required that.

"The characters were very complex. The central figure was very interesting, the union problems were very human. It was a watershed for Theatre of Action and for me. At the same time, our settings were expressionistic. There's an interesting thing: Here we were into a very realistic play about human problems, union problems, a marriage relationship, but our physical expression on the stage was only suggested. The reason for our choice was the hope we would tour it. It would obviously be easier and less costly to move an expressionistic home than a real one. So the steel mill was always seen in the background, dominating the entire production, and the home was a table and three chairs and a window with lace curtains nailed to another small table and a free-standing door for entrances and exits. That was it.

"By this time too, we had quite a number of young people, but we were also attracting older people who came to work with us. We felt that if we could play these characters, well, we were going to be a real theatre company some day."

I asked David if, by the time we produced *Steel*, he felt we were emerging as an acting company with its own acting style, unlike the other little theatre groups.

"Little theatres," he said, "produced superficial plays and therefore their work was more superficial. I think we have to be very careful when we talk about the style of a company. I tend to look upon it a little more carefully. Perhaps it reflects the individual director more than anything else.

"When the adjudicator at the regional festival remarked, 'My, how they listened,' about our performance of *Steel,* that might be interpreted as being our style of acting. But he saw that everybody was interested and involved and had the kind of concentration that comes from wanting to give the most to the production. Our people wouldn't think of not listening. I've seen lots of actors on stage who, when they're not in a scene, look around bored or just stand there. Theatre of Action people just wouldn't think of doing that. In that sense, I suppose, we had something unique."

Before we continued our discussion on *Steel,* I wanted to get David's reaction to the fact that we had a membership to report to in Theatre of Action. Did he find that difficult at all? We had discussions of plays chosen. Sometimes members were critical and questioned certain casting.

"I don't remember it being a negative factor. On the contrary, I considered it as a positive thing where I was learning about democracy, how it worked in a theatre. But there was always a point at which I could say, 'Well, that's the way I want to do it,' and, because the bulk of the members had trust and faith in me, they would accept it. They spoke their minds and I heard them and probably was influenced by them.

"I do recall that for the production of *Steel* we invited three carloads of steel workers to see a rehearsal and they gave their suggestions, which we incorporated in the preparation of the production. They would point out what seemed right and what needed improvement."

There was a special challenge in doing *Steel,* we felt. Here was a play that would give us the opportunity to bring workers to the theatre to see themselves on stage. We took this challenge very seriously. Many of us went out to local union meetings to talk about the play and to appeal to them to get their members to come and see it. We talked about the humor in *Steel,* the fact that it pictured a working class family and their attitude to union organization with truth and sincerity. Most important, this play dealt in human terms and with honesty about the effort it required to bring a union into a plant.

We appealed for support and asked local unions to buy a full house, or half a house, in which case they would be responsible for selling these tickets to their members and, in the process, raise some money for their unions. We did get a good response to those appeals — at least one steel union local bought a benefit evening for the full house. While we didn't keep count of everyone who came to see *Steel,* it was evident that quite a number of workers did come to see it. We played for a week and had very good audiences.

There was also a membership bonus for us when two workers from the Steel Workers' Organizing Committee joined the cast. One of them, Tom Morrison, remained a member of Theatre of Action. He studied with us in our acting class and worked hard both on and off stage in other productions.

A good description of our approach to the script of *Steel* appeared in the *Clarion* and was written by David. He called it, *How Steel Was Made:*

> One of our problems was to make sure that all references, either in speech or in action, to the steel industry or people working in steel mills, was correct and authentic.
>
> Somehow, in our minds, a steel worker was not quite an ordinary human being. For some unaccountable reason, we were always surprised when we discovered that he wore very much the same kind of clothing, behaved very normally, and was not, generally speaking, excessively massive in build and powerful in strength. The feeling that we must find enormous men to fill all the parts of steel workers petered out . . .
>
> Diagrams and charts of open hearth furnaces, Bessemers, blast furnaces and other sections of an average steel mill, became almost part of the actor's script. Fortunately, two men, members of the Steel Workers' Organizing Committee, joined the cast of *Steel* and they knew a thing or two about steel and settled most of our arguments.
>
> Just as rehearsals first began to take shape, Dick Steele, Canadian regional secretary of SWOC, gave the cast a highly instructive and interesting lecture on the organization of the steel industry and the various problems that confront the average steel worker today.
>
> From him the actors learned how the memory of the 1919 walkout and defeat still lingered among the older men and how the different national groups lived and worked together in the various mills, both in the U.S.A. and Canada. We are greatly indebted to Dick Steele for great assistance and advice on the production of the play . . .
>
> After two or three weeks of research, lectures, reading and discussion, the actors began to 'act', as it were. The model of the set, which was brilliantly designed by two of Toronto's most able artists, Sydney Newman and Nathan Petroff, was exhibited to the cast and its style discussed. As usual, a period of healthy, constructive criticism and discussion took place, suggesting various changes.

Setting up an approximate representation of the stage in the rehearsal studio, the actors began to move about either with the scripts in their hands, or improvising the lines. They moved about at will and were often stopped by the director to ascertain the reason for such and such a move, or discuss something that was wrong or right. The actor was continually urged to do things, to act upon impulse, not to be afraid to be wrong, not to rely upon the director to tell him what to do, and to ascertain for himself, as much as possible, the continuity of his physical action on the stage.

The more the actor knows about his character, what his everyday life is like, what his past life was, what his hopes and dreams and desires are, the more the actor's imagination is stimulated, the greater will be his initiative in creating for himself the life on stage.

The Raldny family, that is, the actors, namely, Norval Gray, Toby Gordon, Jules Ross, Helen Coleman, Alex Schatz and Stuart Walton, had many an argument among themselves and their director about their past lives and the things they do between acts that the audience doesn't see . . .

During the middle weeks of rehearsals, the actors move as they please, following basic criticism and suggestions from the director. Here, the director's job is to see that the initial steps are in the right direction and that as many obstacles as possible are removed from the actor's creative path. Later on, he begins to select, to choose and formulate everything that is brought by the actor into a general pattern. Some things are discarded and some are added.

I must admit that for me, playing the daughter of a steel worker who understood the need for unions, and the wife of a steel worker who felt insecure and afraid of union organization, was something I understood well. After all, I was brought up in a union organizer's home and I remembered well the conversations I had heard, the stories my father told about visiting workers and convincing them to join the union. I also knew, from personal experience, from my childhood, what a strike was and how it affected the family. I knew I played this role with conviction. I brought to it all the mixed emotions I remembered from my own home.

"Basically, the one common denominator for set designers is the play, and then there is the interpretation of the play by a director. This is how Syd Newman described the job. "The designer's job is to try and put flesh to his concept, married with the designer's own interpretation of the play.

"The fact that Theatre of Action had little money to work with made it seem impossible to design anything. Yet one didn't feel it as a negative stricture. One wanted more money, but the fact is that those sets were made out of tatty pieces of wood. Occasionally money was available, but a lot of our designs were based on the fact that there was damn little money. For a lot of the sets we used very coarse brown wrapping paper.

"I think part of the abstract and non-representational nature of the sets was a direct reflection of the absence of money. There is no point in trying to do a naturalistic setting because you couldn't afford it. I think it was a kind of nice discipline to cause one to get right down to the essence of what the play was all about and just use little naturalistic bits. I think the economics we were forced into probably resulted in more interesting, more imaginative sets."

All the hard work which had gone into the production of *Steel* was rewarded by the response from the audiences, night after night, for a full week. It also received favorable press reaction.

The Globe, March 19, 1938:

> The Canadian premiere of *Steel* by John Wexley, was presented . . . by the Theatre of Action in Margaret Eaton Hall . . .
>
> This play deals very sympathetically with the process of organizing a CIO union in a large steel plant. It presents the workers in a very attractive manner, and the managers and owners in an equally unattractive way. It is relieved with flashes of humor and has some genuinely moving scenes.
>
> The interest of the audiences was worked up to the climax, which, unfortunately for the play, is rather theatrical and unconvincing, providing no solution to the underlying problem. The director and cast dealt very kindly with the play. It is intended to create interest and sympathy for the union, but fails at times to be good theatre, becoming merely oratory. The players, too, found it difficult to be convincing as husky workers in a steel plant, but brought an earnestness and vitality to their roles which helped cover the defect . . .
>
> The sets were cleverly arranged, so that the sinister steel plant constantly imposed its massive bulk on the audience's attention. The sound effects of the scene in the mill were excellent; the business and grouping of the large cast were good; and the whole production moved with speed and precision . . .

The Telegram, March 15, 1938, Rose MacDonald:

> *Steel*, John Wexley's dramatic brief . . . was given by the Theatre of Action last night . . . From the first, this group has made it clear in its selection of plays that it has a special purpose . . . (The reviewer) is concerned here only with the standard of performance and structural aspects of the play itself.

The action of *Steel* is placed in a steel town in the United States . . . a splendidly effective backdrop with the rolling mill as motif, was not only a backdrop in the usual sense but, following the Stanislavski theory, served also a psychological purpose . . . no attempt was made to relate doors and windows by means of conventional walls.

There was no difficulty in accepting the device. When the rolling mill itself was the scene of the action, an extraordinarily fine dramatic effect was achieved with lights and shadows playing upon the painted backdrop . . . the writer found the off-stage noises suggesting men at labor excellently contrived.

The director, David Pressman, was very successful in suggesting the polyglot character of the workers in such a mill. The accents of Irishman, Pole, Italian, German et al might not have been accurate, but at least the racial types were carefully differentiated . . .

First acting honors were rather equally divided by Alex Schatz and Jules Ross . . . Mr. Pressman himself did a smooth bit of work as the general manager addressing his recalcitrant employees . . . Toby Gordon and Helen Coleman did make a sincere contribution to the local performance . . .

Saturday Night, March 17, 1938, Nancy Pyper:

On Monday evening the Theatre of Action opened a week's run of John Wexley's *Steel* . . . The play . . . is strongly propagandist, but it is an extremely forceful and dramatic vehicle for actors . . .

In the performance it was immediately noticeable that the players here, as compared with their previous work in *Class of '29*, felt that they had something to express. The vitalizing quality of the play infected the cast, and the director seemed to be wisely intent on serving the purpose of the play, while the actors, even in the smallest parts, bent all their efforts to make the performance a complete and concerted whole — something that would preach effectively the doctrine of the author.

As Steve, the son-in-law, Jules Ross gave a performance that might almost be called magnificent . . . Norval Gray . . . made an admirable foil for the older workers . . . In the short part of the father, Alex Schatz . . . played him truthfully. As his daughter, Toby Gordon played a thoughtful, imaginative girl with a fine quality of earnestness and simplicity . . . Helen Coleman portrayed admirably a girl whose fire and independence of spirit matched that of the younger boy to whom she was married in secret.

Perhaps the most heartening review we got was an article by Richard (Dick) Steele, the Canadian regional secretary of the Steel Workers' Organizing Committee, which describes the feelings of the steel workers themselves to the performance they saw. This appeared in the *Clarion* on March 18, 1938:

> 'It's true!'
>
> This is the opinion of hundreds of steel workers and their wives and friends who were the guests of the SWOC, the third night of John Wexley's brilliant play, *Steel*, at Margaret Eaton Hall.
>
> They should know. Every character on the stage had tens of duplicates in the audience. I could look about me and point out a dozen Jim Donovans and Steve Dugans, and in a certain measure, Joe Raldnys. There were likewise tens of Melanias and Betty Dugans. Said one Betty Dugan to me: 'Begosh, Dick — I could have been on the stage meself tonight!'
>
> Says one Jim Donovan of SWOC lodge 1168, 'Remember when we moved in the company union for a general wage increase last June and were told the company had kept its plant running during the depression to provide work for its loyal workers . . . ?'
>
> 'Did you recognize . . . ?' says one steel worker to another in reference to a notorious 'pusher' who is always speeding up the men . . .
>
> The General Steel Wares workers remember how the SWOC helped them organize until they were able to elect the majority of good union men to the executive of the works council, like 'yeast in a barrel of whiskey,' as Jim Donovan explained to his fellow workers at his uncle's wake.
>
> How easy it was to place the sneering superior works manager, Mr. Roberts, by his living counterpart right here in Toronto. And the company detectives — or rats — as they are better known. There were steel workers in that audience who remember meeting in a cellar on Seaton Street a year ago; and who had to climb out of the back window because these 'rats' were standing in a doorway across the street.
>
> How near to many of those in the audience was the feeling of Steve Dugan when he knew that he was going to be laid off. The dread terror of being laid off is a present reality to some 2,000 steel workers in Toronto.
>
> 'If we could arrange to bring out every steel worker in Toronto to see it, we would spare ourselves many hours of worry,' remarked Mr. Heppleston, president of the Toronto joint board. 'Gosh, I should have got another carload of fellows

down from the shop,' said an Acme Screw and Gear worker from SWOC lodge 1452. 'It would do them good to see themselves.'

With the run of *Steel* completed, we decided to enter Act II of the play in the regional festival, which was to take place early in April. Our entry was accepted. Meanwhile, we had been booked to take the production to Oshawa where we would play under the auspices of the Players' Club of Local 222, United Auto Workers. It is worth recording this performance. I had a very special experience there.

Since some people in the cast of *Steel* were fortunate enough to have jobs, we arranged for as many cars and trucks as we could find among members and friends to leave our studio after working hours. Some of the technical staff had left earlier on a truck with the set. Their job was to get everything ready for the arrival of the cast. We were playing on a very much smaller stage in the Legion Hall of Oshawa.

When we all arrived, we had a quick walk-through rehearsal to establish our moves on the cramped stage. Everything seemed to be going well. The hall was filled and as we began playing it was evident that our audience was reacting to what it was seeing. We on stage responded to their enthusiasm.

In Act II there was a short intimate scene in the home between father and daughter who are enjoying a little talk just before the rest of the family arrives from work. When I (as the daughter) greeted the actor who played my father, my nose told me he had had a drink — or maybe two. We started our conversation: father tired, sitting at the table; I at the window, waiting for the others. I started my part of the dialogue, but instead of getting a response, there was silence. At first, it didn't seem to bother me, but I could feel the adrenalin starting to pump.

I repeated what I had said, coming downstage closer to my father. He just stared blankly at me. I began straightening the chairs, brushing crumbs off the table, arranging the tablecloth and dishes in preparation for supper. I wondered out loud why the rest of the family was late getting home.

I could feel the tension backstage. Suddenly there was a hole that somehow couldn't be filled. Try as I might, I couldn't think of anything to say or do that would get a response. Fortunately, my fellow actors heard my plea backstage and came in with hearty greetings for all. From that point, the play proceeded and the actor who had dried up was able to continue. I had a very sick feeling in my stomach for the rest of that performance.

That evening over coffee, when the performance had ended to enthusiastic applause, David asked me what had happened on stage. Of course he knew very well what had happened, but he wanted my explanation. When he got it, he explained quietly that with my training and experience I should have been able to carry on without leaving a hole. His criticism was friendly, but I was upset with myself.

I simply couldn't tell him about the liquor I had smelled. I guess I really was angry with myself for not having done better in the difficult circumstances. I couldn't be too angry at my fellow actor because he was a fine man and did such a good job in the play. I did, however, speak to him before we played *Steel* again. I suggested in a friendly way that he ought not to drink before performances if it caused him to dry up so badly on stage. He apologized profusely and promised it wouldn't happen again ever.

I am happy to say this problem never recurred and our scene together continued to be warm and close without hitches.

Out of that experience, it occurred to me that there are actors, amateur and professional, who need a bit of this false "courage" before stepping on stage. Perhaps, if they are very experienced, they can get away with it. But I can't imagine actors who are at all serious about their work jeopardizing their concentration in this way.

We did play *Steel* again late in April at Margaret Eaton Hall, this time under the auspices of *New Advance*, a Canadian youth magazine.

Grace Gray became secretary of Theatre of Action on a full-time basis at about this time. I, of course, had been doing it on a voluntary basis. I asked her to recall the experience for me.

"I was working with the New Theatre in Winnipeg and had heard of Theatre of Action and its work. Then, my husband at the time decided to come to Toronto. He started to work with the group and I followed later. When I arrived in Toronto, David Pressman was director. I remember that he was working on *Steel*. Shortly after I was hired for $7 a week as secretary.

"I was in charge of the office all day and in the evenings I attended a lot of meetings. At first, I hesitated to talk very much, but as time went on I became more active. I took this job very seriously. It meant a lot to me to do it properly. But it was also part of my social life. After all, most of the people in the theatre worked in the daytime and they would come at night to rehearsal. You met people. What else did you have to do in those days? You didn't have money to spend on movies and this was social and recreational as well. You got to know people very well. You got fond of them. They became very personal friends.

"In *Steel* I was also the famous mill noises backstage. The Steel Workers' Union took over a whole night, providing we cleaned up the language, which of course we did, and it didn't make a bit of difference to the play itself. Some of the steel workers came backstage after the performance to find out how we made the noises of a mill. I remember distinctly having a piece of rope which I pulled back and forth on the rung of a chair, making one of the sounds that might be heard. They found it fascinating to see how we did it.

"They were also absolutely knocked out by the set — the beautiful big backdrop of the steel mill and then just a few pieces for the interior. They were particularly delighted at the way in which we reproduced their lives and their working place.

"I remember the whole cast went to Hamilton to visit a steel mill. They read the play, and liked it very much, except for some of the rough language. By today's standard, the language they objected to would be considered absolutely pure.

"As secretary I attended executive committee meetings, as well as others. We worked as efficiently as any theatre running on a shoe-string could. We had to make decisions, we had to go on financial campaigns. The kids who worked in the theatre were fabulous. They worked all day and what little time and money they had, they put into the theatre. I think that was one of the things that made it so tremendous.

"The time we were in the festival, and eventually won with the second act of *Steel,* they put a very high price on the drama festival and everyone had to be dressed formally. So those people in our theatre who could afford to rent a suit, did. There was a man in the festival committee — he was a dentist, I can't remember his name — who was also interested in photography. His wife, evidently, was the same size as I was. They got me all dressed up in a gorgeous turquoise dress. One of the boys, who worked for a fur company, borrowed a chinchilla jacket for me. The theatre sent my husband and me to the 'do.' They paid for us.

"When David Pressman went, he just went in his navy blue suit, which had quite a shine from long wear. When he went up to receive the award, there was his little shiny behind. It was delightful. Here I was, all dressed up in my finery. It was beautiful — the contrast.

"As for financing the theatre, I know we had financial campaigns. Letters would be sent out to lists of people. I would do the follow-up by phone if someone hadn't sent in their contribution. Then we had various events in the theatre studio to raise money. All members paid a certain amount of dues. That basically is how the money was raised. For a long while we were very popular and we managed to get many contributions. We also had patrons and associate members, who joined for the year.

"Later on, in addition to all my administrative work, I acted in two one-act plays, *Fumed Oak* and *Sunday Cost Five Pesos.* These plays were done in the studio. I did work as Mistress of Ceremony for the studio productions because David thought it would be interesting and different for me to do this, with my pronounced English accent."

How was *Steel* received at the regional festival?

Nancy Pyper in *Saturday Night* on April 9, 1938, wrote of our performance:

"In *Steel* the work was even better than that which a few weeks ago made this production one of the most memorable events of the season . . ."

She went on to reiterate her remarks on the individual acting jobs and ended by saying:

"The entire cast was as good as before and, as before, the teamwork was perfect."

She also quoted Malcolm Morley, the adjudicator, as saying: "This is the best I have seen to date in the Central Ontario Regional Festival this year," mentioning particularly the "living quality of the play."

I recall his excitement as he adjudicated the work of actors and director in *Steel*. At one point, he exploded and said: "My, how they listened!" That *was* the great compliment he paid us. It was what we worked for and we were proud it was recognized. Morley awarded us the prize for the best play in this region and we were to go to the finals in Winnipeg to represent our region there.

Before leaving Mr. Morley, though, here's a clipping from the *New York Times*, in which he wrote on May 22, 1938. He titled his article, *Canada's Drama Festival*. He describes his trip from coast to coast across Canada to adjudicate the regional festivals and the plays presented by the various groups. In the section on Toronto, he wrote:

". . . a high standard is set by the top teams in Toronto . . . a newer organization, the Theatre of Action, in my opinion, gained an ascendancy over these older groups by a performance of John Wexley's *Steel* . . .

"In Victoria, the furthest point west, the Beaux Arts Society, an ultra-English group, contributed a polished performance of the Noel Coward comedy, *Hands Across The Sea*. In the finals it was to follow the ultra *Steel* of the Theatre of Action. The temperature must have changed considerably that evening."

When the excitement of winning top prize for the region wore off, we faced the financial problem of getting actors, director, and set to Winnipeg Our patrons and the friends of the Theatre of Action were pleased that we had won and gave us their support. Some of the employed members of the cast helped by paying all or part of their fares. Needless to say, we found the cheapest way to travel by train — on the day coach.

This meant we slept sitting up for the long trip west. Of course we were young and our group was congenial. We had a fine time together. It was brightened considerably by the fact that we had Richard Bingham in our cast. He brought along the fixings for some Indian curries, at which he was a master. He was also a constant storyteller. I must say a few words about Richard Bingham. He was a very tall, heavy-set man who had obviously been in the army. He was considerably older than all of us, but he moved like a much younger man with a straight back. He had strong, pronounced features, black-turning-to-gray hair which was receding from his forehead. His speech was clear, with an English accent. He played an American labor lawyer in *Steel* and was professional enough to sound American in the play.

He had been in the first World War as an Intelligence Officer for the British. He also spent some time in India before that — and he looked the part. He had had many interesting and exciting adventures, especially in his intelligence work. We would listen eagerly to his exploits in India and, during the war, in the Middle East. His sense of drama made these experiences come alive. It was never dull with Richard around. He certainly made our train trip to Winnipeg a much less tiresome affair. As an actor he always did a fine job, particularly in *Steel.* He added his much-needed maturity to whatever cast he was in.

We arrived in Winnipeg early in the morning of the day we were to perform. This was arranged so that Helen Coleman could leave after the performance and get back to her job. There was no time to rest. When we got to the theatre our set was there and we had to get it up. We looked at the huge stage of the Walker Theatre (very much like the Royal Alex in Toronto) with some alarm. We wondered what our set would look like on this stage, as compared to the one for which it was designed.

Somehow, though, the set was put in place, all actors pitching in. We were fortunate that we had not designed a realistic one, which would have been ridiculous on this stage. We filled in the extra space with dark curtains. It was not too bad.

We had a walk-through rehearsal to adjust to the larger playing area. We spoke our lines to test our projection in this very much bigger auditorium. We then discovered that Ben Lennick had a cold and laryngitis. We began to worry about that. We got in touch with our colleagues in Winnipeg New Theatre and told them all our troubles. They responded with great warmth and efficiency.

A couple of the women took Helen Coleman away to find her a dress and a pair of shoes for the performance — the clothes that had been left on the platform in Toronto. Others took Ben Lennick home to look after his throat so he could perform that evening. We had also written ahead that we would need some food for the show — supper for the family. I went with one of the women to help prepare some shepherd's pie. It had to be ready early enough, so it would not be too hot on stage. Most of the time we ate cold shepherd's pie. It's hard to describe what that tastes like and we still had to make it look like we were enjoying it.

Tired as we all were, when the evening arrived the adrenalin started to flow. We were determined to give as good and energetic a performance as possible. The adjudicator for the Dominion finals was an American (for the first time in festival history, I believe) — Barrett H. Clark, a New York professor, critic, actor and producer.

I don't remember too much about that evening's performance. In spite of all our efforts to relax, we were exhausted, the set seemed lost, it took longer to cross the stage, or to get on stage from the wings, and we were working much harder to project in order to reach the audience. Ben Lennick was truly struggling. But the laughter which reached us gave us some assurance that our audience was responding.

Though we felt we were working hard, it was reassuring to hear the adjudicator, as reported in the Winnipeg *Tribune*, on May 17, 1938:

"In Steel there was an authority and a life, and although but one act of the play was presented, yet the group which offered it did not for a moment let it down. They did extremely creditable work in bringing the act to a climax which simply did not exist.

"While he (Mr. Clark) was not concerned with make-up particularly, yet he felt that in *Steel* it was somewhat overdone in some cases . . . He was amazed at the very fine evidences of good directing that he had seen in the plays presented on the opening night . . ."

The *Tribune's* critic gave us some idea of our work that evening:

"Action plus tensity (*sic*) and dramatic situations are to be found in *Steel* and while the whole of the suspenseful drama could not be realized in the excerpt presented by the Theatre of Action of Toronto, yet if the applause of the audience may be taken as the criterion of judgment, it won high favor . . . it may be recalled by those who have seen the whole play that the act chosen depicts the union meeting in the home of one of the mill workers and affords opportunity for the introduction of a number of diverse characters in the steel workers.

"Of these, Ben Lennick as Tony, was in a class by himself, and surely captured the individual honors for acting on the opening night of the festival. Mr. Lennick has suffered from a severe cold since his arrival in Winnipeg and those who saw his work in the same play in Toronto said his performance here was inferior. If that is so, then his Toronto work must have been surpassingly good, for on Monday evening he proved himself to be a distinctly fine actor with good voice, complete mastery of his role and a nice trick of gesture.

"Norval Gray, former Winnipeg player, was . . . always in character, while Toby Gordon scored heavily in her bit as Melania, and Helen Coleman was extremely good in the emotional role of Betty. Others in the company all played well.

"A feature of this presentation was the use of suggested scenery to indicate the house of one of the workers, with a futuristic treatment of the menacing steel mill as a backdrop. This, with the correct lighting, was particularly effective."

We did not win any awards at these finals, but we had introduced our theatre to a brand-new audience who were perhaps seeing a play about workers for the first time. The festivals were important to us as a showcase of our theatre and the progress it was making. We felt we were making a strong and unusual contribution. And it was comments like Frank Morriss's in the Winnipeg *Free Press* which made us feel that we really did have something special to show. He wrote on May 17, 1938:

The horse and carriage trade came out in full force Monday night — to use an expression from theatrical papers, and the lobby of the Walker Theatre was knee-deep in evening wraps.

The Governor-General sat in the middle of the front row, and some obliging person had provided a special carpet for his party to rest its feet on. His Excellency looked to be having a good time, too, and the timid souls who had been waiting for him to run screaming from the theatre when the Toronto Theatre of Action unloosed its bolts at the state of things capitalistic were disappointed.

He just sat bolt upright, and when there were jokes from the Italian comic, he grinned.

As a matter of fact, the Torontonians were not so fiery as the citizenry had been led to expect, although Toronto must have been scandalized out of its collective wits.

They showed, however, (still using the theatrical trade paper jargon) plenty of class. It was as fine an exhibition of amateur theatrical trouping as Winnipeg has witnessed in many a day. The boys and girls had a snappy ensemble of acting.

XIX

Changing Direction

WHEN WE RETURNED TO TORONTO, our season at an end, David informed us that he would be leaving us to return to New York. He was going to be teaching at the Neighborhood Playhouse. As well, he wanted to try for some further creative work as an actor and director, in his home town. He felt sure, he explained, that Theatre of Action would continue to grow and develop under another director.

Most of us were downhearted at the prospect of losing David. We had come to respect him and his work. We had also become very fond of him as a person who, we felt, was really one of us. It was natural that we should feel this break deeply. Personally, I couldn't imagine working with anyone else. Having worked closely with David, both organizationally and as an actor, I felt we were losing a very special leader.

Still, after the news had sunk in, we understood and knew that one day this would have had to happen. David had stayed in Toronto longer than any of our other directors. He worked with us for two years and the close bond he developed between himself, the Theatre of Action and, one might say, the community around him, made it difficult to part.

"My stay with Theatre of Action was, up to then, the most enormous experience of my life," he told me later. "I could not have become the artist I am without that experience. I think the theatre got from me something in return. Those two years were like ten years of life, because I matured rapidly as only young people can.

"After two years, I felt I wanted to move on. We had often talked about whether I should stay in Canada. I might fall in love with somebody and get married. But that didn't happen. My home was in New York. My family — mother, father, brother, sisters — were all there, and I really was a little homesick for New York in all its enormity. I felt that was really where the major theatre was. I really wanted to take up the challenge in that place. Then, in the mail came a letter inviting me to teach and assist Sanford Meisner at Neighborhood Playhouse. I accepted. I would also be getting a little more money, something like fifty bucks a week."

To replace him, David suggested Danny Mann, who was also a Neighborhood Playhouse graduate. Sanford Meisner also recommended Danny. David talked to him and Danny agreed to come to Toronto.

Perhaps not surprisingly, David, after working on Broadway and serving in the Army, wound up being blacklisted in the fifties. "I couldn't work," he told me. "I was on the blacklist for my activities in the thirties, as well as those around New York after the war. I had been acting, directing and teaching.

"I was a progressive, a World War II veteran who was wounded in an anti-fascist cause which was victorious. I was just getting started in television as well, but I was fired from a lot of television shows, and there were 12 years of very difficult times.

"Still, I don't consider them lost. I went back into teaching and acting. I just was not able to work in television or films. I think if it hadn't been for those years, I probably would be in Hollywood today doing big feature pictures. I might have. Perhaps I tend to blame the blacklist more than necessary; people did emerge from it, you know. But it was a very rough time. Fortunately, Boston University and Neighborhood Playhouse paid no attention to McCarthy. I did, however, want very much to work in television and films. I liked the technology of it and I was beginning to get into it.

"Of course, my income dropped and by this time I had a family to look after. I remember in 1952, the day I was fired from producing and directing on television. I walked out on Madison Avenue and 57th Street and walked up to Fifth Avenue. I felt as if the city had spewed me out. I felt as if I had given my life to something and suddenly, it was bad and had to be vomited out. It felt terrible.

"After a while, of course, you bounce back, as so many creative people have. I do enjoy looking back. In those days in Toronto I paid room rent of $2.50 a week. I remember one day, Jack Creed took me out to dinner. I don't remember where but we were in a little private dining-room. We had a marvellous meal for $1 and I thought that was so expensive. I used to go up to Murray's and for 45¢ I got a complete meal. Sometimes for 55¢ there was fried oysters or a steak. That was in 1937. I'll tell you another thing the Canadian experience gave me. It gave me a political outlook which remained deeply ingrained in me, in spite of all the changes that have occurred in the world. It isn't a question of this government or that, it's a question that the political orientation was a human one. A humanistic social philosophy, that's the heart of it."

Because David was our first teacher-director and set the standards for us, I thought of the many contributions he had made. Since he was aware that he was here only temporarily, he made it his business to encourage those of us he felt had the capacity to try our wings at directing, and to help him audition new people applying for membership. He explained the process of choosing a script and how to approach it as actors and, further along, as directors. His standards were high and he expected as much from us — as actors, directors, technical staff. Every acting class, every rehearsal, was a learning experience with him, yet he never displayed the arrogance of the "superior" director to anyone in the group. He was a warm friend, a dedicated, socially-aware theatre worker, who clearly indicated the path for Theatre of Action to follow, both artistically and socially.

Our new director — Danny Mann — wouldn't be arriving until the fall of 1938. Despite this we began organizing children's classes. Dorothy Cass, one of our members, had some experience teaching children, and she suggested we initiate a Saturday morning class for young children at the studio. We certainly didn't anticipate the response we got. There seemed to be a lot of interest in this field. We decided to enlarge the project and Basya Hunter, who was also a member of the group, expressed her desire to join the teaching staff.

The result was that we had to find another location for children's classes, not only for very young children, but for senior students as well. Norval Gray and I joined the staff as assistants to the two directors of the children's school. I was present at the registration of students and saw the parents who were signing their children up for the school. I realized that most of them were from homes where the depression had had little impact. Our fees were low, it is true, but it was obvious that there were not many students from workers' homes. It wasn't hard to understand this. After all, acting classes for children were a luxury few workers could indulge in during times of lay-offs and unemployment.

Thus it is, even now, that the children who need the kind of enrichment offered by drama have very little opportunity to explore the medium. It is children from homes where they are bound to see plays, participate in music, drama, dance, *etc.*, who are fortunate to be able to explore and discover the cultural world around them.

I must admit I felt this keenly at the time of the Theatre of Action's children's school. I also knew that our theatre could use the income this school provided. As well, we were providing a fresh approach to acting for these young students. That made the project interesting and worthwhile.

I recall Norval and I staged a fairly free-form production of *The Emperor's New Clothes* which the children seemed to thoroughly enjoy doing.

For our own adult summer school in that summer of 1938, Paul Mann and Hazel Okilman were to teach the acting classes. Harold Liskin, who had been a member of the University of North Carolina's fencing team, and was now a member of Theatre of Action, would teach fencing. Lorne Greene was joining the staff as voice teacher.

In the United States, 1938 was the year that *Pins And Needles* was produced by the International Ladies' Garment Workers' Union (ILGWU). The cast was recruited from workers in the shops and the show turned out to be a great favorite with Broadway audiences. It subsequently toured widely in Canada as well. Harold Rome, who wrote the music and lyrics, was "discovered" by the union's Labor Stage, producer of the revue.

The sketches were topical and amusing, the songs tuneful and meaningful. The cast interpreted the material with a gusto which spilled over to the audience. It was marvellously entertaining. *Pins And Needles* showed workers in other unions what they could achieve with theatre, both as participants and supporters.

Professional theatre people and critics greeted the revue enthusiastically. Brooks Atkinson of the *New York Times* referred to the show, as "witty, fresh and box office." He was especially delighted that the musical did *not* deal with strikes or struggles of workers. Certainly the young workers in the revue were delightful and audiences responded warmly. Mr. Atkinson to the contrary, there was sharp bite in some of the anti-fascist and anti-war numbers. I saw the show at the Royal Alex in Toronto and loved it. The talent displayed and the conviction and enjoyment of the workers on stage were to me further confirmation of the possibilities for many more labor theatres, supported by the trade unions. It was certainly an exciting beginning.

I also felt a personal and sentimental interest when I learned that the Labor Stage had been working in the Princess Theatre on 39th Street in New York. That theatre had been used earlier by Artef and I had played a small role in an Artef production there.

In the fall — October 3, 1938 to be precise — Danny Mann arrived in Toronto. While we were very curious about our new director and anxious to greet him, we were also inclined, quite naturally, to measure him against David Pressman, who had just left.

Danny was, though, different in all sorts of ways. He was a tall young man with a strong-featured face. His body was lean, his speech clipped. He had a very interesting kind of intensity. I found his eyes especially attractive. They were always on the verge of twinkling with humor — except when he was laid low by migraines, which we learned about later. His physique seemed to respond to his moods — especially his humor. He could easily and spontaneously break into a graceful little dance.

There was something of the showman in Danny. He could be tough, but always seemed ready in a tense situation to get a laugh, to break the tension. We had little trouble getting to know him and enjoying him as friend and director.

Danny approached the business of finding a place to live and adjusting to life in Toronto on a shoestring salary mostly with good humor. It was going to be an adventure for him and for us.

His first show — *It Can't Happen Here* — opened on December 12. An advance story in the *Toronto Star* on December 8 gave some sense of local feelings. It was written under the pseudonym "The Observer" which was the pen name used by the Rev. Salem Bland, a respected progressive minister in Toronto at the time.

> If there are any decent, kindly, intelligent folk in Toronto and vicinity . . . I would venture to dare them to expose themselves to the play which is to be put on in the Margaret Eaton Hall, McGill Street, next Monday evening, December 12th, by a local company, the Theatre of Action, which distinguished itself last winter in the production of two most striking plays, *Steel* and *Bury The Dead.* This time they are putting on a new version by Sinclair Lewis . . . *It Can't Happen Here.* Whether admirers of fascism agree or not with the picture Sinclair Lewis draws of what would be likely to happen if this epidemic of dictatorship spread to this continent, I can assure them they will be interested. I have found the story, even in the cold text, absorbingly interesting, also disquieting to all who, like me, see in fascism the most dangerous and the most brutal enemy to almost all the things which seem to me supremely lovely and sacred.
>
> I read the original novel when it appeared and found this dramatized version even more pungent. It may be my Canadian patriotism which makes me inclined to doubt that anything as ghastly as what Sinclair Lewis pictures as happening in the United States could happen in Canada, but I confess that this calamity does not look as impossible now as then . . . The play simply shows the sort of things that Lewis thinks would soon be done in a hundred places in America if a dictator were to rise over here. Almost certainly he would not be a duplicate of either Il Duce or the Fuehrer, but a much less unusual or alarming sort of leader, perhaps not one who seemed ambitious at all, but wholly concerned for the welfare of the people, particularly for peace and order, not at all improbably a religious man . . .

In view of what was going on in Abyssinia, Spain, Austria and Czechoslovakia, it seemed right to us to project what fascism would be like close to home — in the United States.

It was, of course, Danny's first production with us. He held many readings for parts and carried on some general discussions in order to better assess the members of the group. A newcomer joined our theatre for that production, the Rev. Reg Thomas, who had studied in our summer school and was ready to participate in production. He was assistant at St. Mary Magdalen Church. He was a bright, intelligent man and contributed maturity to our theatre.

Danny's approach to the acting problems was not unlike what we had

had before. We all felt at ease working with him. He was, I noticed, much more impatient with members of the cast who didn't work hard enough on their roles at rehearsals or at home. In fact, he could hand out sharp criticism to cast members who slacked off. Having done this, there would be a pause. He would look at everyone and his eyes began to twinkle, there would be a little smile and, finally, a little joke to break up the tension. Everyone was ready to work again.

I loved one little anecdote about his grandmother. He started by saying that he adored his grandmother, who was a lovely, warm human being. But she was unable simultaneously to carry on a conversation and tie her shoelaces. But he couldn't criticize her. She wasn't an actor. Everyone laughed. There was a pause. He went on to say that he saw too many actors in the cast behaving like his grandmother. It just wouldn't do. Then we understood his reason for telling us this anecdote.

After this, whenever an actor stopped what he was doing to deliver his lines, all Danny had to say was, "There goes my grandmother again." This phrase stood as a constant reminder of the many things an actor must do at one and the same time on stage.

I for one have always remembered Danny's grandmother in my own work, and in working as a director with others.

In *It Can't Happen Here* I had another "first" on stage — I had to use a hand gun. I must admit, even as a member of the audience, I always worry when an actor has to fire a gun. Will it go off — or will we hear a soft click at the moment of climax. On stage such a worry can loom very large. I had never used a gun as part of a performance before. Certainly I didn't want it to occupy my mind to the detriment of the role I was playing.

We decided to get our permit, plus a small hand gun and blanks, fairly early in the rehearsals so that I could practise to make the action as dramatically smooth as possible. I decided to concentrate on what was leading up to the shooting, to listen well to the dramatic developments that led to it, to prepare deliberately when the moment arrived to use it — and to fire. I think only once at rehearsal, the blank didn't go off. Fortunately, for the run of the play everything went smoothly and the shot was as startling as it was meant to be.

We played to good, enthusiastic houses throughout the one-week run and got a generally positive critical response. In the *Telegram* of December 14, 1938, Rose MacDonald wrote:

> When Sinclair Lewis' *It Can't Happen Here,* grim warning against the dangers of fascism, was first unveiled to the American public, it created quite a stir — remember? . . . Then two years or so ago the play, in its original form, was produced by the W.P.A. Theatre. Toronto is now seeing the play for the first time . . .

It is being done here all week by that very able acting group, the Theatre of Action, and is the first full-length, actually the first publicly-done play that Daniel Mann has done since coming to Toronto at the summer's end to take over the directorship . . .

The place of the play is a 'small American city'; the time — 'very soon — or never.' Huey Long, by the way, was living when Lewis decided it was time to say something forceful . . .

In a drug store, representatives of the citizenry . . . talk of the 'Corpos' in town; the citizens seem not to take them very seriously, to be amused rather at these young men strutting about in uniform . . . Presently we meet Commissioner Swan who seems well-meaning enough, a bit big-headed perhaps, but no harm in him . . . Before the community, the country realizes it, the Corpos . . . are in power, the reign of terror has begun . . .

Richard Bingham, who did such excellent work in *Steel*, is Doremus Jessup and gives a performance which might ornament the professional stage, remarkably convincing at every point. Sydney Banks . . . also gave an outstandingly clever performance, suggesting, as often as not, by expression of the eyes, twist of the mouth, a sly and cruel satisfaction, and finally abject cowardice. A small boy, Garnet Banks, who played Jessup's sturdy little grandson, sometimes almost runs away with the play — has an amazing grasp for so young a lad of the values of his part. One might also mention Rose Kashtan's work; Toby Gordon's, particularly towards the end; Norval Gray as the college youth; Alex D. Schatz's none too scrupulous factory owner; Jules Ross as the commissioner; indeed the cast generally.

With regard to the mounting — the stage exits might have been less awkwardly planned. One would like, too, the radio voices, both of them, to come from the direction of the radio. But these are comparatively minor matters in a strong production.

My husband Oscar, in the *Clarion* on December 13, 1938 wrote:

. . . Last night's showing of the Sinclair Lewis anti-fascist play *It Can't Happen Here* brought the biggest audience ever to attend a Theatre of Action opening; the first-nighters are spreading the word and tickets are becoming as scarce as leaves in Queen's Park.

Theatre of action should be congratulated on its choice of a play of such topical interest and vital importance, on its consistent progress from production to production, on a corps of splendid actors, on its new director, Daniel Mann who, with this one play, has won the right to be known as Toronto's most distinguished theatre craftsman . . .

In Daniel Mann, Theatre of Action has a director whose mind (bolstered by artistic competence) works like a precise machine, and who brings the best out of his actors, particularly in a play which depends entirely on individual and collective performances . . .

The play has several memorable scenes — and that is what makes a play. I refer to the scene between Miss Gordon and Mr. Banks, as Mary and Shad, when he is trying to 'make' her; the scene between Mr. Bingham, the Editor, and Mr. Banks, as Shad, when the lout has become editor and censors the writing of Jessup . . .

Special mention should be made of Elaine Bales and Reg Thomas . . . of 11-year-old Garnet Banks . . . Rose Kashtan . . . whose performances contributed to the general competency of the cast. A salute to Theatre of Action!

And in the *Radio Mirror* of December 22, 1938, Jan Chamberlain wrote:

Three summers ago, during a lazy and peaceful week-end in Muskoka, I read Sinclair Lewis' book, *It Can't Happen Here*. So far as I can remember it didn't fill me with any great fear. I probably catalogued it mentally as 'one of those unpleasant books.'

Last week I saw the Theatre of Action in the dramatization of the same story. It was a startling experience. I found I could not lightly toss Mr. Lewis' play into the heap of 'unpleasant theatre.'

In the two and a half years or so since *It Can't Happen Here* was published, events have moved so rapidly in Europe and in our own country, that one begins to wonder — seriously wonder — just what *CAN* happen here . . .

'There's one thing that can't happen in America. They can't interfere with the freedom of the press.' That's one of the lines that drew a derisive laugh from the audience. That's a dangerous sign. They knew the line no longer rang true — otherwise it wouldn't have seemed funny. Perhaps many of them knew that right here in Toronto a local daily paper was recently barred from sitting at the press table during meetings of the City Council . . .

The Theatre of Action's presentation of *It Can't Happen Here* played to a full house every night. But, as is always the case, the audience was made up of people who are already aware of the problems depicted in the play. While I quite agreed with the group's contention that the theatre offers one of the greatest educational opportunities of our day — it seems to me that somebody now should evolve a method whereby the audience will be made up of the people who need to be educated.

XX

Life And Death Of An American

DANNY MANN'S SHORT STAY with Theatre of Action was highlighted by his spectacular production of George Sklar's *Life And Death Of An American*, with music by Alex North and Earl Robinson. Ours was to be the world premiere of the play, to run the week of March 6, 1939 at Margaret Eaton Hall.

As a matter of fact, before our rehearsals were really in swing, Art and Lillian Messigner, two members of our group, were in New York and went to see Earl Robinson who was, at the time, involved with the W.P.A. production. He had just completed one song that was missing from our script. Robinson gave it to them to bring to Toronto — hot off the piano.

Just about our entire membership was involved in this unusual theatre piece — as actors, as chorus, as bit players, as dancers, some in more than one role. Quite a large number were needed backstage for the technical demands of the show. It was very different from anything we had done before in its swift-moving scenes of song, dance, choral numbers and sound effects. The intricate lighting helped to move scenes from place to place on a series of ramps. It all added up to a highly exciting *tour de force* for our theatre.

Rehearsals were most strenuous physically for all participants, requiring high energy and athletic movement. Everyone was also required to learn the play completely so we could turn up at the right place on the ramp or forestage on time. We had to make our exits swiftly and quietly — all in the flash of a blackout.

I played Kathleen Dorgan, mother of the young American. I had to learn a lullaby by Alex North. The music was beautiful, but rather modern and fairly difficult to sing. This was something new for me. The play opens with the music of the lullaby, and as the lights come up, the mother, sitting on stage and holding her baby in her arms, starts to sing it to sleep.

I had never sung solo for an audience before. I was fearful about what might happen during a performance. What if I open my mouth to sing and nothing happens? This was certainly a shuddering thought. I went to

Danny with my fears. He did a great deal to help me overcome my lack of confidence. He spoke to me about concentrating on what I was really doing with this song — it wasn't just a solo to show off my voice. On the contrary, I was singing a lullaby for a very particular reason — to put a baby to sleep.

Danny worked with me alone while I learned the music and words, until the singing became quite easy and natural. Vera Werrier, our pianist, was very patient in going over the music with me. Between the two of them, I learned to sing and really enjoyed it. I was very grateful to them both. My actual preparation for the opening scene started long before the lights came up. I sat in my chair with the baby in my arms, concentrating on putting him to sleep. Most of the time I rocked him a little. I started softly humming in unison with the backstage electric piano. By the time the lights came up, I just naturally sang my lullaby. I was told by people out front that this scene provided a lovely opening for the play and that my singing had ease and conviction.

My character had only a few scenes early in the script. When they were finished, I changed roles and joined the rest of the company in the choruses, creating the machines in the factory, and generally becoming part of the crowd that filled the stage. These crowd scenes were not used idly and they filled a very important role in the script by introducing the major social events in the life and death of the American.

It's hard to describe what was going on backstage. All I can recall is that we could have used a traffic cop to keep people from running into each other. All changes of costume and make-up had to be done in the wings, for fear of missing a cue. Normally modest types had no time to think about who was watching your state of undress. It could be described as a highly-organized but frantic scene in the wings.

Danny had done such a fine job rehearsing us that we knew the play thoroughly. In addition, the technical staff was so well organized and competent, that we never did miss a cue. The play moved to its climax (as far as the audience could see) smoothly and well-paced. That's why I referred to *Life And Death Of An American* as a *tour de force* for Theatre of Action.

One of the highlights for all of us was a rehearsal visit by Sinclair Lewis. The *Telegram* wrote about it on February 28, 1939.

> If Theatre of Action's rehearsal of *Life And Death Of An American* was particularly fiery last night . . . it might be attributed to the presence in their studio of Mr. Sinclair Lewis . . . He came in around eight-thirty and everything stopped while the players clapped him. 'This is the first time I've ever known the audience to be applauded,' cracked Mr. Lewis . . . And when everybody laughed, he added, 'I think I'll put that line in my show.' For about an hour and-a-half he sat on a straight-backed chair against the wall smoking cigarettes and

watching the performance. Told us he'd not seen any work of the Action group before . . . but was interested in the Toronto crowd because they'd done his play, *It Can't Happen Here.* This is Mr. Lewis' second visit to Toronto, 'I was up here years ago,' he remarked, 'covering the A.F. of L. Convention. I used to be a newspaperman too, you know.'

Sam Dolan, then a young music student and today one of Canada's outstanding composers, saw *Life And Death Of An American* as a "stylized play employing musical effects" which "enhance the dramatic impact to an amazing extent." After seeing a rehearsal, he wrote in the *Daily Clarion* of March 1, 1939 that "in some of the mass chants, the use of an ascending scale starting on a low note and rising to another an octave above gave a terrific punch to the lines. When the entire cast repeats the words 'America for Americans' the effect is indescribable.

"The songs themselves, and there are several really catchy tunes among them, will be sung by the audience when they leave the theatre, for they have everything necessary for a good hit tune.

"Alex North and Earl Robinson, popular working-class composers, collaborated in the composition of the songs and their work is of a very high calibre . . ."

Stuart Walton came from a rather conservative, comfortable home situated on a Rosedale ravine hillside. In 1935, he joined Theatre of Action. He acted in all our productions and, as well, was in a leadership position in many of the theatre's committees.

He was not too keen about *Life And Death Of An American.* At the request of the theatre, he undertook instead a project with the Single Men's Unemployed Association on Duke Street. "They wanted to put on a play to raise some money for their association. The play we chose was *Transit* by Philip Stevenson. It was adapted to mirror the conditions among the local unemployed single men. Their idea was to stage a big show and to take it around to various churches, after which it would tour Ontario cities and towns.

"They also came up with the idea that instead of people buying tickets for the show, they would be asked to pay in kind — razor-blades, soap, socks, *etc., etc.,* to provide much-needed items for the men.

"I remember going to Duke Street, thinking how in the world am I ever going to tackle this assignment? In the first place, I was basically middle-class, there was no getting away from that. How was I going to talk to these youth? Would it look as if I was talking down to them? What could I do?

"I recall vividly going into the place and seeing the lines of grey clothing hanging out to dry, and the little Quebec stove which was used for heating the place. Still, I made friends. I just acted naturally.

"I also remember that the evening before the first performance was to be given, one of the leading characters skipped. I had to play his part at the last minute."

"For me, *Life And Death Of An American* was a traumatic experience because I found I had to do a hell of a lot of running, dashing, prancing back and forth," said Ben Lennick to me later on, using a great deal of energy just recalling the feeling. "I wondered when the hell was I going to start acting, because it was more of a physical exercise, and the place smelled like a basketball arena rather than a theatrical rehearsal hall. The sweat quotient was very high.

"I remember Kenny Peck rolling around on his roller skates, deafening everyone with the noise. You couldn't hear anyone's lines. I also recall one evening Sinclair Lewis dropped in to watch us rehearse, and after it was over he spoke to all of us. I can hear him very clearly saying: 'I have never seen such enthusiastic people working on a play.' He didn't have to say anything, he could just have said 'very interesting' and left it at that. So the enthusiasm came across in a rehearsal situation to Sinclair Lewis.

"Certainly in a play like *Life And Death Of An American* you had to be enthusiastic, but also disciplined. There were troops all over the place, running, dashing around. Danny Mann had migraines at some rehearsals. He would just look in a sort of cross-eyed way at the assembled actors who were ready to perform, saying, 'I just can't do anything with you tonight, kids, I'm off.'

"Another outstanding visitor we had was Norman Bethune. He seemed to come in out of the blue. There he was, obviously on a money-raising tour or something. He came up to 490 Yonge Street, took off his trench-coat and he sat down, very tanned-looking, very healthy-looking too, sort of a bronzed glow about him. He was very, very intent watching us rehearse *Life And Death Of An American.* After the rehearsal he said, 'Oh, that's marvellous spirit you have. It reminds me of things that are going on in Spain.' He was all set to go down to Massey Hall to rouse people for the Spanish cause."

Our week of performances of *Life And Death Of An American* had very good audience support and was received with tremendous enthusiasm. Many people told us it was the best script and stage work they had ever seen. One well-known spectator on opening night of that play was Tim Buck. He was interviewed the following day and his remarks appeared in the *Daily Clarion* on March 9, 1939:

> I changed my mind three times during the play. At times I almost made up my mind that it was pure entertainment and then, like the crack of a whip, a blackout would cut short the humor in the midst of my guffaw and I would see the stark

realism of working-class life during the great panic of 1907, or the post-war crisis. I think that this is really one of the high spots of my general impression of the piece. It is realistic. Being realistic means that it includes the humor which is such a large part of the life of the working people even when they are suffering . . .

I found myself more than once reminded of changes that took place in my own attitude toward life during the periods covered by the play. I, of course, had most of the illusions that young Jerry Dorgan had, was cured of them in the same process that the play illustrates so excellently and during the same years . . .

I had a great evening. I wish I had another evening free this week. I'd go again, if only to hear Jerry gasp: 'Gee, I kissed her.'

Another reporter from *The Clarion* spent some time backstage and described, on March 10, 1939, what he saw there.

. . . Little does the callous audience . . . realize that Jerry Dorgan has exactly seven seconds to change from short pants to football trousers; six seconds from those to long pants; perhaps less from long pants into overalls, and from overalls into pants again . . . from pants into aviator suit and helmet and back into trousers again; and that he has caused the overworked and over-excited electricians and stage crew fits of agony and horror lest the fickle spotlight catch him sans any pants at all . . .

There are whistles up sleeves — hats are shoved up smocks — smocks are hid under dresses and vice versa. In the wings, belts and kerchiefs are waiting in outstretched hands to effect drastic changes — a lowered belt and a different collar . . .

So ingenious and so parsimonious was the costume committee . . . that for the women in the play only one dress was used to traverse a whole period of 37 years . . . Here is where the real cunning came in. By hooks and eyes, three inches of dress are hooked on, and when, in 1927, the shorter dresses are wanted — presto — zip — off the flounce comes — on with the new dickie, a new belt, a change of hair dress and we have an effective . . . costume . . .

The surefootedness with which the whole cast climbs up and down that treacherous ramp is a tribute in itself. It is one of the marvels how there is enough breath left in them to be able to do more than whisper . . .

This surprising group within their own nucleus designed and executed the stage set, designed, cut and sewed all the costumes, applied their own make-up, did their own lighting and sound effects, and still had enough energy and eagerness left to produce a play that in itself is an achievement worthy of a much more mature, more firmly established and financially more secure group.

The press reaction to our effort was again positive. In the *Star* of March 7, 1939, Augustus Bridle wrote:

Theatre of Action presented last night the first performance anywhere of *Life And Death Of An American* by George Sklar. In a few weeks New York will see the Federal Theatre presentation.

Next Wednesday the drama festival will have Theatre of Action's production as one of four full-length plays . . .

The play unites character realism with symbolism and a stylized production. There is no scenery . . . a ramp up to a platform, stairs down the other end to the forestage which also is used for action. These symbolize in turn the names of the two generations of Dorgans, roof-top, a flying field, fair grounds and a steel mill. On these a company of over 30 in period clothes from 1900 to 1936 . . . present in a series of nearly 100 swift cyclonic scenes, with blackouts for scene shifting, the whole social, economic tragedy of the Dorgans. Only a few of the scenes are photographic. There are no streets, no windows, no rooms, and only a little table and two chairs for furniture. Costumes are effective, but not gorgeous.

The play opens with the crescendo chant, 'We want a Living Wage!' This, of 1900 and again of 1936 in the finale, is a sort of slogan theme-song . . .

On this skeleton the author devised an incredible scheme of stagecraft which the producer splendidly executes in an astonishing sequence of mob movements to chants, choric monologues, music and wonderfully effective backstage noises. Scores of scenes present a swift panorama of American life, viewed entirely from one angle. These are skilfully projected in choric movements on a small stage. The central characters, Michael, Kathleen and Jerry Dorgan and Mary, his young wife — are well portrayed by Alex Schatz, Toby Gordon, Norval Gray and Elaine Bales.

In *The Daily Clarion* of March 7, 1939, Oscar wrote:

The *Life And Death Of An American* by George Sklar is a remarkable play, and it was given a remarkable production by Theatre of Action as it opened Monday night at Margaret Eaton hall.

The play is remarkable because of its unusual structure, in which straight drama, musical revue, pantomime, spectacle, Greek chorus and commentator are intermingled and combine to produce a dramatic unity throughout . . .

It is further remarkable because Director Daniel Mann so skilfully unites the varied forms of theatre and integrates the work of a cast of 25, many playing two or more roles . . .

Rose MacDonald too was enthusiastic in the *Telegram* of March 7, 1939:

Life And Death Of An American by one George Sklar was presented last night by those ardent young experimentalists, personnel of the Theatre of Action . . . and for its premiere drew a large audience.

In accordance with the habit and principle of the Theatre of Action, *Life And Death Of An American* is, definitely, commentary on the existing social order. It is not a play at all in the completely conventional sense, rather a swiftly successive series of impressionistically designed episodes . . .

For all its defects this play is distinguished by an uncompromising sincerity and, so far as the present production is concerned, by the choice quality of performance in the instance of the pivotal role . . . Norval Gray gives a choice performance of Jerry, credible at every point, warmly human and fluent. His work is attractively supplemented by young Garnet Banks, who plays the very youthful Jerry, and in turn, his young son, with the same ease which marked him in his more spectacular part in *It Can't Happen Here.* Alex Schatz' Michael Dorgan was a remarkably easy and engaging performance and Toby Gordon's presentment of Mrs. Dorgan had nice quality. Elaine Bales was charming as the youthfully gauche Mary and matured with a sufficiency of conviction, though one would have liked more resilience in her voice, something of color to meet the emotional demands of the part.

The lighting of the piece did a fine dramatic service, as did the unusually successful sound effects, and the ensemble work had vital movement if not always sufficient direction . . . The factory impressions, however, were extremely able in design and in their carrying out as group scenes . . . The finale, however, did not quite come off — last night at any rate.

On March 15, 1939, we presented *Life And Death Of An American* at the regional festival in Hart House. It was the first of several full-length plays being shown. Of the several plays we had entered in the festival, this script was most directly outspoken in depicting what our society does to an individual — especially one who believes in the American dream. The techniques called for in the presentation invade the audience and speak directly to it about the events unfolding.

The night we played, I was particularly aware of the discomfort of the festival audience as they were being confronted, especially at the end, when the complete cast on stage turns to them with a mass chant expressing hope for a change towards a full, free life. Following this "finale," after what seemed like a very long time but was only a few moments, there was a frozen silence. Then, finally, a burst of applause.

At Hart House, the actors and audience are very close. As I faced front with the closing words of the play, I was very conscious of the discomfort. I felt we had given one of our best performances that evening. Thus it was clear to me that it was the content of our play that was causing the unhappiness.

Augustus Bridle, in the *Star* of March 17, had some interesting interpretations of the adjudicator's comments after the performance. The subhead of his story was: "Festival Adjudicator Finds Theatre Of Action Offering Hard Nut To Crack." He then goes on:

> George Skillan, drama festival adjudicator, had a weary look as he took his chair on the Hart House stage last night to give his public opinion about *Life And Death Of An American*.
>
> But in careful language he gave a decision. Obviously, this play, done by Theatre of Action, direction of Daniel Mann, will not reach the finals in London.
>
> This production is the most unusual for a whole evening ever done at the festival here . . .
>
> A festival that presents such plays has a broad-angle democracy in its program much too eclectic for even so fine a little theatre as Hart House . . .
>
> The audience largely agreed with Mr. Skillan, remembering also that *Bury The Dead* by this same group was much more of a stylized anti-war production and much less of a real play . . .

Thelma Craig in the *Globe and Mail* of March 16, also reported on Mr. Skillan's adjudication of our entry:

> With a play that was in no sense of the conventional order but rather a swift succession of impressionistic episodes, the Theatre of Action introduced the first full-length dramatic production into the Central Ontario Regional Festival (CODL) last night . . .
>
> There was considerable difference of opinion as to its merits. Generally speaking, it was felt that the material was excellently handled. But Adjudicator George Skillan felt that there was an

incongruity between the humanistic actor and the impressionistic style that weakened the general effect.

'The scenery, the lighting, the ingenuity displayed in the unit set, and the grouping, were extremely fine. The team work and the movements in the production stood out,' he said. 'But I felt the characterization shrinking beside the impressionistic acting. My general impression of it was of extremely competent handling and imagination and thought. But that was so prolific that it rather confounded the objective. The mass of stylized work and impressionism was so vivid and the scenes so short and in such quick succession, that the idea was rather confused.

'When I read this play through today, I felt that there was a certain drama in the story — a thread of it, but not a strong one,' Mr. Skillan continued. 'I felt the ending was not as well done as it should be. But tonight it seemed to me that the acting side and the story did not come over as they should, due to over-pronouncement, abundance and exuberance, and short periods with the lights coming on and off and on and off. I said to myself: Is it a play or a piece of impressionistic acting?

'But there was a multitude of things so various that the mind was confused. And the actual propaganda came over at times at the expense of the play. It is difficult to mix mediums. But mimetic acting is not new; the Greeks did it and did it coherently.'

The adjudicator declared it was difficult to hold an autopsy on the play. But some of the individual work was remarkable, he felt. 'If the director had chosen a play that depended more on the acting itself, I think he would have given us a remarkable production,' he added.

At the outset, the adjudicator explained that the play was a bit of a novelty to him. 'Under no circumstances do I allow my political or religious ideas to influence my opinions of a piece of work. I keep them locked up in my trunk at home. I look at all stage productions as a man of the theatre judging a work of the theatre. In Winnipeg I awarded the trophy for the best play to a labor group there. It came up to all the required standards of the theatre.

'In a play where there is propaganda, if the play is swamped by it, it ceases to be a play and is not of the theatre. The Winnipeg play was handled as a real drama,' the London, England adjudicator explained. 'In Winnipeg the symbolic effects were not permitted to swallow up the play . . .'

Ben Lennick as Slim was meted out considerable praise by the adjudicator. The musical effects were very effective and the chanting of the voices. Daniel Mann was the director . . .

Mr. Bridle was quite right. We did not get to the final festival, which was held in London, Ontario in 1939, with our "impressionistic" play. We were, of course, disappointed. We felt our spirited, entertaining and unusual show would have added much to the finals.

In the past, it had been the custom in this Central Ontario region to invite the winners of the previous year's festival to go to the finals, providing the theatre group entered a production of high standard. We had been the winners in the 1938 regional festival with an act from *Steel* and had every expectation that our performance of *Life And Death Of An American* would show up extremely well against the other plays presented. Even on the basis of its unusual nature our entry warranted an invitation to the finals.

But it was not to be. An anonymous phone call informed our director that there was some dissension in the regional festival committee on the question of inviting the Theatre of Action to London. We were told that Hugh Eayrs, chairman of the regional committee, had resigned as a result of disagreement with the others on this question. Apparently, dislike of the content of our entry was the determining factor — strong enough to convince the committee to break with traditional courtesy.

There was, however, some good news. We were delighted to hear that New Theatre in Winnipeg were winners in their region and would bring their production of *Rehearsal,* a highly dramatic and vital labor play by Albert Maltz, to London to represent their region. That was the "labor" group that Mr. Skillan had referred to when he spoke about how unprejudiced he was in choosing winning plays for the festival.

We were jubilant that our social theatre movement would be well represented in the Dominion finals with such a fine entry.

It was clearly time for Theatre of Action to move on. And move on we did, to an interesting and, for us, new facet of theatre.

XXI

Moving On

THE *FOOTLIGHT FOOTNOTES* COLUMN was introduced in the *Daily Clarion* by Oscar, who was then a staff member on the paper. It was, to my knowledge, the only Canadian daily to carry such a column of national and international stage news and comment.

March 31, 1939 — "In Process: Michael Brand, who press-agented *Life And Death Of An American,* is at work on a full-length play, tentatively titled *All God's Children* . . . Started the project last October and expects to have it finished in a few months, when he will submit it to Theatre of Action . . . The locale is Toronto, specifically that area around College-Spadina-Bathurst, and the characters are largely young people . . . 'I want to show that a young chap doesn't voluntarily turn to crime but is forced into it by circumstances,' Mr. Brand said. Most of these young people of whom he writes he has known intimately for years, he told the *Clarion* . . . It is, however, definitely not a gangster play, he pointed out . . . In Process: From Hamilton, Frank Love writes a long letter, some of which we hope to reprint soon . . . Mr. Love is at work on a play dealing with the life and times (100 years ago) of William Lyon Mackenzie . . . Hopes to have it ready by the fall . . . also has a play now in rehearsal with the Hamilton Players' Guild . . . There are, Mr. Love remarks, some six producing playwrights in Hamilton . . . Two songs: Frank Gregory (he played the priest in *Life And Death Of An American*) has startled his friends by casually handing them original music and lyrics for two songs . . . Both may be heard next month, it is said, at a Theatre of Action cabaret . . . Notes: Winnipeg New Theatre members (Manitoba festival winners) are planning to visit Toronto for a few days after the London finals . . ."

April 8, 1939 — "Absolutely Final: Through a roundabout route we learn that the Montreal New Theatre Group's musical revue, after many tentative christenings, is finally, irrevocably and more-or-less definitely to be called *We Beg To Differ* . . . Some of the numbers have been tried out at parties and socials and have been voted capital . . . Production date is within a few weeks. This will be the group's last show of the season . . ."

April 14, 1939 — "This Propaganda Fuss: We don't want to stir up the old controversy of Art and Propaganda, but sometimes we question the motives of some people who get themselves into a sweat when a play says something with which they don't agree. Instead of being frank about it and saying they don't agree with the message of the play in question, they launch into full-dress declarations that plays should, in general, never say anything. If a play says anything, it must be propaganda, they argue . . . But when a play does have a message with which they happen to agree, they conveniently forget to label it 'propaganda' . . . Coming events: . . . *Time Lurches On* is the name of the cabaret (April 28 and 29 at the Belvin, College and Spadina, Toronto) when Theatre of Action supplies the talent. Numbers include the now-famous *Chamberlain Crawl,* as well as *Picket-Line Priscilla, We're Socially Insignificant, Waiting For Odets,* etc . . . *Littlewoodisms:* Among the remarks of Samuel R. Littlewood, English drama critic adjudicating the now-concluding Dominion Drama Festival, and voiced at the London, Ontario, Canadian Club this week: 'The tired businessman is the most dreadful person in the world. He ought not to exist.' (In reference to businessmen who prefer leg shows to serious drama) . . . 'The idea of life expressed by Shakespeare, that man is entitled to work out happiness for himself and to help others attain it, is still the most vital thing underlying our civilization.' . . .The theatre (he said) is important as a weapon of social reform."

April 21, 1939 — "Concerning Winnipeg: Joe Zuken, the young lawyer who is chairman of Winnipeg New Theatre, was in Toronto this week with several members of the *Rehearsal* company, stopping off here before returning to Winnipeg from London, Ont., Dominion Drama Festival where their play won second place in competition with 13 other top-ranking groups . . . Winnipeg New Theatre . . . meets Mondays, one meeting a month being set aside for current business, but the other Mondays devoted to lectures, play-readings and the like, open to interested visitors . . . The group was organized in August of 1936 and numbers 100 members. More About Winnipeg: Over 1,000 persons, Mr. Zuken estimates, have seen the group in play-readings before Winnipeg club meetings. Sending group members out to these clubs for private readings of plays has been a valuable means of maintaining contact with audiences between productions and of recruiting additional New Theatre fans. Winnipeg postscript: The group is now planning its second summer school. Last summer's eight-week course was directed by Mercer McLeod, CBC man who directed the Festival award-winner . . . Among other activities, the group publishes a monthly mimeographed bulletin, circulation 300 . . . David Yeddeau leads a Tuesday night make-up class . . . Second Winnipeg Postscript: Four of the winning play's cast of 13 were named by Adjudicator S.R. Littlewood for particularly good performances in *Rehearsal.* They were Frances Goffman, Gordon Burwash, Ruth Segal and Joe Zuken . . . The adjudicator congratulated both Director McLeod and the author, Albert Maltz . . . Before the festival opened, the group received a telegram of greetings and encouragement from Mayor John Queen . . .

More on Manitoba: . . . All in all, it is apparent that we and our readers ought to respectfully doff our bonnets to Manitoba and its capital city and its very capital New Theatre . . . In any event, that's what Toronto Theatre of Action did the other night when they ran a party at their studio for the conquering guests and entertained their footlight friends with excerpts from local productions . . . Notices: . . . Also in Toronto, Sunday night a semi-private full-dress rehearsal of *Transit* at Theatre of Action studio, 490 Yonge Street, by Single Men's Unemployed Association . . ."

And from *The Star* of May 8, 1939:

"Toronto's first political floor-show and cabaret will be presented Sunday night in the studio of the Theatre of Action, Yonge St. Daniel Mann, director of the theatre group, is in charge.

"Acts include satires on the current situation in Europe and the Far East. Included in the program will be four original musical numbers composed by a Toronto boy, Frank Gregory. Mr. Gregory's music will have its world premiere during the evening.

"Dance routines, catchy swing tunes and chorus will be assisted by Lou Jacobi, Francine Shapiro, Dorothy Levine, Michael Brand, Sydney Banks and Jack Kaell. Other members of the cast are Harold Liskin, Toby Gordon, Rose Kashtan, Ray Harris, Gerry Shumer, Elaine Bales, Pauline Drutz, Vera Werrier, Grace Gray, Seymour Adelman."

The floor-show and cabaret was certainly not a new form of entertainment for the well-heeled members of society. What was new was the *political* slant of cabaret which brought theatre techniques of humor, song and dance to bear on the life of the times. Danny Mann's talent, special flair and enthusiasm for this form of theatre made it possible for Theatre of Action to produce a successful series of such popular evenings.

We also discovered that we had some people in the group especially suited for cabaret. Our first discovery was Frank Gregory, who had been writing songs for some time. He joined Theatre of Action in 1937. He reminded me that one of the first plays he was in was Brecht's one-acter, *The Informer*. I had looked over Frank's songs and was impressed with the strong American style that showed up. Frank explained something about it to me later.

"One time," he told me, "when I was writing songs for the cabaret, I wrote one which brought in Canadian politics. Danny didn't respond to Canadian politics, didn't know too much about them. I remember specifically he had me eliminate something about Mitchell Hepburn. If you recall there was a time when it was Hepburn who said to somebody else, 'I'll be the jockey, you be the horse.' It didn't mean anything to Danny and I realized I better stick to what he understood. Actually, the earlier songs, of course, were all kind of Tin Pan Alley, like the *Mason-Dixon Blues*. There was also *Cowboy From Manhattan.* Back in those days we were really suffused with American culture."

Here are some of the songs Frank wrote for our cabarets, reprinted with his permission:

We Get Along

We never travel in Café society,
And Winchell never gives us notoriety —
    I guess we must be
    Socially insignificant
But we get along.

You'll never find us at the El Morocco,
We can't afford the latest Broadway socko —
    It seems we are just
    Socially insignificant,
But we get along.

Don't think we're satisfied
To sit and bide
Our time as we are:
    We're not the patient kind.
For in addition
We've ambition,
But that can't get us far,
    With money and security so hard to find.

So that is why you'll never see our faces
In photographs of all the swellest places:
    You'd think we were born
    Socially insignificant,
But we get along.

This became the theme song of our cabarets and usually opened and closed the performance.

The Syncopated Dictator

Verse: It's the Nineteen-Forties' newest thrill,
You will have no peace of mind until
You get into the rhythm
And join in the crowd,
You start a-swingin' with 'em
And laughin' out loud —
When you're told.

In the Praha streets the abandoned Czechs
Wonder who Adolf will next annex;
They're tryin' like the devil
To swing to the left,
But with the help of Neville
They always are left
In the cold.
Under old Vesuvius
Though a little dubious,
They go to town;
Back in old Vienna
You'll see infant and duenna
who'll be bearin' it down —
wearin' it down — hey!

Chorus: Clap your hands and clatter your heels,
Heil your partner, shiver like eels,
Syncopated Dictator's caught you —
Can't relax while the fascist's got you!

Point your toe and stiffen your knee,
Goosestep round and pivot with glee,
Mussolini's your latest hero,
Ghosts of Caesar and Shades of Nero!
But remember Nero fiddled while old Rome burned,
So don't trust your partner while your back is turned.

Now
On the boulevards of Baden-Baden
Start in shaggin' with a beg-your-podden,
Then as the music gets torrid and torrider
Truck on down along the Polish corridor!

All join hands, don't have to be urged;
Some day you may have to be purged —
You're the victim of — Heaven help you —
Syn-co-pated Dictator-ship!

I'm Just A Puppet Of Passion

What have I got that intrigues men
In such a flagrant fashion?
My love-life is
A perfect WHIZ —
I'm just a puppet of Passion!

When I give out, the ladies faint —
The strongest men turn ashen;
And on a couch,
I'm sure no slouch;
I'm just a puppet of Passion!

Now Mr. Freud
Would be overjoyed
At the progress I've exhibited.
It may be a sin
To mix love and gin,
But it sure helps keep the men
Uninhibited!

The tall, dark, handsome kind are my
Magnificent ob-sash-un;
Like Mata Hari,
Madame DuBarry;
Like Helen of Troy
And Myrna Loy;
Like Diamond Lil
I always will
Be nothing but a puppet of Passion!

Shopworn Sadie

I guess I've got glamour, in a sort of a way;
And I've got personality — or that's what they say;
But at the Five-and-Ten
In the bargain basement section,

I never see the men
Take a look in my direction!

Chorus: Shopworn Sadie, that's how they call me;
Shopworn Sadie, gents never fall for me.
Night and day, I utter this prayer:
"Oh, Good Lord, send along a millionaire
To me — to Shopworn Sadie!"

I don't smoke, I don't drink, nor commit indiscretions,
Gents don't go for my type like they do in True Confessions;
Nothing's wrong with my technique,
And my face won't crack a mirror;
Hell, on thirteen bucks a week,
Can you look like Norma Shearer?

I'm quite literary — *The Times* I see a lot,
And what do I lack that Vivien Leigh has got?
I'd make a perfect wife,
But it seems like little Sadie
Will spend her future life
Saying: "Something for you, lady?"

This ballad was sung by Miriam Levy in the cabaret:

Each Day The Same Again

Why do I lie and dream of things
That never can be?
Why can't I realize that nothing comes from dreaming?
Each day the same again,
I go to bed at ten,
The whistle blows and then
Back to work.

Sometimes I wish I had the wealth
To take me on a long vacation.
But while I still have my health,
I'll have to keep working along — too long.

Only a miracle can set me free,
And till it appears,
I'll have to be content in my imagination.

Upper Left: Toby Ryan, 1931; Above: Oscar Ryan, 1932; Left: Toby and Oscar, Toronto, 1932.

Members of Theatre of Action in Queen's Park, 1939. Left to right, Lou Jacobi, Grace Gray, unidentified member, Oscar, Toby, Michael Brand.

Toby in The Inspector General, *1939.*

Toby and David Pressman, 1938.

COUVER PLAYERS
DRAMA FESTIVAL

YING BACKGROUNDS OF GROUPS
MPETING FOR ACTING HONORS

By Canadian Press
A, April 21.—Among the
ups of amateur actors and
who arrived in Ottawa the
of the Fourth Dominion
Festival,
opened at
awa Little
e Monday
were play-
om the ex-
east: Saint
and Kent-
N. S., and
extreme west:
couver.
nd as far apart
their homes are
e backgrounds
organiza-

Garfield King

Vancouver came 17 young
but three out of work.
direction of Garfield King,
r lawyer, and Guy Glover
Vancouver Little Theatre,
ounded last August the Prove Arts Club and a Workers'
re and played "Waiting for
to packed theatres for 25 per-
at home. They play here
y night.
ree performances in Van-
y were closed by the police
to open again by publi

worked their way acros
try playing en route
s, Regina and Winnipe
ain concern has been
of time but how to get "
and things" necessary
he journey.
Saint John came five
f the local Theatre Gui
ve club which is open
ibers.
lawyer, a member of
ent of Militia and a
d woman director were
who gathered for rehe

NSERVATIVE EAST

"We are hoping to arouse more in
terest in the Little Theatre at Home"
one member confided, then remarked
sadly: "We have so little backing,
everyone is so conservative down
east."

Other players who arrived today included three from Edmonton, five
from Regina, seven from Winnipeg,
three of them small boys who had
never been away from home before;
six from Toronto, seven from London,
Ont., three from Montreal and 12
from Quebec.

The first Canadian play in the
found favor Monday night
Granville-Barker, the
playwright who
year's

ville-Barker discussed the plays, Sir
Robert Borden, president of the festi-
val committee, read messages from
Lord Bessborough, founder of the
movement, and Hon. Vincent Massey,
Canadian High Commissioner to
London and chairman of the com
tee, wishing the festival all su

Mr. Granville-Barker's re
were general, rather than direct
ticularly to discussion of the
plays given.

These were "Come Out o
Cage," by Mary Plowman,
of the Players Guild of H
"Judge Lynch," by J. Y. R
presented by the Sixteen-Th
Montreal, and "Nellie Mc

Canadian press clipping, 1936.

Promotional logo for Vancouver Tag Day, 1936.

Vancouver's Waiting For Lefty *as performed in Ottawa, 1936. The photo is by Karsh.*

Above: *Joe Zuken of the Winnipeg New Theatre, 1940; Below:* Six Men of Dorset, *Winnipeg New Theatre.*

he programme f Eight Men peak *in Toronto,* *33.*

Professor Mamlock

By FREIDRICH WOLF

GRAM

Professor Mamlock, *Winnipeg New Theatre, 1942.*

Bottom: Sybil Cherniak and Ruth Segal, members of the Winnipeg New Theatre, meet with Dominion Drama Festival chairman, Col. Osborne in London, Ontario, April, 1939.

ub

e

K”

Lilian Mendelssohn, director of Montreal's New Theatre.

The cast of Relief *arrive from Saskatchewan for the DDF finals.*

David Pressman, DDF finals, Ottawa, 1937.

WORKERS THEATRE

in first Ontario tour

presents

a series of –

PLAYS

sketches

and – mass recitation

ALSO

AVROM

foremost CANADIAN proletarian cartoonist

Sun., June 25

8.30 p.m.

EMPIRE THEATR

Above: Syd Banks and Frank Shuster in the Theatre of Action production of The Inspector General; *Right: Lou Applebaum in the same production.*

orkers' Theatre tour poster, 32.

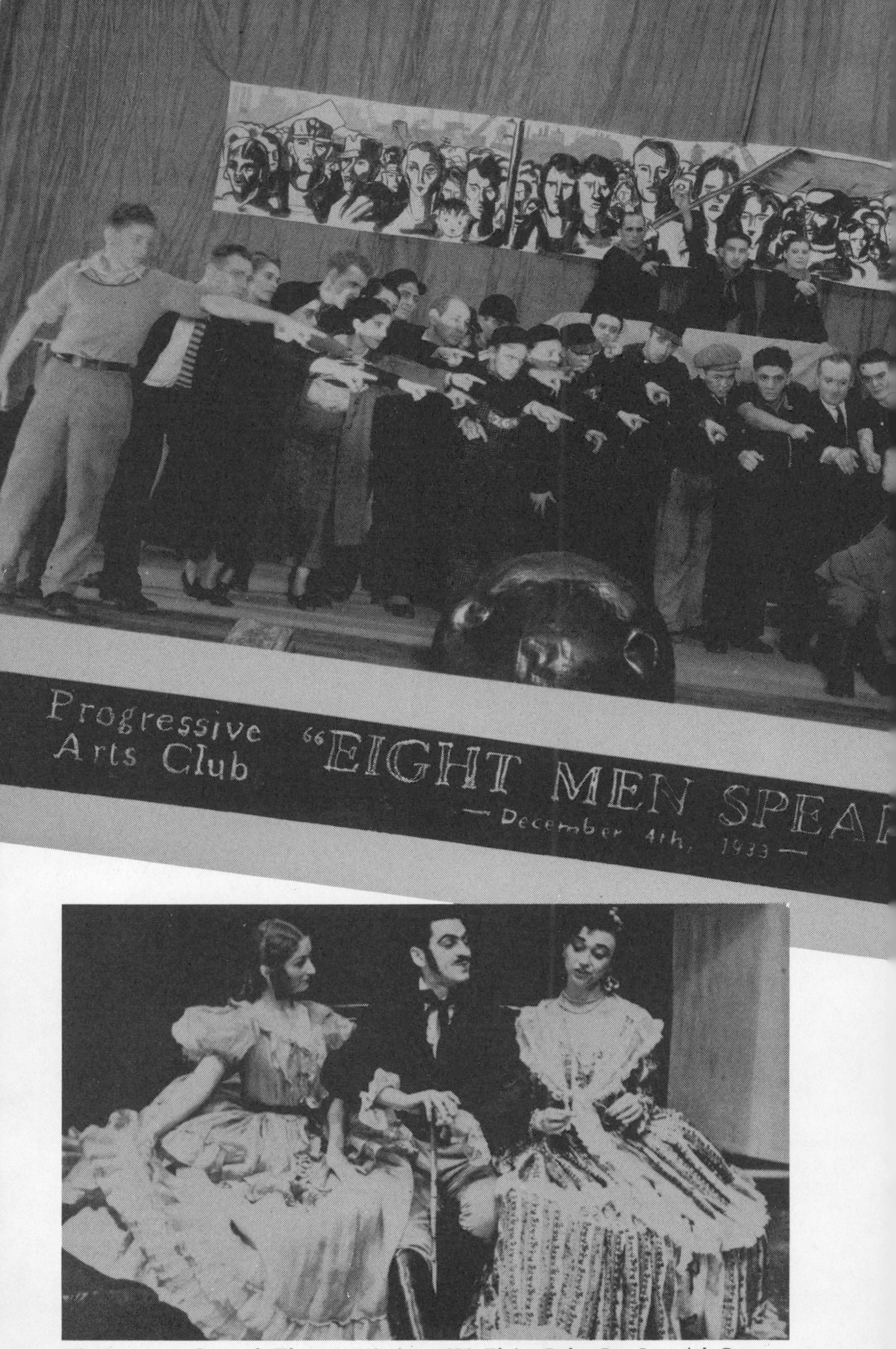

The Inspector General, *Theatre of Action, 1939. Elaine Bales, Ben Lennick, Basya Hunter.*

David Pressman as Mascarille in The Affected Young Ladies, *1936.*

Set design for Of Mice and Men, *Theatre of Action, 1940.*

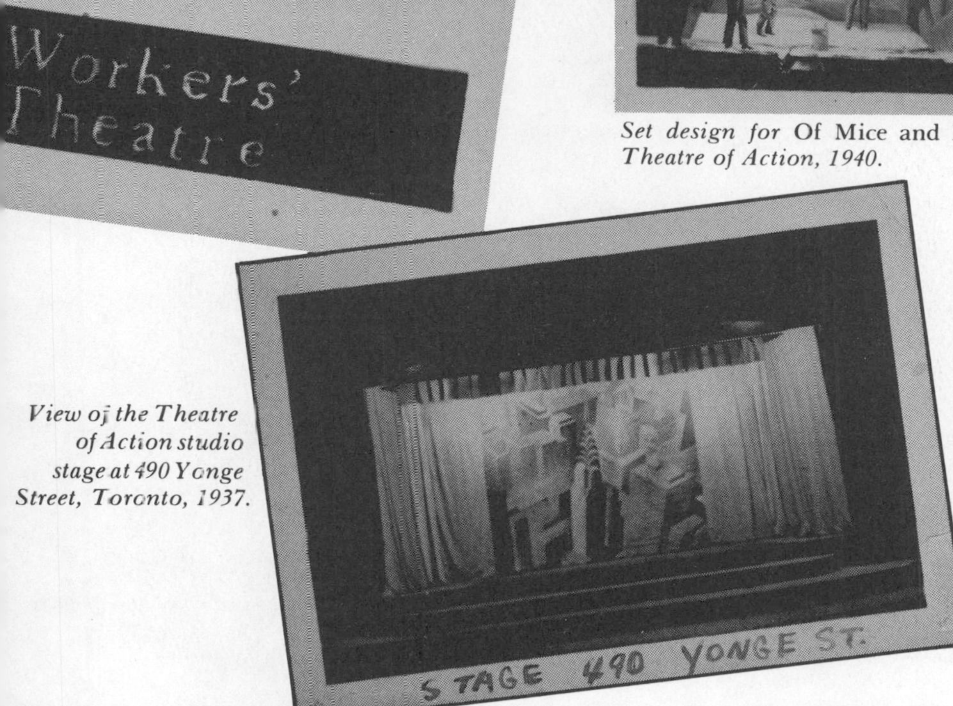

View of the Theatre of Action studio stage at 490 Yonge Street, Toronto, 1937.

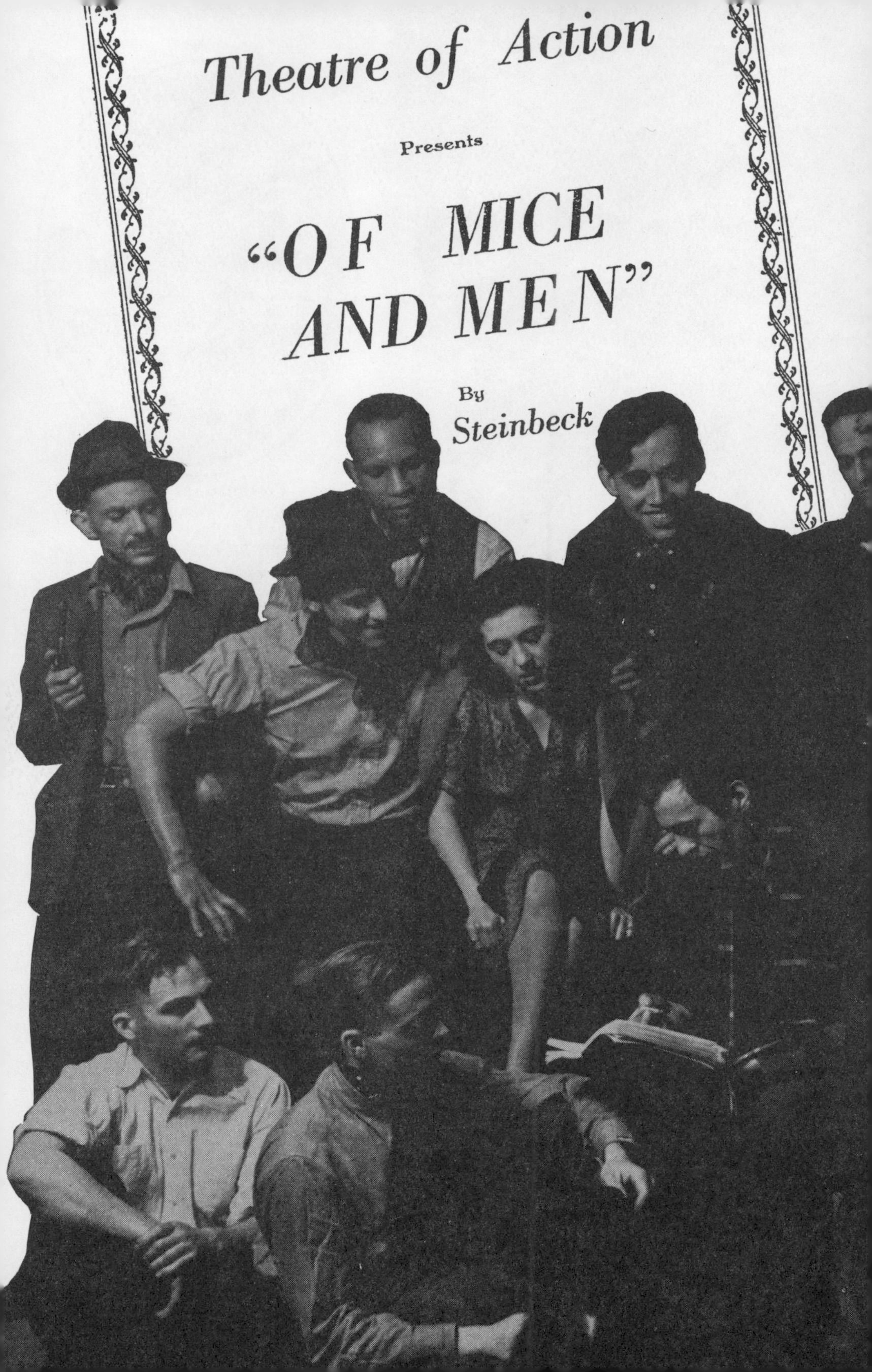
Theatre of Action
Presents
"OF MICE AND MEN"
By
Steinbeck

Scene and set design, Steel, *Theatre of Action, 1938.*

Artwork for cover of Theatre of Action's It Can't Happen Here, *1938, as designed by Lawrence Hyde.*

Director Syd Banks, (holding book) and the cast of Of Mice and Men, *Theatre of Action, 1940. Toby is in the centre. At right in white shirt, Ben Lennick.*

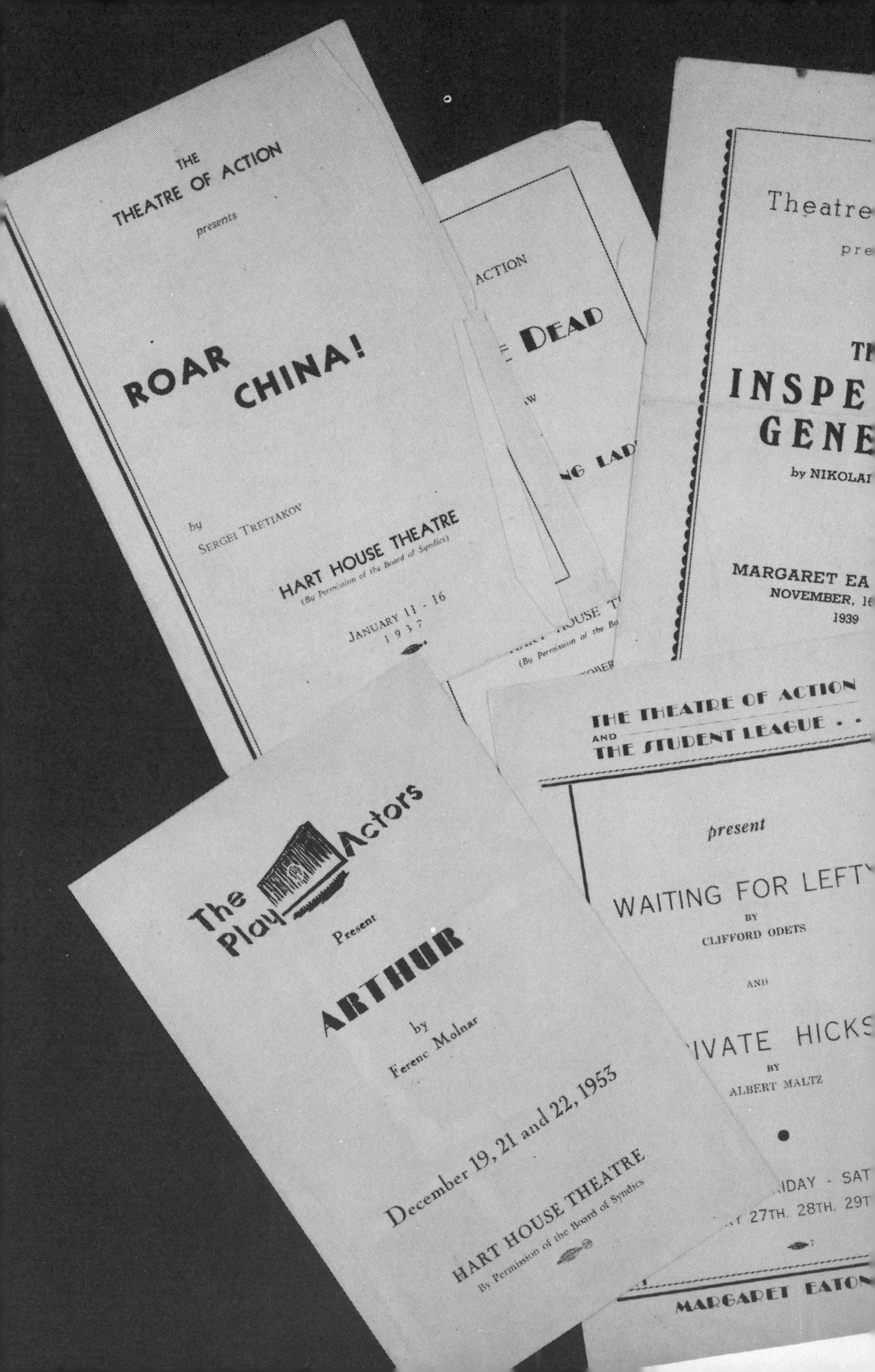
THE THEATRE OF ACTION
presents
ROAR CHINA!
by Sergei Tretiakov
HART HOUSE THEATRE
(By Permission of the Board of Syndics)
JANUARY 11 - 16
1937
ACTION
DEAD
NG LAD
Theatre
INSPE
GENE
by NIKOLAI
MARGARET EA
NOVEMBER, 16
1939
THE THEATRE OF ACTION
AND
THE STUDENT LEAGUE . .
present
WAITING FOR LEFTY
BY
CLIFFORD ODETS
AND
IVATE HICKS
BY
ALBERT MALTZ
IDAY - SAT
27TH, 28TH, 29T
MARGARET EATON
The Play Actors
Present
ARTHUR
by
Ferenc Molnar
December 19, 21 and 22, 1953
HART HOUSE THEATRE
By Permission of the Board of Syndics

Above: Paul Mann and David Pressman, Theatre of Action, 1937; Below: Scene from Theatre of Action cabaret, 1939. Michael Brand as Hitler, Syd Banks as Chamberlain, Jack Kaell as Mussolini.

Jean "Jim" Watts, director of Toronto's Theatre of Action, 1936.

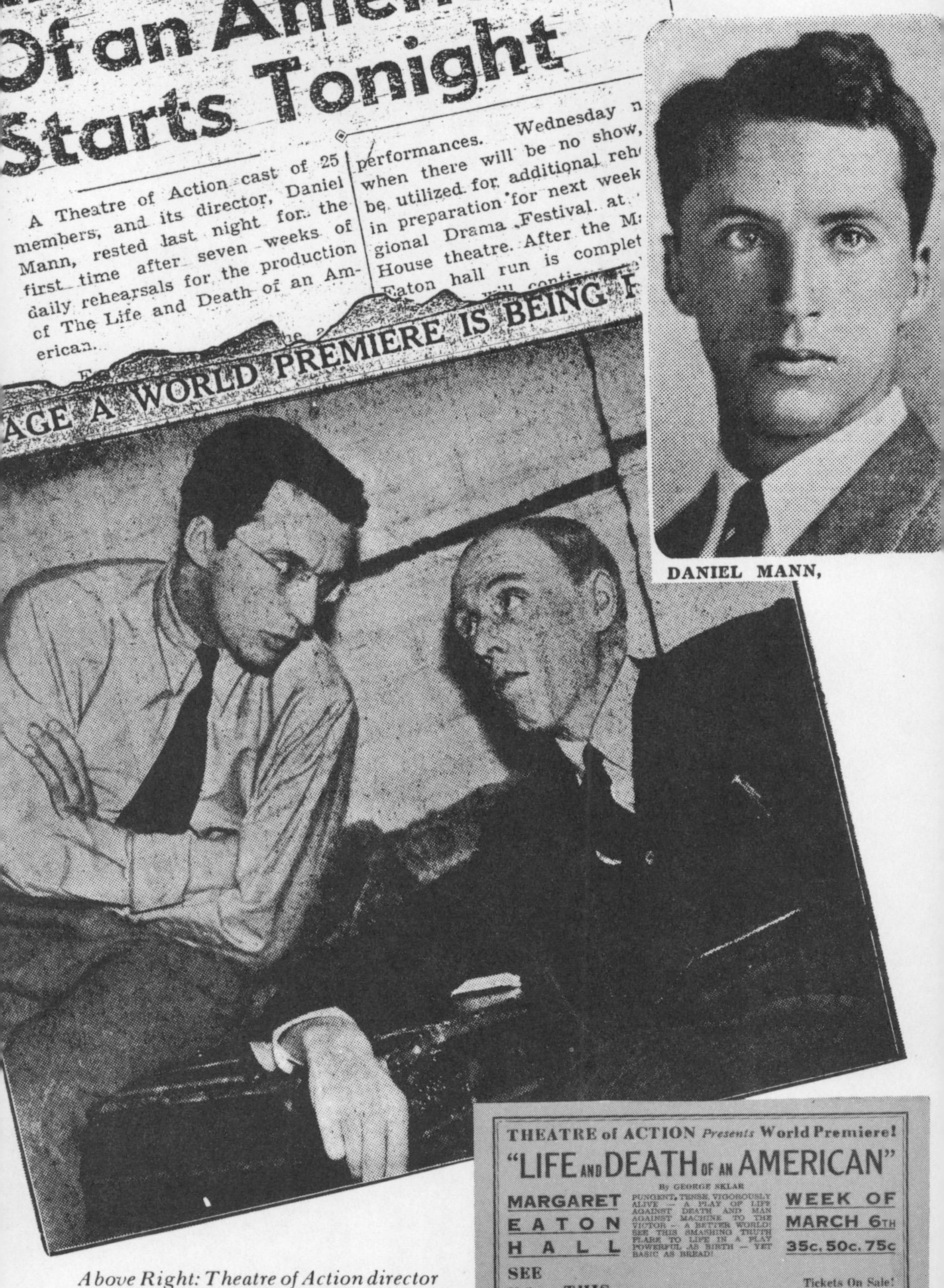

Of an Americ
Starts Tonight

A Theatre of Action cast of 25 members, and its director, Daniel Mann, rested last night for the first time after seven weeks of daily rehearsals for the production of The Life and Death of an American.

performances. Wednesday n
when there will be no show,
be utilized for additional reh
in preparation for next week
gional Drama Festival at
House theatre. After the M
Eaton hall run is complet

AGE A WORLD PREMIERE IS BEING F

DANIEL MANN,

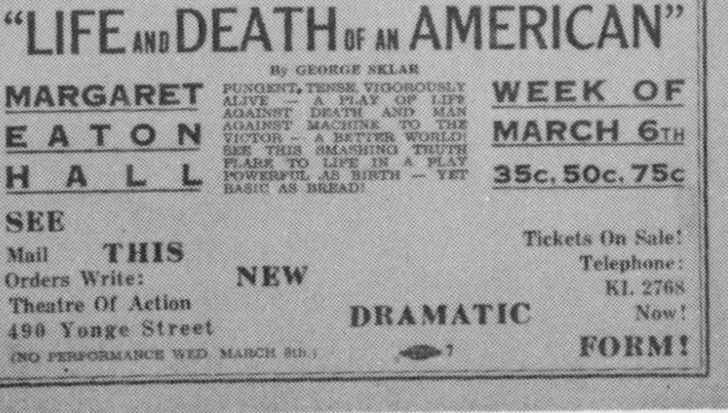

THEATRE of ACTION *Presents* World Premiere!

"LIFE AND DEATH OF AN AMERICAN"

By GEORGE SKLAR

MARGARET EATON HALL

PUNGENT, TENSE, VIGOROUSLY ALIVE — A PLAY OF LIFE AGAINST DEATH AND MAN AGAINST MACHINE, TO THE VICTOR — A BETTER WORLD! SEE THIS SMASHING TRUTH FLARE TO LIFE IN A PLAY POWERFUL AS BIRTH — YET BASIC AS BREAD!

WEEK OF MARCH 6TH

35c. 50c. 75c

SEE THIS NEW DRAMATIC FORM!

Mail Orders Write:
Theatre Of Action
490 Yonge Street

Tickets On Sale!
Telephone:
KI. 2768
Now!

(NO PERFORMANCE WED. MARCH 8th.)

Above Right: Theatre of Action director Danny Mann; Above: Danny Mann, left, with Sinclair Lewis in Toronto for a rehearsal of Life And Death Of An American, *1939; Right: Theatre of Action promotional handout, 1939.*

"I took part in the cabarets and did some skits. I enjoyed that." Syd Banks was commenting on that aspect of his work with Theatre of Action. "Whether it was agit-prop material or cabaret material or theatrical material, it didn't matter. It was all a learning experience."

Grace Gray discovered she was a singer.

"I sang some of the songs that Frank Gregory wrote. I recall rehearsing with him in the studio. I was also in the chorus. I must admit I enjoyed those cabarets very much."

"I remember one Christmas or New Year's cabaret vaguely, probably because I got drunk after it," Stuart Walton told me. "I took part in them doing skits and songs and had great fun doing it. A ham is always a ham and there is a touch, I hope, of zaniness in me. Or there was at that time."

Irving Hoffman smiled broadly when he thought of those evenings. "I was in a lot of the cabaret sketches, *Waiting For Odets* for one."

I had never done cabaret before, but was an eager participant in those shows. I loved being part of the chorus, singing and dancing and acting in some of the sketches. It was great fun and very refreshing to work in a new way on very different material. It was especially enjoyable to receive the warm and happy responses from audiences. We showed something new about our theatre — the ability to laugh and have fun.

Most of the cabaret evenings were held in our studio. Some of them were sponsored by organizations (*New Frontier* magazine was one of them) to help raise money. When we had a sponsor, we played in a larger hall. One thing was certain, whether we played for ourselves or for some other organization, the audiences enjoyed them thoroughly. They were also financially successful.

In terms of staging, we took pains to turn our studio or rented hall into a night club setting. We decorated the place appropriately, arranged small tables around the room for intimacy, and served fruit punch, cold drinks, sandwiches and sweets. In those days, liquor and beer couldn't be sold in Toronto nightclubs. This didn't particularly bother our audiences. We created enough of an easy-going atmosphere so that people would enjoy themselves while watching a contemporary, fun-filled show.

As word got around about Theatre of Action cabarets, we attracted larger audiences. In fact, we had to repeat performances to accommodate all the people who wanted to attend.

The Daily Clarion, Footlight Footnotes:

May 5, 1939 — "Northern Bulletin: From Jim Tester, educational director of the Workers' Cooperative of Northern Ontario, comes this very welcome announcement datelined Timmins: 'The Workers' Cooperative of

Timmins, Ontario, announces formation of the Workers' Cooperative Drama Group, sponsored by the Educational Committee of the Co-op . . . Participation in this group is not confined to co-op members, but, it is intended, will be on a city-wide basis, this group being in the nature of a service to the people of the Porcupine Camp by the Workers' Co-op . . . Membership is free and open to everyone . . . The Director: The group is under the direction of Bert Marcuse, of the Co-op Educational Department. Mr. Marcuse has had four years of experience in the Drama Guild at Queen's University and is well acquainted with the progressive theatre movement."

May 19, 1939 — "We Have The Writers: Despite rude asides heard from time to time when mention is made of Canadian writers, there are nevertheless many men and women in this country who spend a great deal of their time writing and there is a good number of Canadians who make their living by it . . . But few of them are writing for the theatre, whose literature is undoubtedly the weakest and quantitatively the lowest of all Canadian literature . . . whereas in some countries authors have been accorded fellowships, scholarships, or employment on government theatre projects, we have done nothing in Canada to enable a playwright to make a living out of his writing . . . Canada needs plays if a genuinely native theatre is to flourish. That is a commonplace, of course, and in the meantime the various groups must use what they can get . . . Certainly among the radio script writers, fiction writers, newspapermen and poets, there are men and women who have something to offer to the stage . . . Perhaps this very lack of a Canadian theatre tradition may result in some novel stage forms — and experimentation, unless it becomes a fad, is always healthy . . . There are groups throughout the country to which playwrights should attach themselves in order to grasp the nature of theatre writing. And above all, there is a great country, with great traditions and great problems about which to write. Nova Scotia fishermen, Alberta miners, Ontario lumberjacks, Manitoba farmers — Quebec and Prince Edward Island . . . 1939 and 1837, North West Rebellion and pioneer days — workers and middle class on prairie and mountain country — there we have the material. It ought to be written about."

And Oscar kept us in the news. From the *Clarion* of June 2, 1939:

Reunion in Toronto: This must be Neighborhood Playhouse Old Boys' Week. Over at the Theatre of Action studio, which has been requisitioned as H.Q., there has been an invasion by graduates, denizens and fans of the illustrious New York theatre school. Present the other afternoon were Sanford Meisner, head of the Playhouse faculty of acting; David Pressman, former T. of A. director and now Mr. Meisner's assistant; Daniel Mann, present T. of A. director and Playhouse graduate; Paul Mann, Playhouse graduate, who has taught Toronto and Montreal summer schools; Lorne Greene, recent N.P. graduate; Sholom Gelber, who has completed one year at N.P.; and John Wilson, also an N.P. student ... Mr. Mann (Paul), also a Torontonian, is now occupied with TAC (Theatre Arts Committee) in New York, in both acting and organizational ends of this enterprising body which has made the political cabaret so popular in North America ... About Mr. Meisner: One of the founders of the Group Theatre. Has played in most of its productions . . . Has been a theatre worker 12 years ... About building the Canadian theatre (Meisner says): 'You have a real fight here. We'll help you, but eventually you must find your own leadership here.' About Theatre of Action: 'We got very good reports about it.' Mr. Pressman: David Pressman is studying as well as teaching, he told the *Clarion*. He maintains close contact with Canada through constant correspondence and merciless quizzing of visitors from Canada. 'I am happy to be here to see T. of A. on its feet,' he said. 'Maybe some day I'll be back here again.' . . .

June 9, 1939 — The Timmins Workers' Cooperative Drama Group made its first public appearance on Friday, May 26. The feature of the *stage-fest* was *Remember Pedrocito*. A capacity audience responded in striking fashion to this anti-fascist play, so much so, in fact, that the play was frequently interrupted, not only by spontaneous applause, but as well, by shouts from the audience itself, particularly from some of the Mac-Pap vets who were there. The play was directed by Bert Marcuse of the Workers' Cooperative educational department . . . Meanwhile *Steel* is being carefully considered and will in all probability be presented to the northern public this winter. A play of this nature will undoubtedly receive tremendous support and evoke great enthusiasm from the gold miners of Northern Ontario, who are now organizing into their union under similar conditions to those depicted in Wexley's play . . . Comings and Goings: In town for Theatre of Action summer school is Hazel Okilman, instructor, back home from New York . . . Returned to New York is Daniel Mann, until recently T. of A. director. In a brief interview, Mr. Mann told the *Clarion:* 'Proximity of the United States greatly influences the Canadian theatre movement, since the artistic problems are very similar . . . Canada itself has little theatre tradition and it remains for Canadian playwrights to create the native basis, with the aid of native directors and technicians. Theatre of Action in three years has come tremendously to the fore through its contemporary approach and far outshines other theatre organizations. Objective for Canada is development of a people's art theatre.'

June 16, 1939: "Vancouver: Some of the old-timers of the Progressive Arts Club (regional winners and Dominion second-placers in the drama festival several years ago) and more recently of the Vancouver Theatre of Action, are working with the hope of getting up a permanent progressive theatre on the coast. A letter received here a few days ago reports that for the past year they have been conducting study classes, producing a few skits, and even a one-act play. Now they are planning to buckle down to more ambitious things . . . Toronto Notes: . . . Theatre of Action summer school opens June 26, with elementary, intermediate and advanced classes . . . T. of A. cabaret numbers will be seen and heard again tomorrow night at the youth centre garden party, 40 Cecil . . . More Cabaret: The first section of the program of the new cabaret to be put on by the Theatre of Action next month will, it is reported, deal with the outstanding events of Canadian history as remembered from school days. Laura Secord will be there with her cow, and Madeleine de Verchères, surrounded by Indians giving a college yell as well as war whoops. Sir Francis Bond Head will rub shoulders with John Cabot, while the finale of this section is to be entitled *Moscow Gold Rush* . . .

It was at the end of the season, as Oscar had noted, that Danny Mann regretfully informed us that he was returning to New York to resume his own work there. Regretfully, we had to accept his decision.

Without him, Theatre of Action moved on to the organization of its 1939 summer school.

Where was our work at that point? I quote the *Star* of June, 1939.

Summer schools of drama will all be in full swing next week. Theatre of Action opens its fifth on Monday. Four years ago this group held its second school in a stable on Grenville Street, with a hayloft for a workshop. Its growth into the most aggres-

> sive play group in Canada is one of the most interesting phases of a nationwide movement traced graphically in *The Star* last week by George Skillan, adjudicator.
>
> Twice this theatre has come near the top in Drama Festival awards. Its chief hindrance to getting first place has been mainly the sort of plays the T. of A. choose to put on. As a rule, these are social-economic plays with a propagandic class-interest slant. Inside that pattern, the group has achieved wonders: at first in mass action and tableaux, more lately plus individual acting; always with expert emphasis on effective light and color, along with mob vocalism and movement; often with allegorical presentations. Such things as the T. of A. does are the result of concise ideology plus hard work and enthusiasm. The summer school will illustrate this.
>
> . . . No other little theatre corps in Canada has quite such a record in theatre dynamics. But a 'national' theatre in Canada, as understood in various degrees by most of the hundreds of groups across the country, is possible only on a basis of absolutely free drama; freedom to present any sort of play, not only as to nationality but as to ideology. A theatre tied to a particular set of ideas may take first place here, as the T. of A. does, in all the dynamics of theatre art; but because it is tied to a particular set of ideas it is not a free theatre, in the complete democracy of drama.
>
> The T. of A. has remarkable facility for expressing ideas in drama. For three years it has engaged a professional director from New York. Under David Pressman, the group made wonderful progress, in all but individual acting. Under Daniel Mann, his successor, it has carried on all that Pressman taught with considerable emphasis on personal acting. The summer school of 1939 has already engaged Miss Hazel O'Kilman, graduate of the New Theatre School in New York, as teacher-director of plays; Mr. Lorne Greene of the Neighborhood Playhouse, New York, as voice instructor; Mme. Lasserre of Toronto Conservatory as teacher of Dalcroze eurhythmics. The Stanislavski system of acting, as practised most efficiently in Moscow, is the method to be used by the faculty. This phenomenal system is known here mainly in Theatre of Action productions . . .

The above, I believe, is one of the clearest estimations of our role as a theatre in Toronto. But, more than that, it also pays tribute to and recognizes the high standard of the group's training programs. Clearly, we are praised for our theatrical presentation, but our scripts are the disturbing element. I would say we made the proper impact.

As for Danny Mann, like some of the others in our group, I too believe he contributed much to our development. He had, of course, the sound foundation that David Pressman had built, but he did add some new qualities. The skilfully-orchestrated production of *Life And Death Of An American* was an outstanding example of his enormous talent as a director.

His other contribution, new to our theatre, was the revue form and its satire, expressed in song and dance as well as in acting. There is no doubt also that he added new dimensions to our theatre in performance and technical capabilities.

Danny Mann has traveled a long way since those Theatre of Action days. He has been and still is a very successful movie director, with many fine films to his credit. Most recently I saw his production of the Fania Fenelon autobiography, *Playing For Time* on television. It was a moving, sensitive portrayal of a desperate group of women who rely on their musical talents to stay alive in a Nazi concentration camp. Danny directed this harrowing story with head and heart. He exposed the fascists for what they were and for the monstrous acts of which they were capable. He pilloried the pretense of their "artistic" cultivation of musical taste.

Danny did tell me on the phone not long ago, that he considered his brief stay with Theatre of Action as one of the more exciting and educational times of his young life. I must admit it's a great feeling to know that we had made some contribution to his development as a director.

XXII

1939-1940

WITH OUR 1939 SUMMER SCHOOL LAUNCHED, we now turned to the real problem at hand. Who would be our next director? We had several discussions on the subject. Finally, it was decided to write to New Theatre League in New York again for assistance.

Sometime during the summer we heard from them. They had a young man from New Jersey who had done some directing. He was willing to come to Toronto. His name was Leo Tepp.

On the Sunday of the Labor Day weekend in 1939, a group of us were spending the holiday at Lake Simcoe, just before returning to Toronto to greet our new director. It was a very hot day and we sat on the porch of our cottage, being lazy, listening to the radio. Suddenly the music was interrupted. A serious voice brought the news. As a result of Hitler's invasion of Poland, Britain had declared war on Germany. Although we had known that war was imminent, the announcement hit everyone hard. A state of war had been declared — what would this mean to us, to Canada, to the world? We knew it would bring major changes to individuals, to organizations, to cities, to countries. What these changes would be was not yet too clear. Late that night, we piled into a car and headed back to Toronto, worried and upset, but prepared to continue our activities as planned.

A week or two later we met our new director. He seemed quite an affable young man, a little on the shy side. Looking at it from his point of view, it must have been even more difficult for him to come to a strange country to work as a director with people completely unknown to him.

We did our best to make him feel at home with us and to help him get settled. It did seem a bit harder to warm up to Leo, I felt, than it had been to either David or Danny. The fact is that I was more mature and undoubtedly was measuring our new director against the training and experience I had had already.

We had been reading scripts and had recommended to him that we do Gogol's *The Inspector General*. It was, of course, one of the great Russian classical plays and a delightful social satire. It also had a large cast of exceptionally interesting characters for actors to explore — some bigger roles and quite a few smaller ones to work on. The make-up and costuming would require special attention. Finally, it would be a refreshing departure for Theatre of Action to present to its audiences. The milieu was different and the time was the past.

All this was discussed with Leo and he agreed with our decision.

When we were ready to begin casting, I suggested I would like to stage manage this production. I had thought about it and felt I could be helpful to our new director in this capacity. I hoped he would feel more comfortable in his first production with someone who knew the members of the group very well. Leo accepted my offer eagerly. When he cast the play, he also offered me a small part.

From the beginning of rehearsals, which I attended regularly, I felt that Leo was more than a little uncertain in dealing with the actors. Those playing the major roles had had considerable experience in a variety of productions, but he seemed to find it hard to give direction to their efforts. The characterizations seemed to be taking shape through the efforts of the actors themselves. But most of all, it seemed to me, what was lacking was some stylization which would give directorial unity to the production, as well as underscoring the satire.

From my position as stage manager, I felt good that our company of actors were achieving so much on their own. Obviously, our training had made it possible for the performers to work independently. Still, I worried, because Leo's hesitant kind of direction — suggesting a lack of confidence in himself — could hurt the production. He was turning to me more and more, for advice or approval in working out the script. It was then that I began to feel that perhaps we had reached the stage in our development where we could handle this play without a director from the States.

As I think about it now, we were, at that time, suffering from a disease which, to this day, still infects some of our theatres. Canadians believed then, as now, that somehow we were not good enough to take over the major job of direction. We could direct studio work, but for major productions we needed outside help — American or British.

In Theatre of Action, of course, we needed to develop and grow at the beginning. We had excellent director-teachers in David and Danny. By 1939, I believe, Theatre of Action had in its ranks people who could direct *The Inspector General* as well as, if not better than, our American director.

What Theatre of Action had left out of its discussions of a successor to Danny Mann was the idea that one of our own group could be assigned to the task. Somewhere, in the deep recesses of my mind, the thought was there. I was afraid to voice it, because I had questions: would we be successful with one of our own members as director? We now had a reputation to live up to. Would the members be as disciplined and dedicated to someone from their own ranks? Was it too soon? These questions seemed unanswerable at the time. So the matter had never been discussed.

Syd Banks expressed similar ideas: "I thought choosing one of our own as director came too late. I thought we could have done it when David

Pressman left. We were ready, we were *gung ho*. I'm not taking anything away from Danny, but I think we were quite capable of handling it. We might have made a mess of it, I don't know, but, we were ready.

"Our new director, Leo Tepp, found it difficult to work with us because we realized we knew as much as he did. We were obnoxious, no question. We became arrogant and he wasn't capable of handling that kind of arrogance. Danny Mann would have handled it. He would have put us in our place, but Leo was a gentle guy. He was confused, no doubt.

"As for going it on our own, people were a little afraid, I guess. But, I think, at the same time, a corollary to that — even though I say we could have done it, we lost nothing by having a Danny Mann, by having a Leo Tepp. We gained yards. Certainly I personally did, no question."

All this is not to say that finally the production of *The Inspector General* was a fiasco. On the contrary, when we played it in Margaret Eaton Hall, November 16-18, it was a bright, colorful, funny show with some very good performances. Members of the cast brought to this script some very interesting and stylish performances — some of them contributions from the director, and some brought by the actors themselves.

I must admit I drool when I think of what David Pressman, with the same cast, would have done with this play. Or Danny Mann. There was, nevertheless, some fine acting, especially by Ben Lennick, as the inspector general; by Stuart Walton as the foolish and women-dominated mayor; and by Syd Banks and Frank Shuster as the twin toadies of the town; by Basya Hunter who, as the Mayor's wife, played to the hilt the pretentious social climber; and all those other interesting characters in the town, small parts that contributed to the total picture.

Among the interesting characters of the local bureaucracy was a member of Theatre of Action who, in his first real acting assignment was transformed into a typical beholden apparchnik. His name was Louis Applebaum and he played the Charity Commissioner.

I asked Lou years later who he came to be in this production.

"I was originally offered a walk-on in *Roar China*," he recalled. "I was a white sailor boy with rouge on my cheeks and a white uniform. There were a couple of places where I had to stand guard. I don't think I had a line to say. I'd grunt. I spent a lot of my time in the wings, watching and waiting.

"I think I was caught up very deeply. As I say, the rehearsals and all the involvements adversely affected my academic career. Between that and the pool hall at Hart House, I put in a lot of time in non-academic pursuits. I do know that my performance in *The Inspector General*, as Artemi Philipovich, still brings peals of laughter to anybody who saw it. Apparently I did a lot of shifting from left foot to right foot, every time I had a line to say. That's what my wife tells me and her family tells me. In fact, they still imitate me. I don't recall how I got the role. It might have been desperation on the part of the director.

"I had to learn lines, which was very tough. I remember the costume try-on. That was very impressive. I think I was pretty conscientious about attending rehearsals. But the real difficulty was that I had no training at all. I remember hanging around scene painters and carpenters and sitting around chatting. I also recall, vaguely, trying to understand the director and what he was trying to do, and what a director meant. I became very impressed with Pressman in *Roar China* for the depths of his insights and the way he handled people and that sort of thing. . . . those times were very difficult. But, on the other hand, unless you did something of that kind, life became very tough to live. So I think there was a natural compensation, a natural draw towards an activity that would allow you to expend your stored energy on something productive. It meant something special to come to rehearsals and work hard. Obviously I was hooked.

"There was a great sense of the pleasure of it all, the joy of it all.

"Theatre of Action certainly had an impact on the theatre life of the country. Didn't we go to the Canadian Drama Festival? That became a very important factor, given the times."

There was another rather interesting first in *The Inspector General.* When I mentioned this play to Syd Newman, he smiled and quickly added: "I was in it. I acted in that one. I'll never forget it. Somewhere I have a photograph. It was a tiny part, something with one line. I remember the sets, they were all sort of gold and red, a highly decorative set, done almost as a farce comedy. That was the first and only time I was on stage. Did I enjoy it? Oh no. I was self-conscious, stiff as a board, no good at all. I never really wanted to be an actor."

When the production of the Gogol play was concluded, we had to deal with the problems that arose between director and actors during the rehearsal period. Leo felt very unhappy, and the cast that worked with him were also dissatisfied. It was important to talk about this rather quickly, before we moved on to anything else.

A reading of the Production Council minutes, written by Stuart Walton, Secretary, will help to get a clearer picture of the way in which this matter was handled. The Council met within five days after the performances had ended:

"**Nov. 21, 1939** — All present. Also attending, Syd Banks and Toby Gordon.

"Most of the discussion took place on the last production. After a prolonged and thorough discussion, the following basic report was more or less agreed upon by all members.

"It was agreed that while the production would not be termed a flop or failure from the viewpoint of popular applause, from the standpoint of our own standards and self-criticism, the production would have to be written down as a bad one.

"The main drawbacks were its lack of a clearly defined line; that it failed to interpret Gogol adequately as a social document; its mechanical effects rather than spontaneous living, the fatal lack of belief in the play itself by the actors and the lack of inter-relationship between the characters themselves. The acting itself was inferior, inadequate and a retreat from previous standards, rather than an advance to new.

"These faults were, of course, the result of ten weeks of rehearsal and much discussion took place on how and why the rehearsals had not been successful.

"The faults of the production were the result of what took place at rehearsals. Many reasons and many criticisms were given. Summarized they could be put as follows:

"1. The basic essentials were not sufficiently insisted on, *i.e.* talking, listening of the actor, knowing why and where he was going; what he was doing and why.

"2. That obvious false notes and half-hearted work was allowed to slip through.

"3. That the actors either could not or would not adapt themselves to a new way of working and that consequently a gap was created between director and actors which had fatal results in creating a lack of harmony and understanding.

"4. That as a consequence, the actors scamped their creative work, lost morale and allowed themselves to slide into a lack of discipline which, in the case of our more responsible people, must be censured whatever the cause.

"5. Because of these happenings, together with others which were not specified but could be understood, a certain disillusionment and discouragement took place in the attitude of our director which, however understandable, contributed further to a certain disintegration.

"Upon these main points all were more or less in agreement. Naturally the key point to the whole discussion lies in the gap that existed between actors and director. This involved questions of acting technique and theory. Summarizing again the two viewpoints, it could be said that:

"The viewpoint of the acting body on the Production Council was that Leo's method of directing was too mechanical, rigid, and was directed to the producing of carefully thought-out effects rather than guiding of the actor towards an understanding of his part and his action in order that the effects may occur of themselves and become an organic part of the actor and the play. That sufficient attention was not paid to the problems of each individual actor and that the pitch to be reached was set too early on, resulting in external show of energy which was completely false.

"Leo took the floor. He said that the greatest fault he had found with members of the theatre was a lack of ability to do things, to physicalize a part or an action. Because of an 'intellectual' approach to acting they allowed themselves to become obsessed with internal feelings and psychoanalysis rather than acting — or 'externalizing' — the play so that it would get over the footlights. He criticized the actors for their lack of courage in doing things, and pointed out that business had only been given them because they themselves brought nothing to the rehearsals. He admitted he was disappointed in the level of acting shown in the theatre, but that certain criticisms of the play as a whole were justified.

"The Production Council was then forced to discuss what could be looked for in the future as it was quite apparent that no future production would be carried on under the same conditions. A candid discussion revealed that few were willing to concede that there was any possibility in them altering their attitude towards the acting problem and that, consequently, there was slight hope of the gap between actors and director being bridged. Leo suggested that there was apparently only one thing to do and that was for the theatre to look for another director, more in tune with its level and methods. After some discussion the Production Council felt it necessary, though regretfully, to take this step and, accordingly, passed the motion unanimously.

"In passing this recommendation to the Executive, the Production Council wishes to make clear that there is here no question involved of Leo's capabilities as a director, nor of the merit or demerit of the views put forward by both sides. The question that concerned them was whether or not the differences could be so bridged over as to make a suitable atmosphere in which director and actors could work creatively to the satisfaction of each. It was felt this could not be achieved, and on these grounds, the recommendation is made.

"The members then recognized that the following actors deserved a word of commendation because they felt that, while the result was not necessarily correct, nevertheless they felt that these people had worked more or less correctly and conscientiously along the right lines. Names of the members were Elaine Bales, Frank Gregory and Ken Peck.

"The backstage staff were commended for an all-round good job . . ."

Interestingly, *The Star* review by Augustus Bridle noted the production style changes in a different way:

> Theatre of Action struck a new note last night at Margaret Eaton Hall in the first production of a Gogol play in Toronto. *The Inspector General* is named as one of four distinctive works by the 'father of Russian realism' . . . Gogol was the G.B.S. of Russian drama . . . he was also a sort of minor Dickens in realistic character-studies.
>
> The play is a satire on Russian bureaucracy. It has 25 characters; a tremendous job to costume and make up such a curiosity-shop of caricatures . . . A still larger theatrical chore to teach so many young amateurs how to act and speak so that these queer

Russian folk of 100 years ago seemed to live in the scene and not just gab and strut through it.

Leo Tepp, the young director, did something quite notable in this; he broke away from the mob technique of his predecessors into the freedom of individual characterization and the comedy of everyday folk. To make them all true to form in a satirical drama with less action than the average Shaw play was a gigantic task. That they did so well is a tribute to hard work, able direction and a clear perception of the comedies in the scenario. The costumes were cleverly contrived and picturesque. The dialogue was generally animated and natural. These Canadians, most of them Anglo-Saxons, created a folk scenic comedy almost as distinctive as any of the racial dramas produced here by foreign 'nationals', a real achievement in the art of amateur theatricals.

With Leo Tepp's return to the States in mid-season, once more the question of a director, particularly for the next production, had to be considered. Again, according to the minutes of the Production Council of December 11, 1939, there was a letter from New York with an offer of another director. There was discussion. It was felt that the present financial situation of the group was such that an imported director was out of the question.

Syd Banks had been reading scripts and took over as director, though not yet officially. At that meeting it was formally decided that he should direct the next major production.

I find it interesting that, even at this stage, the appointment of one of our own members as director came about for financial reasons, rather than as a conscious act expressing confidence that we could handle this job on our own. Nevertheless, the step was taken.

A later meeting of the Production Council recommended to the membership that we produce John Steinbeck's *Of Mice And Men*. This was subsequently confirmed by the membership and casting for the play began.

I felt there was a good feeling in the group assembled for the casting. We knew Syd, he had worked with all of us and thus would recognize our talents and abilities. Still, he was now seeing and hearing us in a new capacity.

Of Mice And Men had a small cast. Its distinguishing feature was that it had only one female role. It's obvious that this kind of competition for a single role is bound to bring serious jealousies to the fore. It also placed great responsibility on the director's decision in casting the role. It was clear from the script that the play depended completely on the acting, with a number of difficult characterizations among them. Syd was well aware of the challenge he had undertaken.

He proceeded with the casting of the male roles. Since he knew the actors well, the process was quickly completed. He left casting of the lone female for the last. He finally boiled down his choices to four women — and I was one of them. I must admit that more than any other part I had played, I wanted very much to do this particular one. It was a complex and colorful role and I felt confident that I could do it well.

I kept my feelings to myself, however. My confidence came from the fact that of all the women trying for the part, I had had the most experience on stage, and I hoped this would count in my favor.

Syd announced his final decision to the Production Council, informing them he had cast me in the role because he felt I was "suitable for the part, had no great problems, and could work sufficiently well alone to leave him free to work with other" more difficult roles in the script.

I deal with this particular casting because there was something new here. Neither David nor Danny had ever felt it necessary to justify the choice of an actor for any role that was assigned. Syd felt some compulsion (because he was one of us?) to explain his choice.

At the same time, problems surfaced in our ranks. They were sharper for this play because of the competition for one role. Actors who read for parts are always disappointed when they aren't chosen. That's quite natural. But in Theatre of Action it was established from the start that the important thing was the *play*. Towards this end actors, as well as technical staff, were expected to combine their efforts to successfully perform and interpret the script.

I began to think: why was this happening now? Was it because one of our own members was director and was making the choices? Was it easier to question his decisions? Possibly there was some of that attitude within the group. But I detected some additional difficulties surfacing.

The war, of course, was on, but in a rather strange way. Many historians have referred to that early period as the "phony" war. After the merciless bombing of Poland, nothing much was happening in Europe. Still, war was having its effect on people and organizations. We noticed first that some members now found jobs and were not able to contribute as much time to our theatre. Some joined the armed forces and left our ranks. Suddenly, young people were needed again, whether in plants to produce for the war, or in the manpower needed to fight the war. The change seemed to take place suddenly — after ten years of rejection of people's talents and of abilities lying dormant. Young people especially, now felt they were needed for something more important — to defeat fascism.

For Theatre of Action it meant that we lost members, and also experienced difficulty raising money for our various projects. But we were committed and we carried on with rehearsals for *Of Mice And Men*.

I found working on this play a special experience. The small cast made it possible to relate to each person in a much deeper way. All the relationships were interwoven. We found ourselves working together better than we had before. Most of us were determined that this production would be a great leap forward on a creative level. Somehow we knew *Of Mice And Men* would be a test of our theatrical maturity.

The tragic ending in the play depends on the special relationship which develops between Curley's wife and Lennie, the mentally impaired itinerant farm worker, played superbly by Frank Gregory. I felt this relationship growing with each rehearsal. By the time we were on stage, our scenes together had achieved real depth. I know I played with ease and complete absorption in what was happening on stage. This was possible because Frank was so completely believable.

In the last scene together in the barn, our concentration was so complete that I was conscious only of our voices and a very deep silence around us. I could never, at any performance, remember what I did — only what I felt. It was a memorable role, in a very beautiful, socially aware, humanist play.

I wanted to supplement my own reaction to the appointment of Syd Banks as director. I spoke with Ben Lennick about the changeover.

"I thought: 'About time. Good!' I thought it was a good idea that someone who had grown within the theatre, had developed in the theatre, had sunk his roots and committed himself to what we were trying to do, should take over that position. It was clear to me that we didn't have to import, no matter how sympathetic and knowledgeable our teachers and directors had been, that we could trust someone who worked alongside us. I had utter and implicit trust and faith in Syd. I think it was a sign of our maturity.

"*Of Mice And Men* was probably the most difficult play we had tackled. To me it was a challenge. I played another strange old character. It was a damn good play, rich in characters, and it had a good story to tell about humanity on the fringes, about an alienated personality and how he could make his way under difficult circumstances.

"Even though it wasn't a labor play, we were dealing with humanity. We were well-versed in the foibles of humanity and that understanding was what we brought to this script."

Syd Newman designed the set for the Steinbeck play. It had special importance for him.

"I think the actual working arrangement I had with Syd Banks as set designer was very similar to the one I'd had with David, but there were several differences. One, I was working without Nat Petroff; two, Syd and I had a personal strain going; finally, I think in my own mind I felt a sort of lack of glamor in being associated with Syd Banks as against David Pressman or Danny Mann. Perhaps everybody felt that. When it was all over, it was a splendid working relationship. I admired the production very much.

"I used the word 'glamor' quite deliberately. David Pressman was a very glamorous man, and I've kept my association with David all these years. Danny Mann was even more attractive than David in a rather more flamboyant way. Syd had a lot to overcome.

"The big problem of the set was the painting of a totally artificial perspective. There's nothing original about false perspective, but it was a picky thing to paint actually. The stage was shallow at Margaret Eaton, and that was the biggest thing to overcome."

Frank Gregory played Lennie in *Of Mice And Men* and it was our scenes together that were crucial in the script. His comments were of interest to me so many years later.

"*Of Mice And Men* is a memorable production for me." Frank Gregory says this fervently.

"With this new play I went two miles deeper into the character than I had ever gone before. I had a feeling of control, at least of my area of the stage, that I had never had before. I had relationships with other actors on stage that went deeper, a 500 percent change for the better. I should say right away that working with you, Toby, the relationship with you as Curley's wife, was a fantastic thing for me. I believe we had matured considerably. Generally, this cast, since it was small and very compact, did develop a certain ensemble feeling which, perhaps, no other play had before.

"When I think back to Theatre of Action now," Frank continued, "there's no question that it was the seminal influence in my life. I was active in that theatre for less than two years, but in that short space of time, I'd taken giant strides as an actor, writer of songs — those two particularly. But I'd come a long way in so many directions with the help and guidance of the people at Theatre of Action."

Finally, it was to Syd Banks I turned to find out what experiences he had had as director. I asked him how he felt members of the company responded to him? Whether he felt they were happy to work with him?

"I think many were," he told me. "There were a few who weren't too cooperative. I guess my personality bothered them. I made no bones about it, the fact that I was quite confident. Sometimes that can be misconstrued. In other words, I didn't worry. I didn't go home and have nightmares. I was quite comfortable and that can be misunderstood, and as a matter of fact, was.

"*Of Mice And Men* was a very difficult play to do. The problem I had was with the few people who were bucking me in the cast. It was not an easy task. Most of the people worked well and hard. The few who didn't made my life miserable. But what was more important was the fact that I beat them. I proved what we were doing was correct and that we had a winner going. Everybody loves a winner. We came of age, I would say. On opening night I knew it."

I must admit that I was not aware of the few people Syd referred to as giving him a hard time. If he felt that, I must assume there was some resistance, although I didn't notice it. Certainly the people I worked with were determined to give their best for this director in this play.

It seems that just about every role I played provided some unusual experience for me. *Of Mice And Men* was no exception.

I referred earlier to the scene near the end where Lennie and Curley's wife play out their dreams while they sit together in the barn. Towards the end of that scene, Curley's wife calls attention to her lovely, silken hair and urges Lennie to feel it. He does so, hesitantly. He enjoys the sensation — he loves soft things. Because he is big and strong, the pressure of his hand on her head becomes unpleasant. She asks him to stop. When he doesn't respond, she raises her voice and starts to squirm in fear. Lennie is terrified and confused. He continues to hold on because he doesn't know what to do. By this time Curley's wife is shouting. In an attempt to stop her — he doesn't want any trouble — he takes hold of her neck with one hand and presses the other over her mouth to stifle the sound. She actively fights him and gets up to escape him. His grip on her neck gets tighter and he presses his hand harder over her mouth. Finally, she stops moving. Lennie removes his hand and she drops to the floor — dead.

Well, the floor of the barn was covered with straw and when I fell there were two problems: first, the straw was sharp and scratchy if I didn't fall properly; second, if I fell with my face into the straw, there was a good possibility that I would start sneezing. These problems were compounded by the fact that I had to lie there for what seemed to me an eternity before the scene ended. Credibility dictated that I should fall with my head and body facing upstage. Just the mechanics of this one small moment took some time to work out. At the same time, it had to look spontaneous.

Frank Gregory and I rehearsed that particular section of our scne together until we had it running smoothly. Yet each night of performance, as I was on my way down to the floor, I suddenly remembered what I had to avoid. When the fall was completed and I managed it satisfactorily, I lay there concentrating hard on anything but where I was, so I could forget how uncomfortable it felt as I lay on scratchy straw with my cheek pressed down on it. Sometimes I felt the scene would never end. To this day, that memory — as much as any other — is so very vivid.

We opened on March 6, 1940. The reviews were again positive. "T.C." in the *Globe* wrote:

> The Theatre of Action has a habit of staging better-than-average productions and last night it lived up to its reputation

when it presented John Steinbeck's *Of Mice And Men* in Margaret Eaton Hall. While the play did not attain the heights of polish and poignancy that productions such as *Steel* or *Bury The Dead* have done, this full evening's presentation had considerable merit both in the character of the acting and the effectiveness of the mounting.

Continuously intensive training in the technique of acting has, no doubt, been responsible for the finished way in which such young men as Norval Gray, Frank Gregory and Don Moore, and such young women as Toby Gordon, play their parts. The direction was a credit to Sydney Banks. Frank Gregory, as the mentally helpless, physically powerful Lennie, was excellently cast. Toby Gordon, as the flitty young wife who wanted to get to Hollywood, did a regular bit of professional acting in the scene in the haymow. Don Moore, as the colored stable buck, gave a smooth performance and Norval Gray carried the heavy load of the smart laborer with the dream of ten acres of land with genuine finesse . . .

There were moments when the play possessed a tremendous dramatic quality such as the death of the dog and during the soliloquies and colloquy of Curley's wife and the 'dumb guy'. The sets designed by Sydney Newman were brilliantly conceived, particularly the one of the bank of the river and the one of the haymow . . .

The other papers were almost as enthusiastic. In *The Tribune* of March 9, 1940, "M.F." wrote:

This week's performance of Steinbeck's *Of Mice And Men* by the Toronto Theatre of Action is directed by Sydney Banks, who has been working with the company for some years, but has not hitherto directed any of its chief productions. He is to be congratulated on an outstanding piece of work. The opening scene made it clear that actors and producer had entered completely into the author's intention, and further, had mastered a theatre technique which could best express it.

The play is tragic with a lyrical quality. The opening and closing scenes 'rhyme,' and all through there are repetitions of incident and speech. George's dream of the happy future, repeated three times to Lennie, Lennie's rhythmical life of affection and destruction, the drawing of Candy and Crooks with their identical needs, into the circle of the dream, all these give intensity and power to the central theme: the stranglehold of society as it is upon the lives of men like George and Lennie.

'Nobody ever gets to heaven,' says Crooks, 'and nobody gets no land . . .' The playing of this part (George) by Norval Gray showed a tension and a control worthy of a metropolitan professional theatre. And over against him was Frank Gregory's faultless acting as the idiot, Lennie . . .

This week's performance of *Of Mice And Men* was a deeply sympathetic interpretation of a very moving story.

And Canada cannot wash her hands and say: a way of life is unknown here.

From *The Telegram* of March 6, 1940, by Rose MacDonald:

It has remained for the Theatre of Action to play Steinbeck's *Of Mice And Men* in Toronto, and a firm-textured performance this acting group give of a difficult play . . .

Steinbeck, in his own dramatization of his grim, yet curiously touching story . . . has employed practically in its entirety the original dialogue . . . The language is harsh, for this is a play about elemental people . . . The piece moves inexorably to its tragic end. But the inner theme has a tender beauty — selfless protective loyalty of the strong character George toward the poor, wit-lacking hulking creature he has known from boyhood; on the other hand, the dog-like trusting devotion of the witless one towards the other . . .

For the first time the Theatre of Action players are directed by one of their own number, Sydney Banks, whose first attempt at directing this is. A most rewarding experiment for the theatre. Mr. Banks has a rarely imaginative quality of mind, a singleness of purpose, and apparently, those practical qualities which enable a director to get things done. He has under his guidance a most eager group, possessed of no little talent and apparently tireless.

So this young man . . . has been enabled to give us a play imaginatively set forth, and perhaps the most artistically presented play which this little theatre group has yet presented.

A sheaf of palms must also be presented to Sydney Newman for his remarkable sets — executed by members of the group . . .

Casting has been excellent, with first honors going to Frank Gregory's interpretation of the witless Lennie, a strikingly truthful portrayal, the characterization consistent to the end. Norval Gray is scarcely the hard-bitten George one might expect, but, physical considerations aside, he plays with discernment, firmness and sincerity . . . Don Moore, playing the lonely and embittered Negro stable buck . . . has a voice eminently responsive, subtly variegated in tone; this, together with his smoothly coordinated stage movement, made his small part one of the outstanding achievements of the evening. Ben Lennick has accustomed us to good performances and his wistful old wreck of a Candy was admirable . . . Calm as a stage veteran, his amiable dog-companion, by the way.

The play has but one feminine character and . . . Toby Gordon was chosen to fill the role of the over-bold young woman, known simply as Curley's wife. Miss Gordon, on the whole, made a good job of it . . . The straight capable Slim was successfully undertaken by Harold Liskin and Jack Kyle's Carlson was good, if a bit too heavily underscored in the scene over the dog . . . Tommy Morrison, Kenneth Peck and Stuart Walton were also competent performers.

And lastly, *The Varsity* review of March 6 written by Herbert Cowan:

The Theatre of Action, our local troupe of socially-conscious thespians, has turned its attention at last to John Steinbeck, a writer who seems, as the idiom has it, to be right down their alley. Usually the theatre's peculiar talents are unloosed on something a little noisier, but their current production of *Of Mice And Men* at Margaret Eaton Hall is in some ways one of the best things they have yet done . . .

Of Mice And Men is a good play. I need not here discuss its value as a social document or as a study in various kinds of frustration, but as a tragedy, it is a remarkable achievement . . . (It) makes considerable use, not too obviously, of that old favorite, dramatic irony. The dog-shooting episode is the best instance of this; I may be wrong, but I think that it is almost certainly intended as an anticipation of Lennie's approaching fate; . . . It's a difficult scene, splendidly done . . .

There are several distinguished individual performances in this production. Frank Gregory as Lennie heads the list; much of his part consists of being silent, but he never loses his hold on the character. The runners-up, Ben Lennick as Candy, Toby Gordon (Curley's wife) and Don Moore (Crooks). The rest are, on the whole, not less than adequate. The director, Sydney Banks, has not left his mark as unmistakably as some of his predecessors have done — not altogether a bad thing. Sydney Newman's sets are impressive and decidedly realistic; I've never seen quite so much real hay on a stage before. Make-up and costumes are also much above average. The sound effects by some horrible record-playing contraption, are both unnecessary and regrettable.

Don't go to this just to be entertained; it's strong stuff . . .

XXIII

Disintegration

OF MICE AND MEN WAS THE LAST MAJOR Theatre of Action production.

The Minutes of the Production Council record rehearsals of one-act plays, both for studio presentation and outside bookings. The children's school was still functioning, but the Minutes make it clear that no major production with children was now feasible. It was suggested that an informal demonstration of work for parents be held.

A reading of those Minutes reveals that things were not going too well with Theatre of Action. I quote from the Minutes of April 18, 1940:

"The general state of the theatre was discussed and it was agreed that a state of disintegration was apparent. Members seemed to have no sense of responsibility toward the theatre, if they were not engaged in a major production.

"It was agreed that we should call a (membership) meeting — using whatever means necessary to insure a large attendance — at which the question of discipline and morale could be taken up."

At one of the Production Council meetings, at that time, it was recommended that Syd Banks become permanent director of Theatre of Action.

I asked some people what, in their opinion, had caused the disintegration of the group.

Irving Hoffman: "I think the times had changed. The Theatre had more or less served its purpose and a new voice, a new type of theatre, was necessary. It had done what it had to do for the time and said what it had to say. Everybody at that time had already branched out. Also, in the years in between, people matured. I guess in the depression they had more time. I remember you could go up to the theatre any afternoon and there were always actors around. It was almost like a meeting place, a refuge, in a sense. You could get away from the horrible bleakness of the outside world. Think of people who had gone to university and had nothing to do. How horrible it must have been for them. With the advent of prosperity after the war, everybody got their jobs, proceeded to professions which they had worked so hard for, and didn't have the same time to devote to theatre."

Ben Lennick: "I think political circumstances were such that it became perhaps too much for some of the people. I think some were running scared by the late 30s. We were known as a radical group. Not that we were all that radical, but we had a history perhaps of that sort of thing because of the plays we had done. Many people were asking the question, 'Are we going to stand condemned?' Some were joining the armed forces and our ranks were thinning quickly. I just wanted to go on being involved in theatre as long as I could, prepared to do any plays that were valid, that I thought presented a challenge to me as an actor, and that had something to say, even if it was said in terms of Gogol's *The Inspector General*.

"To me it was a blow to see the theatre disintegrate. The last chance, I thought, was the rallying around Syd Banks when we did *Of Mice And Men*. I think it was a successful production. I don't know what happened thereafter, whether the heart went out of a lot of people, who felt they were fighting great odds, or maybe people felt they'd had enough.

"There was so much difference of opinion about which path the theatre should take — should we go on being an unpopular voice in the wilderness at this time? There was official disapproval inveighing against the theatre all around us. We were a suspect minority there and perhaps it didn't end with a bang, but almost with a whimper. That was too bad.

"Syd called me either in late fall or early winter. It was a new group called Theatre Project that Syd had hoped to form along the basis of what had existed previously, but with him as its guiding genius. I don't know where he got the money, he may even have mortgaged his home. He got a studio down on Yonge Street below King. He called me and asked would I like to get involved in a theatre. I said that was great. I came down and Lou Jacobi came and my wife-to-be, Sylvia, was there. That was the first time we met. I can't recall who else was involved. We eventually did Sidney Kingsley's *The World We Make*."

Grace Gray: "I think it was the times that contributed to the demise of Theatre of Action. It was the time when war broke out and also it was the time of the 'phony' war. A lot of the small theatres had to fold anyway, because people had far more on their minds, then, than raising money for theatres. Ours particularly was hit. This whole period, people who had been interested in workers' theatre all of a sudden got a little leary about it and didn't contribute any more. It was one of those things where one couldn't carry on any longer. And, of course, there would be a division among the people in the theatre as well, in their own thinking. I would say those were the reasons. If it hadn't been for those circumstances in that particular period, the theatre would have gone on. It was a very disturbed time and this was the cause of it."

Syd Banks: "There was a tendency for it to become a political animal and I was dead set against it. The war came along and we were suspect, because we were a left-wing group. We were suspect and the war had taken people's attention."

Stuart Walton: "I think the theatre was getting a little big for itself. It was agonizing over giving everybody something to do. There was now a fairly wide membership of people who had been trained. We were getting more and more young people for whom we had no place and we didn't know what to do with them. It was getting almost too much for us.

"If I recall rightly, we tried to organize into two theatres — the less experienced who would be given their own type of show to do — and the regular productions of the theatre in which we now had a very skilled personnel to cast and call on. I think it was too much for us to handle.

"The direction was also faltering and the air was starting to splinter before the war came, but I think it was the war that gave it its death-blow. It's very hard for us to go back to those times, but the issue was: What were we going to do? Obviously we couldn't put on an anti-war play then. Besides, as I recall, there was very little anti-war sentiment. The struggle with Nazi Germany had come and we had been expecting it for years."

I agree that it was the times and the events taking place around us that contributed to the demise of Theatre of Action. I don't agree that we were somehow under pressure because we had a different, or radical, approach to the social problems of our day. Theatre of Action, judged by the content of our plays, was a dissenting voice, a true alternative theatre, which brought to our audiences — working class as well as others — an understanding of the times they were living in. In addition, we introduced new forms which entertained and inspired the hope that people could change the prevailing conditions. In this sense, we were different, and different at that time meant radical. We reflected our times with the best possible artistic standards. That is what made our theatre unique and important.

If there was one major reason for the disintegration of Theatre of Action in 1940 it was that the leadership of the group simply could not agree on our role during the war. I was one of those who felt we could continue, on a much reduced scale, to provide programs for a touring theatre which could get bookings from organizations and trade unions.

Our membership would be reduced, as would our finances, but I felt we could find sufficient one-act material to keep a small number of people active. It would be possible, as well, to continue our studies, with some emphasis on training for work on classical plays, with an eye to the future. This would now be possible, without the pressure of doing major presentations.

Unfortunately, not too many members in the leadership of the theatre agreed with me. At that point, I withdrew from Theatre of Action. Several others followed me.

The majority of members, those who were still taking the summer course in 1940, felt that Theatre of Action should change and go on to other kinds of scripts which would be more acceptable. A small number of others even suggested we do anti-war scripts as a mobile theatre.

It was obvious that these divisions could not be reconciled. The majority prevailed and were now free to go on with whatever program they had in mind.

I did not attend the summer course. Instead, I sought paid employment. I managed to find myself an interesting secretarial position. My salary, compared to what we had been living on, was more than modest.

This was the first time in many years that I had considered my own well-being. The first luxury for Oscar and me was renting a small apartment. No more rooming-house landladies to tell us when to bathe and how much hot water to use. What freedom!

These changes in life-style did not prevent me though from missing the active life I had led in the theatre and the kind of excitement it had provided. But I forced myself to channel my energy into other activities.

I did get the occasional call to direct a play. I even tried working with another group. But I couldn't take the undisciplined attitudes that prevailed — rehearsals never started on time, or people didn't show up at all so that everyone wasted an evening. The scripts didn't appeal to me and the approach to acting was very superficial. The work this particular theatre group was doing didn't seem to matter very much. It was not my style of work at all and I quickly gave it up.

Having recalled many of their experiences in Theatre of Action, I asked some of my close colleagues and leading participants in the group, to comment briefly on that period in their lives.

Ben Lennick: To me, Theatre of Action was the only wheel in town. I just felt that any theatre that dedicates itself to training, inviting people practically off the street and welcoming them to grow and learn — that was a really challenging theatre. It was a marvellous approach because it had continuity. I always thought of Theatre of Action as a growing thing. We, of course, grew with it.

Lillian Messinger: It was a marvellous school for what we went on to, not only in the theatre field, but often quite unrelated to theatre. It was really one of the most productive and enriching parts of my life.

Art Messinger: It was a place for us to grow. It was not something that we ever found a chore to do. We just couldn't wait to get there.

Syd Banks: Our group was daring. We had an intensity none of the others had. We were the only ones who had schools attached to our theatre. I think we were unique in that sense. It was very logical for us to have continuous training, because students could see a light at the end of the tunnel — there was a company towards which they could move.

Stuart Walton: Some of the happiest years of my life were in the Theatre of Action. You became a more human person because you were mixing with so many different kinds of people at different stages of their development. I wouldn't exchange that experience in Theatre of Action for anything. It was thrilling, stimulating, stretching. You were doing something worthwhile and realizing yourself in the process.

XXIV

The Meaning Of It All

WHAT DID IT ALL MEAN TO ME?

My experience in Workers' Theatre and later, in Theatre of Action, trained, developed, educated and molded not only my personality but also my interests, social awareness, relationships to others and gave me an abiding interest in all forms of theatre, and the arts generally. Obviously, it meant a lot to me as it did to most of those whose lives it all touched.

One of its major weaknesses was its inability to find and produce many Canadian scripts. But the very reason for the existence of this theatre — a theatre dedicated to plays that spoke for our desperate times — made it difficult to find the playwrights (very few in number in the thirties) who were interested in that kind of writing. Even with the explosion of professional theatres that has taken place in the last decade or so, there are not too many scripts being produced that deal with the unique problems facing us in this place and in this time.

As well, we didn't really succeed in attracting large numbers of working people — especially those in the labor unions — that we would have liked. We did, however, make a start in this direction through our mobile theatre presentations and, especially, with our production of *Steel.* The fact was, there were too few people doing the necessary organizational spade work to make this part of our work entirely successful.

In Theatre of Action we did work hard to create a theatre collective dedicated to productions of high standards. Members knew from the start that, in our group, the play we were doing was the important element, rather than the personal glory. We were not able, however, to completely eliminate ego. Clearly, we didn't do enough at our membership meetings to solve this touchy theatrical problem.

In a personal sense, Theatre of Action trained me as an actor in a variety of plays that spoke of our times, sometimes harshly and many times eloquently. Directors helped me to grow in each role I played, large and small. They encouraged me to work at forms which I never thought I could do. I learned how to work on a role independently, to relate to other actors, to work with directors in a disciplined and creative fashion.

As secretary of the theatre, I learned to work in administration and organization. This put me in a leadership position and for that valuable experience I am also grateful.

As part of the acting company, I was made aware of what formidable power the theatre can wield over large numbers of people — entertaining them, lifting their spirits, sharpening their awareness, touching their emotions.

In all, my participation in Theatre of Action was a joyful experience, using my youthful energies and commitment in a positive venture, at a time when young people were generally dispirited about the future.

It is part of me, as it is still part of those people I talked to, and, I'm sure, many others I didn't reach.

XXV

Postscript

TO COMPLETE MY PICTURE OF THE social theatre movement in Canada, I must include a later attempt to bring into being a theatre focussed on its own period — the fifties.

Witch-hunting McCarthyism was at its height in the United States, with one of its major targets the arts, and especially theatre and film. This disease spilled over into Canada.

Three people — Virginia MacLeod, Louise Sandler and I — started talking about the need for a theatre to voice opposition to those attacks on people involved in the arts. We decided to call this new theatre, The Play Actors. On January 16, 1953, we held a public casting for a script by Howard Fast. Called *Thirty Pieces Of Silver*, the title accurately describes the content of the play.

I was to direct, Louise was our technical director and Virginia was to play in it, as well as to help organize and do publicity. We attracted some experienced people at our casting, as well as some who had done little previous work on stage. Our rehearsals were held in the United Electrical Workers' Union Hall, which they generously allowed us to use. We had no money. One of the first things members of the group had to turn their attention to therefore was the raising of the necessary funds for this production. Isabel Bevis joined us specifically to help in financing.

Thirty Pieces Of Silver is not a very well-constructed play. We were aware of that, but we worked very hard to make it believable and convincing because of its important contemporary theme which, we felt, needed to be made widely known. We played for three nights at the end of April, 1953, at Hart House, where, much to my surprise, I was greeted by Jim Hozak, whom I hadn't seen since Theatre of Action days.

The press, however, was quite severe in its criticism of the play. As for the acting, the inexperience was noted, but on the whole *it* was favorably reviewed.

Beginning with this play, I noticed a marked difference between the attitude of the press toward The Play Actors and to our earlier Theatre of Action. I can only assume that the political and social climate in the country had made them less tolerant of our dissenting voice. Theatre of Action in the thirties was part of the growing opposition to things as they were. Even when our scripts were not approved by some critics, the need for them was recognized.

Audiences for *Thirty Pieces Of Silver* were quite large, though, and they enthusiastically greeted our new theatre and the script.

Our next production was a sophisticated, somewhat satirical, comedy by Ferenc Molnar called *Arthur.* This script required a very special professional style of acting and direction. At our stage of development, most of the actors lacked the polish and crispness to do justice to this social satire about a con man and his daughter in high society. As director, I realized too late that it was not my kind of script at all. Perhaps it was too early in our experience to meet its special demands.

Neither our audiences, which were small, nor the press, received it well.

The script that followed was by George Tabori. It was called *The Emperor's Clothes.* Using the children's story theme, it was an allegory on contemporary society.

The locale is fascist Hungary in 1930. The leading character is a professor who, in his younger days had been involved in radical activities, loses his job and is blacklisted. His fear has made him cautious of any such activity. To his young son, though, he is a hero still. At the end, when the professor must make a difficult choice, it is this young boy who strengthens his will to do the right thing.

The outline hardly does justice to the structure and writing of this script. It was a strong play and offered splendid opportunities to the actors and the director for characterization and developing theatrical relationships. Together, we achieved a moving and absorbing theatre experience.

Henry Orenstein, a young artist, designed a functional and beautiful indoor-outdoor setting, which aided the mood of time and place.

I believe we introduced a "first" with that production. We had two fine black actors in our group — Kathleen Livingstone and Aubrey Forbes. They both read for parts in *The Emperor's Clothes.* Strictly on their ability, they were both cast in leading roles. What was interesting is that people who saw the show spoke about their acting without any reference to their color. We were delighted at this reception of their work.

Audience response to Tabori's play was excellent and we played to filled houses. The press, in general, received the production well.

We entered *The Emperor's Clothes* in the regional drama festival and were accepted. We were, however, given a very poor time slot for our presentation — a Wednesday matinee — for which we had great difficulty obtaining an audience. Since we had a rather complex set to put up, we spent most of the night, after the previous group had struck their set, working on ours. And after our matinee, all of us had to work quickly to get our set off and leave the stage ready for the next group. It seemed that things were made very hard for us.

With all of that, the adjudicator, Andre Van Gyseghem, from England, was impressed with the quality of our production and the script. He signalled this recognition by awarding the Edgar Stone Challenge Trophy jointly to me and to Mrs. D.F. Roberts, director of the Sudbury Little Theatre Guild who directed Jean Anouilh's *Antigone*.

For a struggling new theatre, this was welcome recognition.

In the summer, The Play Actors conducted classes in acting, movement and stage management.

We continued in the fall with several one-act play programs, at least two of them written by Canadians. These were done with new and original members as well as with new directors taking charge.

Our programs were clearly hampered by lack of money. We did several readings of plays to help raise funds and several good friends of the group lent us their homes to make fine social evenings for invited guests. Somehow, though, our efforts were never really sufficient and drained the energies of our leading members, who were involved in all of these activities.

The final production of Play Actors was the Dutch classic, *The Good Hope*, by Herbert Heijermans. This play had its premiere in Amsterdam on Christmas Eve, 1900. Heijermans wrote passionately about the exploited, poverty-stricken and endangered Dutch fishermen and their families. Men were sent out to sea in leaky old ships by owners who knew the fishermen might never return to port. It was a strong working class play, in which the author firmly took his stand with the fishermen and their cause.

We developed a very fine relationship with the Dutch community in Toronto as a result of the work on this script. They were invaluable in gathering authentic costumes, props and make-up, as well as offering advice for our set and furnishings. They also provided a fairly large audience, who were delighted to see this classic on stage.

The play called for a large cast, which created problems of getting everyone out to rehearsals. Our lack of money made it necessary for us to find available rehearsal space free. We rehearsed at Bathurst Street United Church, through the generosity of Rev. Gordon Domm. We had to use whatever space was available for each particular night. Mostly, we found ourselves in small rooms — sometimes the board-room with a long table in the middle of it. That was fine for rehearsing individual scenes with a group of actors. But it made it almost impossible to get the whole cast together, except occasionally.

For me, as director, the play presented some challenges. Heijermans supplied situations in the script which were highly emotional, as they dealt with life and death matters. It was essential for the actors to play with conviction and passion, and not cross the fine line into melodrama and its superficial emotions.

It took a great deal of individual effort on the part of everyone to find the fine line and play the situations for their true qualities. I met with the leading actors in private sessions to get to the true theme of the script.

When we finally got *The Good Hope* on stage, I was pleasantly surprised to see how many very moving performances there were. Audiences responded with genuine deep silence at the most emotional moments. We all felt that we had — together — met the challenge of this difficult script. The people we played for signalled their agreement by the reception they gave each performance.

Following this production, we set up another summer school, but the load of running this theatre was just too heavy for the few of us involved. It was decided to disband The Play Actors.

Yet this group was another important part of my life. It had given me an opportunity to work with children in at least five of the productions. I found working with them and using their natural qualities very rewarding. As a result, I began to explore the field of children's drama.

I was excited by the new concepts of child drama demonstrated by Brian Way at a workshop he gave, and the subsequent reading of Peter Slade's work. Their approach to drama for children as a developmental creative process, not at all related to "child performers," started me thinking.

The idea that all children, as part of their development, rich or poor, could participate in this art appealed to me. I began further reading in this field and I attended many workshops subsequently. It wasn't difficult for me to relate to this outlook. My own theatre training was not too far removed from this basic approach.

I took up teaching drama to children, first as an after-school activity in my neighborhood school, on a voluntary basis. The children I worked with were delighted and happy to participate in this free-form drama and never asked or thought of doing performances. They were just happy to work out their own ideas and occasionally to do a demonstration for their parents.

A program of this kind that I carried on at the Duke of York school was later filmed by the National Film Board. It is called simply *Mrs. Ryan's Drama Class.* The filming was done while I was working out the sessions "live", as it were. The film, I am told, is appreciated for its honesty and forthrightness — different from some films where the children seem so perfect.

Eventually the Inner City Angels came into being in Toronto with the idea of promoting the arts in the inner city schools. I was one of the early artists who went in to do drama with children, this time as part of their school activity in school time. Later, as a member of the Canadian Child and Youth Drama Association, I was fortunate to be chosen as one of the teachers at the Children's Creative Centre at Expo '67 for a period of six weeks. That too was an unforgettable experience.

Today, I still enjoy my work with children. I am still involved in exploring and discovering new approaches, new ways of using my experience and training in that unique theatre which produced so many creative people — the Theatre of Action.

Part Four:

APPENDICES

A.

The following credits are from the Dominion Drama Festival's B.C. Regional program.

Fourth
British Columbia
Regional Festival

Empress Theatre
31st January and 1st February, 1936

Adjudicator:
Allan Wade

Friday, 31st January
"Waiting For Lefty"
Philosophical Drama by Clifford Odets

Scene: Labor Union Hall

Harry Fatt, Head of the Union .... Lynn Gibb
Miller .... G. Turner
Phillips .... Harry Louis
Gunman .... M. Nichols
Joe, a hack .... Edward Lauk
Edna, his wife .... Stevi Semkowich
Sid, a young hack .... D.T. Kristiensen
Florence, his girl .... Florence Hayes
Irv, her brother .... Wm. Kunka
Clayton, a labor spy .... Harry Hoshowsky
Clancy .... M. Kunka
Dr. Barnes .... Theodore Boresky
Dr. Benjamin .... Ben Sochasky
Agate Keller .... Guy Glover
Members of the Union .... J. Davidson, Wm. Semkowich,
Bob Waldman, Fred Lawrence, P. O'Neil

Directed by Garfield A. King and Guy Glover
Presented by Progressive Arts Club of Vancouver.

B.

Beer and Skits — Winnipeg

The following are excerpts from some of the songs written for Winnipeg New Theatre's Beer and Skits *evenings. The numbers were, of course, costumed and theatrically staged. Readers are asked to indulge their imaginations and to visualize the staging. I think the lyrics may convey some of the spirit and flavor of the comments on topics of the time.*

It Can't Happen Here

It can't happen here,
It can't happen here,
It can happen over there
But it can't happen here.
Oompah, oompah, etc.

Down on the Ford assembly plant
A certain guy named Jones,
Went on the picket-line,
And six policemen broke his bones.

But it can't happen here,
It can't happen here.
It can happen to a Libyan,
Far beyond the blue Caribbean,
But the *Free Press* and the *Tribune*
Say it can't happen here.

Dictator nations are so broke,
They've put a tax on taxes,
In Rome, Berlin and Tokyo,
They're flat upon their axis.

But it can't happen here (*Chorus repeated*).

Cock-a-Doodle-Doo

Cock-a-doodle-doo
Day is breaking.
Cock-a-doodle-doo,
Time you were waking.
Get out of your bed,
You smug little ostrich heads.

Cock-a-doodle-doo,
Out of the darkness,
Cock-a-doodle-doo,
Out of the blindness
Of night and despair,
Tomorrow is dawning fair.

If you're not out to end abuses,
You can stew in your own fat juices,
We don't care
What you doodle, doodle, doodle, doodle, doo.

Joe Worker

Joe Worker just drops right
At his work he drops,
Weary, weary, tired to the core.
And then if he drops out of sight
There's always plenty more.
Joe Worker must know
That somebody's got him in tow.
But what is the good for one to be dear?
Oh, it takes a lot of Joes to make a sound you can hear!
One question inside me cries:
How many frame-ups, how many shake-downs,
lock-outs, sell-outs
How many times machine-guns tell the same old story,
Brother, does it take to make you wise?

Nero, Dante, Columbus and Caesar

We're Nero, Dante, Columbus and Caesar,
Scions of sunny Italy.
Caesar, Columbus, Dante and Nero,
Dead, lo, these many years are we.

But since our day, our land has changed,
They've purified the race.
Yes, things are sadly re-arranged,
Since the Duce became the Ace.

Chorus: You've got to be Aryan,
You've got to be pure.
Though your skin is dark
And your nose is hooked,
If you ain't Nordic, your goose is cooked.
You've got to be Aryan today.

Nero: In Rome I played the fiddle
Chorus: And were you lousy, sire.
Nero: When things got bad
I swung my Strad,
Till I set the joint on fire.
But if I were in Rome now,
I wouldn't be so free.
If Mussolini hates Toscanini,
What the hell would he think of me!

Chorus: You've got to be Aryan *(repeat)*

Columbus: Back in 1492
When I sailed the ocean blue,
I was never seasick once
In those frail sloops.
Tossing waves would never get me,
Stormy seas could not upset me.
But each time I hear Benito talk
— — — — — — — — I whoops!

Chorus: You've got to be Aryan *(repeat)*

Caesar:	I thought I'd known The very worst of hells, When I was staged By Orson Welles.
All 4:	We're Nero, Dante, Columbus and Caesar, Forgive our irreverent hee-haws. Caesar, Columbus, Dante and Nero, We're turning in our graves because —
Chorus:	You've got to be Aryan, You've got to be pure. Though your skin is dark, And your nose is hooked. If you ain't Nordic, Your goose is cooked. You've got to be Aryan today.

C.

Montreal Press Comments On New Theatre Group Productions

The following excerpts (even those which don't have dates or the names of the newspapers they came from) are sufficient, I think, to shed light on the response to New Theatre Group's productions by some of the Montreal critics.

The Montreal Herald, October, 1936:

Bury The Dead is a play that requires many quick changes of scene and tempo. On a stage somewhat cramped these were managed with celerity and intelligence which speak well for Lilian Mendelssohn's direction. Mr. Louis Mulligan's settings, stark but impressive aided not a little in the overcoming of a serious fault — the tendency to lag which was painfully evident in earlier productions.

The individual players are uneven. Serious errors in diction detract from the work of some of the best of them. Little fault, however, could be found with the Captain of Irving Moscovitz or the First General of Murray Black. Some of the women, notably Isabella Lipkin, Erna Allet and Lillian Gargan were lyrical in their attack and carried off their little scenes with something approaching finesse . . . it may be said that each one did his bit effectively. Some merely had greater opportunity than others, despite the Group's disdain of the star system.

The New Theatre group has a lot to learn and I am confident that they will learn and will improve. Meanwhile this earnest, jesting, rueful, savage document they are presenting is worth your patronage. *Bury The Dead* makes you stop and think. In view of the headlines from abroad, stopping and thinking should be on everybody's order paper these days.

— *W.D. O'H.*

Montreal Gazette, (undated), *Theatre Group Stages Three Social Dramas:*

There were three plays on the program given by the New Theatre Group in Victoria Hall last night. Without wishing to minimize the work expended on the first two, one might say, nevertheless, that they served as curtain-raisers to *What It Takes,* the third play.

What It Takes, by Philip Stevenson, is the tragedy of a little man crushed in the mechanics of a big business. Its scene is the home of an automobile salesman on a Sunday morning. Its characters are the salesman, his family, his boss and a fellow-salesman . . .

With brilliant irony the playwright makes the son deliver his speech-day paper to the audience in his preparations for school. The speech is on the subject of 'Social Security.' From that point the play moves swiftly to a tragic climax.

The work of the whole cast was excellent. The major weight falls upon Morton Cohen, as the salesman, who conveyed the full situation admirably. In support, the sympathetic performance of Erna Allet as the wife, the beautiful timing of Ada Span as the daughter and the sensitive quality suggested by Hilliard Crown as the son, made this play one of the most effective ever offered by this group.

— *H.W.W.*

Montreal Star, March 29, 1940, *New Theatre in Odets' Play:*

Clifford Odets, the playwright, found himself during the depression years. He touched the bottom and has not forgotten how it felt. In many plays, the social conscience he developed during that period is most marked. But nowhere has he interpreted the spirit of those first desperate years with such vigor as in his favorite work, *Paradise Lost,* which the New Theatre Group presented at Victoria Hall last evening.

This is a vivid portrayal of the futility and discouragement of those years . . . The New Theatre Group, certainly in their leads and in many of their supporting characters, interpreted the play with a depth of feeling that make this final presentation of the season a notable one . . . Lilian Mendelssohn directed with a rare sense of the play's values, building her atmosphere solidly and consistently through the first act to give the second act, the play's most powerful portions, a strength and pace which brought out all the power of its drama . . .

Montreal Gazette, (undated):

The New Theatre Group returns to Clifford Odets for its latest play, *Awake And Sing,* given at Victoria Hall last night . . .

Awake And Sing has for its characters a family living in the Bronx in New York. . . . These are not pleasant people. But it is brought home strongly that they are what they are because of the conditions forced upon them by an existing economic structure. . . . The New Theatre Group finds here something into which they can get their teeth. They play the first two acts at the top of their voices and pound every point home. The treatment is heavy but the value of such handling is shown in the later scenes when contrasting methods are employed in scenes of straight tragedy with very moving results.

The cast is good, gaining its special strength from the playing of Erna Allet in the role of the mother. This is an unsympathetic role, but the actress in her few lines of justification makes the character as much a victim of these same conditions as the son and the daughter. . . . The staging employed was similar to that used by this group in *What It Takes,* but in this case did not prove as interesting — or as helpful in creating the atmosphere of a home in the Bronx.

— *H.W.W.*

The following is from an unidentified newspaper clipping of March, 1940:

In the New Theatre Group's production of Odets' *Paradise Lost* at Victoria Hall last night theatre-goers were given an opportunity to enjoy an example of this dramatist's work which includes much of the best he has to offer while disclosing his more marked weaknesses.

This frequently bitter satire of a disintegrating American Jewish family . . . is a play that is often harsh, often very funny indeed, but one that at every turn tightly holds its audience.

The piece contains some of its writer's best dialogue . . . The fault in the play lies rather in the lack of development of its characters . . .

The New Theatre Group turns in one of its finest performances here. The playing of Erna Allet as Clara Gordon, the mother, and Irving Moscovitz, as her husband, were outstanding. But several others of this bright lot of actors handled their roles ably . . .

Altogether an excellent show and the New Theatre deserves high praise for bringing it to us . . .

— *P.N.*

D.

Songs From *We Beg To Differ*

Several songs, music by Mel Tolkin, lyrics by Reuben Ship, as recalled by Malcolm Samuels, from the revue We Beg To Differ, *Montreal.*

Theme Song

We beg to differ,
We don't agree with so-called facts we've been told,
Time-honored maxims, long-established truths
Are taken with a grain of salt
By up-to-date youths.
So if you are for us
Join us in chorus
And let us all agree to differ.

Excuse It Please

We are gentlemen from Japan,
We are the highest type of man.
We abhor a fight or quarrel,
And we hold this for our moral:
Do to others just as you would have others do to you.

So we'd like to make amends
To our honored English friends,
And we open wide the door
To the Sir Ambassador. *(machine-gun rattles)*
Ambassador . . . no more.

A Doctor A Day

We're a blessing to our science,
We're the greatest men, you see.
We're a blessing to our clients
(slash 'em, stitch 'em).

We're a blessing to our clients,
We prescribe all sorts of pills,
Red and white and pink and blue,
But you'd better pay your bills —
If you know what's good for you.

Spanish Lullaby

The sun is now descending over war-torn Spain,
Another day is ending of horror and of pain.
So how can I sing of fairies that dance in the night,
How can I sing when the air is a terror and a fright?
How can I sing when the aeroplanes roar?
This, my child, is a lullaby of war.
Sleep my little non-combatant,
Shut your eyelids tight.
If you're very lucky,
You may live through the night.
Aeroplanes fly through the sky,
Bombs will break your lullaby.
God is waiting,
God is watching, babes in every town
As He guides the bombs that Mussolini's sons drop down.

E.

Waiting For Lefty — Toronto Press Reaction

The Globe — February 28, 1936 by Pearl McCarthy:

Waiting For Lefty, by Clifford Odets, that American playwright who drew the attention of most conservative people to the left-wing theatre, was given the first of three performances in the Margaret Eaton hall last night. This one-act drama lived up to the highest praise that has been written of it . . .

The Odets play is so good, so genuine in craft and spirit, that not even its propaganda flavor can mar the enjoyment. With reason, sincerity and the most acute use of dramatic possibilities, it shows how exasperation with an existing economic system may drive men to drastic action. Every step is given motive by true, basic human feelings. It was well directed by Miss Jim Watts and Martin Loeb, and consistently well acted by a large cast.

An engaging device of the play is the union of auditorium and stage, the stage scene being a hall platform, and the hecklers of the meeting speaking from the audience.

Private Hicks by Albert Maltz dealt with a young American soldier who refused to shoot strikers. It had no reason beyond a boast of block-headedness expressed in blasphemy.

F.

Press Response To *Bury The Dead*

From *Varsity* — October 27, 1936:

There were cheers, along with the accepted forms of theatrical applause as the curtain closed on *Bury The Dead* . . . The cheers were for the excellence of the production but certainly no one left the theatre without considerable mental applause for a play and a sentiment . . .

The plot is based on a story of six men killed in a war and who refused to lie down and be buried. The pleas of generals, beloved women, and priests cannot convince the wakened corpses that there is not something still on earth for them to see and do, something that would change the world so that others would not have to lay down their lives for the profit of others, for generals, 'paying for real estate with lives of young men.'

The play is exciting, gripping and stimulating when looked at in retrospect. There are parts in the play which, for dramatic effect, are unsurpassed anywhere in theatre literature. Other parts show an unfamiliarity with the requirements of a stage . . .

The acting is commendable, each part being done adequately if not always outstandingly. There are some of the cast, however, who are easily among the best actors and actresses in Toronto . . .

As the curtain raiser, *Les Precieuses Ridicules,* or *The Affected Young Ladies,* was appropriate. It is well produced — the main feature being the stylized costumes by Margaret Boultbee. Moliere would be a bit surprised at some of the liberties taken with his little gem of social satire, but there is still the pointed humor of the French master. Jocelyn Moore and Ruth Coleman did some fine work . . .

This long review is evidence that we consider the play worthwhile. It is an artistic event which promises to be one of the most important of the year.

— *M.B.L.*

From *The Globe,* October 27, 1936, by Thelma Craig:

Bury The Dead, an allegorical play by Irwin Shaw, was produced by the Theatre of Action under the direction of David Pressman at Hart House last night, and given for the first time in Canada.

The play is one of the greatest indictments of war that has ever been produced on the stage. It is powerful propaganda for peace in drama form. Yet withal, it does not savor of the traits that cause propaganda so often to defeat itself. It is a picture that is presented and that leaves the onlooker to draw his own conclusions as no sermon could do.

When at the end the folly of war and futility of youth laying down its life had been fully demonstrated, and the youthful dead refused to be riddled with bullets and put back to the grave but marched forth to seek the pleasures of the world which they had missed, the audience fell into cheering and burst into a frenzy of applause.

Every member of the cast deserved credit but particular commendation should go to the women who played the parts of the wives, sisters and sweethearts that went to the side of the grave to plead for the dead men to 'lie down', and to those dead men . . .

Saturday Night, October 31, 1936, W.S. Milne:

Of *Bury The Dead* much might be written — much has, of previous productions — but it all comes down to this: *Bury The Dead* is alive, timely, provocative, unconventional, theatrical. It is presented by a cast whose collective enthusiasm makes up for much that is crude and slipshod in individual performances. It is playing to an audience that goes there because it wants to see a play which says something that seems needing to be said, and says it in terms of today. In some ways, to one accustomed to the dowager decorum and languid condescension of a typical Hart House first night, perhaps the most dramatic thing about *Bury The Dead* was the audience. They did not come late. They listened to the play. They were not ashamed to laugh loudly, to groan and hiss. At the final curtain they rose and cheered. They cheered the cast and cheered till the young producer, Mr. David Pressman, came on the stage. They went out hotly discussing the play, and repeating the final tag: 'Stand up and do something!'

The Theatre of Action . . . is doing something with a vengeance. It is tossing a bombshell, I hope, into the dramatic complacency of Toronto Little Theatre groups. After seeing *Bury The Dead* I feel I never want to witness a blurred copy of a passé London stage success again. In view of the definite leftist slant of the Theatre of Action, perhaps I had better make it clear that I do not belong even to the CCF.

What is it all about? It is an anti-war play, expressionistically constructed, the central theme of which is the macabre notion that certain young American soldiers, killed in action, and buried after two days, refuse to stay in their graves until they have discovered the answers to certain questions . . . Throughout a succession of short, tense scenes the six corpses stand silhouetted and immovable, halfway out of their graves. At last, moved to jeers by the attempted performance of rites of exorcism, and shot at by the panic-stricken generals, they leave their graves and go out into the world, a world in panic, a world in which the down-trodden living are also beginning to think about standing up . . .

There is much that is merely hysterical in the play, and much that is gratuitously shocking with a small-boy sort of indecency, but if that sort of thing is needed to drive home the idea, I am not at all sure that the end does not justify the means. At any rate, *Bury The Dead,* as presented by the Theatre of Action at Hart House is living theatre, and should be seen by everyone who cares enough for the theatre to hail signs of life with joy.

G.

Chronological List of Theatre of Action Major Productions

February 27, 28, 29, 1936 — *Waiting For Lefty* by Clifford Odets and *Private Hicks* by Albert Maltz (double bill) at Margaret Eaton Hall.

October 26-31, 1936 — *Bury The Dead* by Irwin Shaw and *The Affected Young Ladies* by Moliere (double bill) at Hart House.

January 11-16, 1937 — *Roar China* by Sergei Tretiakov at Hart House.

April 1, 2, 3, 1937 — *The Marriage Proposal* by Anton Chekhov and *What It Takes* by Philip Stevenson and *And The Answer Is . . ?* by Mary Reynolds at Margaret Eaton Hall.

November 22-27, 1937 — *Class of '29* by Milo Hastings and Orrie Lashin at Margaret Eaton Hall.

March 14-19, 1938 — *Steel* by John Wexley at Margaret Eaton Hall.

December 12-17, 1938 — *It Can't Happen Here* by John Moffitt and Sinclair Lewis at Margaret Eaton Hall.

March 6-11, 1939 — *Life And Death Of An American* by George Sklar at Margaret Eaton Hall.

November 16, 17, 18, 1939 — *The Inspector-General* by Nikolai Gogol at Margaret Eaton Hall.

Week of March 5, 1940 — *Of Mice And Men* by John Steinbeck at Margaret Eaton Hall.

(This list does not include plays done for the mobile section of the theatre, nor studio productions of one-act plays, Living Newspaper, readings or cabaret performances.)

H.

Interviews

People interviewed for this book during 1978 and 1979:

Vancouver: Ted Boreski, Guy Glover, Harold Griffin, Harry Hoshowsky, D.T. Kristiensen.

Winnipeg: Max Golden, Fred Narvey, Imbert Orchard, Joe Zuken.

Montreal: Erna Allet, Joe Golland, Rose Kashtan, Rosalind McCutcheon, Irving Myers, Malcolm Samuels.

Toronto: Louis Applebaum, Syd Banks, Helen Coleman, Bernard Cowan, Grace Gray, Irving Hoffman, Miriam Hoffman, Jack Kaell, Phil Knibbs, Ben Lennick, Frank Love, Paul Mann, Art Messinger, Lillian Messinger, Jocelyn Moore, Syd Newman, Oscar Ryan, Frank Shuster, Stuart Walton, Johnny Wayne, Avrom Yanovsky.

New York: Frank Gregory, Ken Peck, David Pressman.